AN OFFICIAL FAN'S GUIDE

2002–2003

John MacKinnon &
John McDermott

FIREFLY BOOKS

ABOUT THE AUTHORS

JOHN MacKINNON has reported on hockey for over 18 years. A longtime Montreal resident, he covered Les Canadiens during his eight years with the *Canadian Press*. He was a staff writer with the *Ottawa Citizen* from 1988 to 1995, chronicling the city's successful expansion bid. He now lives and works in Alberta.

JOHN McDERMOTT has been editor of several national sports magazines over the past 10 years. In 1995, he helped launch *NHL PowerPlay*, the official magazine of the players and teams of the NHL. He lives and works in Michigan.

Published by Firefly Books Ltd., 2002

Picture Credits:
Getty Images / NHL

First Printing
National Library of Canada Cataloguing in Publication Data

MacKinnon, John, 1953–NHL hockey : an official fans' guide 2002-03 /
John MacKinnon & John McDermott.

ISBN 1-55297-662-9

1. National Hockey League—Miscellanea. I. McDermott, John II. Title.

GV847.8.N3M368 2002 796.962'64 C2002-903175-3

Publisher Cataloging-in-Publication Data
(Library of Congress Standards)

MacKinnon, John. NHL hockey : an official fan's guide 2002–03 /
John MacKinnon ; John McDermott. –1st ed. [128] p. : col. ill. ; cm.

ISBN 1-55297-662-9 (pbk.)
1. Hockey – Miscellanea. 2. National Hockey League. I. McDermott, John. II. Title.
796.96/ 264 21 GV847.5.M33 2002

First published in Canada in 2002 by
Firefly Books Ltd.
3680 Victoria Park Avenue
Toronto, Ontario M2H 3K1

First published in the United States in 2002 by
Firefly Books (U.S.) Inc.
P.O. Box 1338, Ellicott Station
Buffalo, New York 14205

Project editor: Luke Friend
Project art direction: Darren Jordan
Picture research: Marc Glanville
Production: Sarah Corteel
Printed in Canada

Contents

INTRODUCTION

The transformation of the National Hockey League from a parochial league into an organization with a global vision began with the 1972 Summit Series between Canadian stars and the great national team of the Soviet Union—the Big Red Machine.

After years of seeing their understaffed team whipped by the Soviets at the Olympics and World Championships, Canadians were finally given the chance to see their best players, their professionals, the stars of the NHL, supposedly deliver an overdue lesson to the big, bad Russians. It didn't work out quite that way.

The Canadians won, but it took some desperate, last-minute play and a goal by Paul Henderson with 34 seconds remaining in the final game to give Canada a 6–5 victory in the game and a slender series triumph—four games won, three lost, one game tied. The Canadian-invented sport—and the NHL—would never be the same.

NHL teams soon began to copy the superior Russian training methods, to blend their intricate, purposeful drills into often unimaginative North American practices, to pay more attention to the game's technical aspects.

The Russians, and other European teams, grafted the North Americans' never-say-die competitiveness and physical courage onto their highly skilled brand of hockey.

As the NHL expanded, first from six to 12 teams, then to 14, then 18, then 21 after absorbing teams from the World Hockey Association, and now to 30 this season, teams have had to cast their nets wider and wider in search of major-league talent.

The NHL, dominated for its first half-century by Canadian stars like Frank McGee, Howie Morenz, Aurel Joliat, George Hainsworth, Maurice (Rocket) Richard, Gordie Howe, Glenn Hall, Bobby Hull, Bobby Orr and Frank Mahovlich, was adjusting to an influx of European talent.

NHL fans grew to admire players like Borje Salming, Anders Hedberg, Ulf Nilsson, Peter, Anton and Marian Stastny and, in the 1990s, Sergei Fedorov, Pavel Bure, Jaromir Jagr and Teemu Selanne.

Now the NHL has entered the 21st Century and it boasts five times as many teams as it had just three and a half decades ago. There are 17 US states represented, as well as the District of Columbia and four Canadian provinces.

The cliché that the NHL appeals merely to regional interests in the US simply does not apply any longer.

In the fall of 1996, the inaugural World Cup of Hockey was held, a joint venture involving the NHL and the NHL Players' Association. Team USA beat Canada in a best-of-three final series, stunning the favored Canadians in the process.

The 1998 Olympic hockey finals was a triumph for the sport and enabled millions worldwide to watch some of the NHL's greatest stars in action. They reveled in the exploits of Wayne Gretzky, Joe Sakic and Patrick Roy of Canada; Finland's Teemu Selanne and Saku Koivu; Pavel Bure and Alexei Yashin of Russia; Brian Leetch, Keith Tkachuk of Team USA and, of course, the incomparable Dominik Hasek and Robert Reichel of the Czech Republic. The finals also showed that the once dominant North America stranglehold had weakened to such an extent that neither the USA or Canada took a medal home with them. The Czech Republic's stunning victory against Russia in the Final was proof that hockey was truly a global game.

In 2002, the NHL's finest again displayed their skills during the Olympics in Salt Lake City, where Canada pipped Team USA to gold.

The NHL has come a long way indeed since Henderson's legendary goal on a cold September night in Moscow in 1972. The ongoing progress should be great fun.

The Detroit Red Wings' Brendan Shanahan celebrates with the Stanley Cup after defeating the Carolina Hurricanes in five games.

STANLEY CUP
A

BIRTH OF A HOCKEY LEAGUE

The whole world was not watching when a small cluster of men met in a downtown Montreal hotel on November 22, 1917 and formed the National Hockey League. The National Hockey Association, a forerunner of the NHL, had suspended operations, so the heads of the Montreal Canadiens, Montreal Wanderers, Ottawa Senators and Quebec Bulldogs attended a founding meeting and formed a new league.

A single reporter—Elmer Ferguson, of the *Montreal Herald*—reported on the somewhat shaky launch. For starters, the Bulldogs, a poor draw in Quebec City, decided not to operate in the NHL's first season, so the Toronto Arenas were admitted to the league as a replacement.

The league was down to three teams early into the first season, though, after the Westmount Arena, home to the Montreal Wanderers, burned down. With nowhere to play, the Wanderers, too, dropped out. The NHL, then, featured the Original Three for most of its initial season, not the Original Six, a term that would gain common usage years later.

The first president of the NHL was Frank Calder, a soccer-playing British émigrée to Canada who had grown to love the Canadian game of hockey. His name would eventually be etched onto a trophy given annually to the best first-year, or rookie, player in the NHL.

In that first season, the league held the first of many dispersal drafts to distribute the players from the Bulldogs, including their scoring star, Joe Malone, who was chosen by the Canadiens.

In one of two opening-night games for the new league on December 19, 1917, Malone scored five goals as the Canadiens defeated Ottawa 7–4. Malone went on to score 44 goals during the 22-game regular season, easily winning the scoring title and setting a scoring pace never equalled in NHL history. The new league had its first superstar.

The league suffered its first major setback the following season, 1918-19. An influenza epidemic enfeebled many of the players on both finalists in the Stanley Cup playoffs—the Montreal Canadiens and Seattle Metropolitans of the Pacific Coast Hockey Association. Joe Hall, one of Montreal's star players died of the disease and so many players were stricken that the series was cancelled with no winner declared.

Building a Following

Interest in NHL hockey grew appreciably through the 1920s and 1930s, but the popularity curve was far from smooth.

In 1919, the Mount Royal Arena was built as the home of the Montreal Canadiens and five years later, the Montreal Forum was constructed to house the Maroons, the other NHL team in that hockey-mad city. In Ottawa, Frank Ahearn built a 10,000-seat arena called the Auditorium in 1923. And in Toronto, Maple Leaf Gardens was completed in 1931.

When Ottawa met the Canadiens in the 1923–24 playoffs, 11,000 jammed into the Auditorium to see the Canadiens, with Howie Morenz, defeat the Senators 4–2. The Canadiens went on to defeat Vancouver to win the Stanley Cup, the first of 23 they would win in the NHL's 80-plus years.

The Forum, the Canadiens' home for most of the century, was actually built as the home of the Maroons. But a warm spell spoiled the natural ice at the Mount Royal Arena in the fall of 1924, so the Canadiens asked to play at the Forum, which had artificial ice. So it was that the Canadiens opened the Forum on November 29, 1924, whipping the Toronto Maple Leafs 7–1.

The 1924–25 season witnessed the first labor-management dispute when the players of the Hamilton Tigers, where the Quebec Bulldogs had shifted in 1920, went on strike before the playoffs. They wanted to be paid an extra $200 Cdn. per player for work during the playoffs, a seemingly reasonable request since Hamilton had made a record profit.

Fans' Target: NHL president Clarence Campbell enraged Montreal fans in March 1955 when he suspended their hero, Maurice (Rocket) Richard.

League president Calder, though, acted in support of the owners, in the belief that giving in to the players would put at risk the owners' "...large capital investment in rinks and arenas, and this capital must be protected."

Accordingly, Hamilton was disqualified from the playoffs, and the players were suspended and fined $200 Cdn. each. The Hamilton players' stand on playoff pay would be echoed in a similar stand later in the century by all NHL players, but at the time it seemed a minor obstacle on the league's pathway to success.

By the 1927–28 season, the NHL had grown from three teams to ten, split into two divisions: the Canadian and American. The Canadian division included the Toronto St. Patricks, the Ottawa Senators, the New York Americans, the Montreal Maroons and Montreal Canadiens. The American division consisted of the Boston Bruins, the New York Rangers, the Pittsburgh Pirates, the Chicago Blackhawks and the Detroit Cougars. This two-division alignment remained intact for 12 seasons, although this era was hardly immune from franchise shifts.

After winning the Stanley Cup in 1927, the Ottawa Senators, increasingly cashstrapped as the Great Depression approached, slid downhill. In 1930, the Senators sold star defenseman Frank (King) Clancy to the Toronto Maple Leafs for $35,000 Cdn., the largest sum ever paid for a hockey player. But even that cash infusion couldn't staunch the financial hemorrhage and, after suspending operations for the 1931–32 season, the Senators moved to St. Louis. The Eagles, as they were called, staggered through one season, before folding. Franchises also sprung up, struggled and folded or moved, in Pittsburgh and Philadelphia.

There was no shortage of star players in this era, which featured the scoring exploits of Nels Stewart, Cy Denneny, Aurel Joliat, Babe Dye, Montreal's incomparable Morenz, Harvey (Busher) Jackson, Charlie Conacher, Bill Cook and Cooney Weiland.

The game was evolving, finding itself, through the NHL's early days. Forward passing of the puck was not permitted at all until the 1927–28 season, when a rule change legalized this radical change in the defensive and neutral zones. When another rule change in 1929–30 gave players the green light to pass the puck ahead to a teammate in all three zones, goalscoring doubled. Ace Bailey led the league with 22 goals in 1927–28, compared to 43 goals for the league-leading Weiland the following season.

Play in the NHL was often vicious in the early days, but no incident horrified fans quite like Eddie Shore's attack on Ace Bailey on December 12, 1933 at the Boston Garden. Shore had been bodychecked into the boards by Red Horner and got up seeking revenge. He skated up to Bailey, who had his back to him, and knocked his feet out from under him. Bailey's head smacked against the ice and he went into convulsions. Horner responded by knocking Shore out with one punch, opening up a seven-stitch cut. Surgeons had to drill a hole in Bailey's skull to remove a blood clot that had formed near his brain. He remained unconscious, near death for 15 days and never played again.

The NHL of the 1930s produced many sublime evenings, also, but none like the Longest Game, a playoff encounter that began March 24 and ended March 25 in 1936.

That night, the Montreal Maroons and the Detroit Red Wings faced off in a Stanley Cup semifinal series opener that lasted 176 minutes 30 seconds. The only goal was scored by Detroit's Modere (Mud) Bruneteau at 16:30 of the sixth overtime period, provoking momentary stunned silence among the 9,000 fans at the Montreal Forum, followed by a huge ovation of relief. The game that began at 8:34 pm had ended at 2:25 am the following morning and all in attendance were utterly exhausted. None deserved a rest more than Detroit goaltender Norm Smith, a Maroons castoff, who stopped 90 shots in his first NHL playoff game.

The Forum was also the scene for one of the saddest days in NHL history—the funeral of Canadiens great Howie Morenz on March 10, 1937. Morenz had died from complications arising from a broken leg. More than 25,000 fans filed past the coffin at center ice in the Forum.

As the 1930s progressed, teams began to die as well, as the NHL shrank from a ten-team, two-division league to a one-division league with seven teams by 1940.

The War Years

In the early 1940s, a rule change introduced a center red line to the NHL ice surface. The idea was to speed up play and reduce offside calls. The change marked the onset of the league's so-called Modern Era.

As the NHL moved into this new phase, one player dominated the transition—Maurice (Rocket) Richard. Playing

Mr. Hockey: Gordie Howe's marvellous career stretched over five decades. His legendary longevity permitted him to play in the NHL with his sons, Mark and Marty.

Russian Bear: Anatoli Tarasov has been called the father of Soviet hockey. In fact, he studied the hockey writings of Toronto's Lloyd Percival.

right wing with center (Elegant) Elmer Lach and left winger Hector (Toe) Blake, Richard was the scoring star for the Montreal Canadiens, a symbol of competitive excellence for all French-Canadians and one of the most fiery, combative athletes ever to play any professional sport.

In the 1944–45 season, Richard scored 50 goals in 50 games, setting the standard for scoring brilliance for years to come. Lach (80 points), Richard (73) and Blake (67) finished 1-2-3 in the scoring race, earning the nickname, the 'Punch Line'.

Richard set a single-game scoring record that season, too, by scoring five goals and adding three assists as the Canadiens whipped the Red Wings 9–1 in Montreal on December 28.

The Stanley Cup highlight of the World War II period had to be the Toronto Maple Leafs' dramatic comeback victory in 1942, the only time in NHL history that a team overcame a 3–0 deficit in games to win a seven-game final series.

The Maple Leafs, second-place finishers during the 48-game regular season, found themselves in that predicament against the Detroit Red Wings, who had finished fifth in regular-season play.

At that point in the series, Maple Leafs' manager Conn Smythe, the man who built Maple Leaf Gardens and whose hockey credo was: "If you can't beat 'em in the alley, you can't beat 'em on the ice," took extreme measures.

Smythe benched right winger Gordie Drillon, the Leafs' top scorer, provoking outrage among Maple Leafs' supporters.

ICE TALK

"I HAVE NEVER SEEN A BETTER PLAYER THAN RICHARD FROM THE BLUE LINE IN."

TOMMY GORMAN, MONTREAL CANADIENS GENERAL MANAGER (1940–41, 1945–46), SPEAKING OF MAURICE (ROCKET) RICHARD

Rubbing salt in the fans' wounds, he replaced Drillon with Don Metz, a raw rookie, putting him on a line with Nick Metz, his brother, and Dave (Sweeney) Shriner. The trio dominated the rest of the series as the Leafs, who got spectacular goaltending from Turk Broda, did the seemingly impossible and won the Stanley Cup. Drillon never played for the Leafs again.

Many NHL stars of this era enlisted in the Canadian armed forces and served in the war, including Broda, Syl Apps, Bob Goldham, the Metz brothers, Jimmy Orlando, Sid Abel, Mud Bruneteau and Bucko McDonald. The league operated throughout the wartime era, but the quality of competition was thinned by military service.

It was in the 1940s, too, that the NHL stabilized as a six-team league, its constituent members coming to be known as the 'Original Six.' The general managers, the sporting architects of those teams, became as legendary as the players: Frank J. Selke in Montreal; Toronto's Smythe; Jack Adams, who built the great Detroit Red Wings teams of the 1950s; Tommy Ivan with the Chicago Blackhawks.

The Richard Riot

Sports journalist Rejean Tremblay once said: "The Rocket once told me that when he played he felt he was out there for all French Canadians."

Accordingly, all of French Canada was outraged in March 1955 when NHL president Clarence Campbell suspended Richard from the final three regular-season games and the entire playoffs for slugging a linesman in a fracas during a game in Boston.

Campbell, who embodied Anglophone dominance for many French-Canadians, attended the Canadiens' next game, against Detroit, at the Montreal Forum and quickly became a target for the irate Montreal fans seeking revenge for what they perceived as unjustly severe treatment of their hero.

At the end of the first period, a young man approached the NHL executive, extending his hand. But when Campbell held out his for an expected handshake, the man slapped his face. Moments later, a tear-gas bomb was set off behind one of the goals and soon after, the city's fire chief stopped the game, which was forfeited to Detroit.

The 15,000 fans filed out onto Ste-Catherine Street and a procession of pillaging unfolded along the street for several blocks.

The next day, Richard went on radio and television to appeal for calm in Montreal. The incident resonates to this day in Quebec. Many cite it as the spark that touched off the so-called Quiet Revolution, a period of profound and peaceful social change in the early 1960s.

The league entered the 1950s with its depth of talent restored, its membership rock solid and the quality of play impressive.

ICE TALK

"IT WAS BOBBY CLARKE WHO BROUGHT THEM THROUGH. WITH THE SERIES TIED, 3 TO 3, HE CALLED THE FLYER PLAYERS TOGETHER, PUT THEM ALL IN A MOTEL LAST NIGHT AND LAID IT ON THE LINE.

"THEN HE WENT OUT ON THE ICE AND SHOWED THEM HOW TO DO IT. HE DESERVED TO BE THE STAR OF THE GAME BEFORE HE EVEN STEPPED ON THE ICE."

ISLANDERS GERRY HART ON THE FINAL GAME OF THE 1975 STANLEY CUP PLAYOFFS SEMI FINAL

The Rocket and Mr. Hockey

If the overall quality of play was high, two teams stood out head and shoulders above the pack—the Detroit Red Wings and the Montreal Canadiens. Between them the Red Wings and Canadiens won ten of 11 Stanley Cups from 1950–1960. From 1951 through to 1960, the Canadiens made the Stanley Cup finals ten straight times, winning the Cup six times, including five in a row from 1956–60.

Beginning with the 1948–49 season and ending with the 1954–55 campaign, the Red Wings finished first in the regular season seven straight times, topping things off with a Stanley Cup victory four times during that run of excellence.

The Red Wings were constructed around Gordie Howe—Mr. Hockey, a prolific scorer and physically powerful player with a legendary mean streak he often expressed by delivering a pile-driver elbow to an opponent.

The Canadiens' leader was Maurice (Rocket) Richard, a passionate star with a burning desire to win at all costs. Richard's eyes, it was said, lit up like a pinball machine as he crossed the opposition blue line and homed in on the net to score.

In the Stanley Cup semifinals against Boston in 1952, Richard scored one of his most memorable goals. After a thunderous check by Boston's Leo LaBine, Richard left, semi-conscious, for the Forum clinic to have a nasty gash to the head stitched. He returned to the game late in the third period, with the score tied 1–1. His head bandaged, still groggy, Richard fashioned an end-to-end rush that he completed by fending off defenseman Bill Quackenbush with one hand and shovelling a one-handed shot past goaltender Sugar Jim Henry.

With two spectacular stars like Howe and Richard, the NHL's popularity soared, and television broadcasts of NHL games only added to its appeal.

It was a period of consistently fat profits for the club owners: Conn Smythe in Toronto; the Norris family, which owned or controlled the Detroit Red Wings, Chicago Blackhawks and New York Rangers; Weston Adams in Boston; and the Molson family in Montreal.

Some of the players, notably Ted Lindsay of Detroit and Doug Harvey of Montreal, did some figuring and estimating and concluded that they were reaping a small slice of a revenue pie that was much larger than the owners let on.

In 1957, Lindsay was the driving force behind the formation of the National Hockey League Players' Association. The group wanted to take control of the players' pension fund, and channel broadcast revenues from the All-Star game directly into the fund.

The owners were, to say the least, hostile to the players' efforts. Jack Adams, the Red Wings' GM, traded Lindsay and goaltender Glenn Hall, both first-team All-Stars, to the Chicago Blackhawks. The Canadiens, unwilling to lose their best defenseman, waited three years before trading Harvey to the New York Rangers. Ownership battled the players every step of the way and in 1958 the players dropped their attempt to form a legally recognized association.

The exciting on-ice wars between the Red Wings, Canadiens, Bruins and Maple Leafs obscured the decade-ending labor-management skirmish. Far more prominent in the public imagination was the dominance of the Canadiens, who won a record five straight Stanley Cups to close the decade.

The Fog: Fred Shero coached the Philadelphia Flyers to two straight Stanley Cups in the 1970s but couldn't rekindle that magic as coach of the New York Rangers.

The Canadiens of that era were so proficient on the power play they forced a rule change. In 1956–57, the NHL ruled that a penalized player could return to the ice if the opposing team scored a goal in his absence. Previously, a player had to sit out the full two minutes, during which time the potent Canadiens power-play unit sometimes scored two or even three times.

As the league moved into a new decade, Richard retired, but another brilliant player emerged with the Chicago Blackhawks—Bobby Hull. Actually, it was Bernie Geoffrion, one of Richard's ex-teammates, who became the second player to score 50

Skill Set: Anders Hedberg, who played for the Winnipeg Jets as well as the New York Rangers, helped to change the way hockey is played in North America.

ICE TALK

"THERE IS NO WAY (THE CANADIENS) CAN BEAT US WITH A JUNIOR B GOALTENDER."

GEORGE (PUNCH) IMLACH, TORONTO MAPLE LEAFS' GENERAL MANAGER AND HEAD COACH ON ROOKIE MONTREAL GOALIE ROGATIEN VACHON ON THE EVE OF THE 1967 STANLEY CUP FINAL SERIES

goals in a season. Of course, Geoffrion recorded the feat in the 1960–61 season, a 70- not a 50-game season. Hull recorded the first of his five 50-plus goal seasons the following year.

Hull and teammate Stan Mikita were at the top of an impressive list of 1960s scoring stars that included Frank Mahovlich, the still-impressive Howe, Jean Beliveau, Andy Bathgate, Red Kelly, Alex Delvecchio, Rod Gilbert, Ken Wharram, John Bucyk and Norm Ullman.

The Toronto Maple Leafs supplanted the Canadiens as the dominant team in the early 1960s, winning three straight Stanley Cups from 1962–64, but the Canadiens won four in five years from 1964–69. They might have won five straight, except for Toronto's stunning upset victory over Montreal with an aging team in 1967.

That Stanley Cup final was truly the last of an era, because the NHL was preparing for unprecedented growth as the decade wound down.

A Victory for the Aged—Toronto's 1967 Stanley Cup Win

The Montreal Canadiens had won two straight Stanley Cups and seemed a solid bet to win a third as they prepared to meet the Maple Leafs in the final pre-expansion final series.

The Maple Leafs, third-place finishers during the season, had surprised lots of people by knocking off the first-place Chicago Blackhawks in the semifinals, but the younger, speedier Canadiens had swept the New York Rangers in four games, going with rookie goalie Rogatien Vachon.

The Maple Leafs' lineup had an average age of more than 31 years that included 42-year-old goalie Johnny Bower, and 41-year-old defenseman Allan Stanley. Twelve members of the roster were over 30—seven of them over 35.

When the Canadiens won Game 1, 6–2, with Henri Richard recording the hat-trick and Yvan Cournoyer scoring twice, it seemed to confirm the experts' analysis—the younger, quicker Canadiens were simply too good for the aging Leafs.

Then the ageless Bower went out and shut out the Canadiens as Toronto won Game 2, 3–0. The Leafs won Game 3 in overtime 3–2, with Bower brilliant again, making 60 saves. But when he strained his groin in the Game 4 pre-game warm-up, Maple Leafs' coach Punch Imlach had to insert Terry Sawchuk in goal.

The Canadiens seemed to solve Sawchuk, winning 6–3 to even the series 2–2. But Sawchuk only gave up two goals in the final two games—as Toronto stunned the hockey world by winning the series 4–2. The ageless wonders had turned back the clock and rediscovered their prime.

"I felt sick for a month afterwards," said Montreal defenseman Terry Harper. "To lose the Stanley Cup, that was horrible, but to lose to Toronto and have to live in Canada afterwards, oh man—everywhere you'd go you'd run into Leafs' fans, well, that was like losing twice."

ICE TALK

"A MISTAKE HAS BEEN MADE."

NHL President Clarence Campbell, after mistakenly announcing that the expansion Vancouver Canucks would select first over the Buffalo Sabres in the 1971 Entry Draft

Broad Street Bullies

"We take the shortest distance to the puck and arrive in ill humor." That was the Philadelphia Flyers credo, as enunciated by head coach Fred Shero. He wasn't kidding.

The Flyers were constructed around a core of stellar players: goaltender Bernie Parent; defensemen Jim Watson and Bob Dailey; centers Bobby Clarke and Rick MacLeish; and wingers Bill Barber and Reggie Leach.

The supporting cast included some honest checkers like Bill Clement, Terry Crisp and Ross Lonsberry and a platoon of enforcers like Dave (The Hammer) Schultz, Bob (Houndog) Kelly, Don (Big Bird) Saleski, Jack McIlhargey and Andre (Moose) Dupont.

The blend of goaltending brilliance, team defense, toughness and scoring punch helped make the Flyers the first expansion club to win one Stanley Cup, let alone two.

Shero was nicknamed 'The Fog' by his players because he was given to cryptic sayings.

On the day of Game 6 in Philadelphia's Stanley Cup victory over the Boston Bruins in 1974, Shero wrote this message on the chalkboard in the dressing room: "Win together today and we'll walk together forever."

The Flyers won, and carved their names into the Stanley Cup.

So Long, Original Six, Hello Expansion

The success—artistic and financial—of the Original Six had attracted interested investors as early as the mid-1940s. In 1945–46, representatives from Philadelphia, Los Angeles and San Francisco had applied for franchises. The Original Six owners, jealously guarding their rich profit margins, were hostile to the notion for years.

But envious of the lucrative TV contracts U.S. networks were signing with the National Football League, American Football League and Major League Baseball, and recognizing that such riches were definitely beyond the grasp of a six-team, Canadian-based league, the league governors decided to proceed with expansion. The decision was spurred, in part, by aggressive efforts by the Western Hockey League, a development league, to push for major-league status.

The NHL governors received 15 applications for new franchises and in February, 1966, granted teams to Los Angeles, San Francisco, St. Louis, Pittsburgh, Philadelphia and Minnesota. The new franchises cost $2 million US each.

The new teams were grouped together in the West Division, which enabled them to be competitive amongst themselves, even if they weren't really competitive with the six established teams in the East Division. The first three years of expansion, the St. Louis Blues, coached by Scotty Bowman, and staffed with aging stars like Glenn Hall, Jacques Plante, Doug Harvey, Dickie Moore and others, advanced to the Stanley Cup final. Each year, the Blues lost in four straight games.

The third of those three four-game sweeps of the Blues was administered by Bobby Orr and the Boston Bruins. Orr had become the first defenseman in NHL history to record 100 points in 1969-70, when he scored 33 goals and added 87 assists for 120 points to win the scoring championship. Many thought it was the first Stanley Cup of a Boston dynasty, but Orr's career was foreshortened by a series of knee injuries. He left the NHL before he was 30, with just two Stanley Cup rings—1970 and 1972.

Expansion coincided with the establishment of the NHL Players' Association—ten years after Ted Lindsay's effort had failed. A Toronto lawyer named Alan Eagleson had helped striking players on the minor-league Springfield Indians win their dispute with Eddie Shore, the club's president and manager.

That victory helped him win the players' support when, led by a core group of Toronto Maple Leafs players, the association was established in 1967, with Eagleson as its executive director. Players' salaries, kept artificially low for decades, were about to

King of Kings: After Wayne Gretzky was traded to Los Angeles in 1988, it suddenly became chic to be seen at an NHL game in La-La Land.

increase dramatically, but it was a rival league—the World Hockey Association—far more than the Eagleson-led NHLPA that would be responsible.

The Winnipeg WHA franchise provided instant credibility for the rival league by signing Bobby Hull for $1 million Cdn. Then they borrowed Hull's nickname—The Golden Jet—to name their own club. Other high-profile players who followed included J.C. Tremblay, Marc Tardif, Gerry Cheevers and Derek Sanderson.

Many clubs signed players to lucrative contracts rather than lose them to WHA teams.

To combat the upstart league, the NHL kept on expanding, adding Vancouver and Buffalo in 1970. That year, the great Gilbert Perreault was the prize available for the expansion club fortunate enough to choose first in the entry draft. To decide between the Sabres and Canucks, the league brought in a wheel of fortune apparatus, the kind popular at country fairs. The Sabres were assigned numbers one through ten, with the Canucks getting 11-20. The wheel was given a spin and came to rest at the number 1—or so it seemed. Clarence Campbell, the league president announced that the Sabres had won, prompting elation among the Buffalo supporters. But the wheel had stopped at 11. Campbell stepped back to the microphone and uttered this phrase: "A mistake has been made."

Perreault played 17 seasons for the Sabres and scored 512 goals, while Dale Tallon, selected by the Canucks, had a solid, but unspectacular career with Vancouver, Chicago and the Pittsburgh Penguins. Expansion continued in 1972, when Atlanta and the New York Islanders were added, and in 1974 the Kansas City Scouts and the Washington Capitals joined the league. The NHL had tripled in size in just seven years, severly depleting the talent base.

The dilution was made more apparent by the 1972 Summit Series between Canada and the Soviet Union. Canadians expected their pros, who had been banned for years from competing in World Championships or Olympic competitions, to drub the Soviets, but were stunned when the Soviets beat Canada 7–3 in the opening game at the Forum. The Soviet game, with legendary coach Anatoli Tarasov directing its development, had caught up to and, in many areas, passed the Canadian style. That realization stunned a country which prided itself on producing the best hockey players in the world.

Canada, playing on pride, guts and determination, won a narrow series victory with four victories, three losses and one game tied. But the game had changed forever.

On the expansion front, meanwhile, not all the franchises took root where they were first planted. The California Golden Seals moved to Cleveland in 1976, then merged with the struggling Minnesota North Stars in 1979. The Kansas City Scouts moved to Denver, Colorado in 1976 and then in 1982 to East Rutherford, New Jersey, where they remain as the Devils.

In the early expansion days, Montreal general manager Sam Pollock took advantage of expansion to build a 1970s dynasty in Montreal. The Canadiens, rich in solid talent throughout their farm system, swapped good young players, and sometimes established but aging players, to talent-starved expansion clubs for high draft picks.

In this fashion, the Canadiens obtained Guy Lafleur, Steve Shutt, Bob Gainey, Doug Risebrough, Michel Larocque, Mario Tremblay—the building blocks of the six Stanley Cup champions during the 1970s.

Super Mario: The Pittsburgh franchise was struggling when it made Mario Lemieux the first overall draft pick in 1984. Eight years later, he led them to their second straight Stanley Cup.

Many complained that the rapid expansion drastically diluted the talent in the NHL. The Philadelphia Flyers, the first post-expansion club to win the Stanley Cup, certainly weren't overloaded with talent. Their canny coach, Fred Shero, made the most of a small nucleus of excellent talent, led by goalie Bernie Parent, center Bobby Clarke, and wingers Bill Barber and Reggie Leach, and a belligerent style of play that intimidated the opposition.

That formula led the Flyers to back-to-back Stanley Cup championships in 1974 and 1975. By 1976, the Canadiens load of drafted talent—particularly Guy Lafleur—had matured, and Montreal rolled to four straight Stanley Cup championships to close out the 1970s.

The turn of the decade also saw the ten-year war with the

ICE TALK

"I REALLY LOVED EDMONTON. I DIDN'T WANT TO LEAVE. WE HAD A DYNASTY HERE. WHY MOVE?"

WAYNE GRETZKY, ON HIS BEING TRADED TO THE LOS ANGELES KINGS IN 1988, A TRANSACTION THAT SENT ALL OF CANADA INTO A STATE OF MOURNING

WHA resolved, when the only four surviving teams from the rival league—the Quebec Nordiques; Hartford Whalers; Edmonton Oilers; and Winnipeg Jets joined the NHL. The teams were stripped of the talent they had recruited, often in bidding wars with NHL clubs, and denied access to TV revenue for five years after joining the NHL.

As a result, the Jets lost stars Anders Hedberg and Ulf Nilsson, both of whom played for the New York Rangers thereafter. The Oilers were permitted to keep Wayne Gretzky, who had signed a personal services contract with Oilers owner Peter Pocklington. And the Whalers iced a lineup that included 50-year-old Gordie Howe, playing with his sons, Mark and Marty.

The Nordiques' response was be to creative in its recruiting efforts. Club president Marcel Aubut arranged for Slovak stars Peter and Anton Stastny to defect from Czechoslovakia, and the pair were joined one year later by older brother Marian. The Stastnys, especially Peter and Anton, became the scoring stars on the rebuilt Nordiques.

The success of the Stastnys helped convince NHL managers that there were rich veins of talent in Europe that had to be tapped. Communism was one major obstacle to doing so immediately, however.

There were few large impediments to importing Scandinavian talent, though, as the New York Islanders found out. They won four straight Stanley Cups, beginning in 1980, with some talented Scandinavians, like Tomas Jonsson, Stefan Persson, Anders Kallur and Mats Hallin, playing important roles.

The European influence really took hold in the NHL, though, with the Edmonton Oilers, who supplanted the Islanders as the NHL's pre-eminent team in 1984, when they won the first of five Stanley Cups in seven years.

Glen Sather, the Oilers' general manager and coach, sprinkled some talented Europeans like Jari Kurri, Esa Tikkanen, Reijo Ruotsalainen, Kent Nilsson and Willy Lindstrom around the Edmonton lineup, with good results.

But Sather went one step further, borrowing much from the flowing, speed-based European style and adapting it to the NHL. Sather once described the Oilers' style as the Montreal Canadiens (of the 1970s) updated for the 1980s.

The style of play—executed by great players like Gretzky, Mark Messier, Glenn Anderson, Paul Coffey and Kurri—helped Sather construct a Canadiens-like 1980s dynasty.

Thinking Globally

As the NHL moved toward the 1990s the governors began to develop a larger vision. This was not an easy process. The traditions and mind-set of the Original Six had continued to dominate the league well after expansion had transformed a small, regional league into a continental one, albeit a weak sister compared to major-league baseball, football and basketball.

The NHL had evolved into a 21-team league but was controlled by the triumvirate of league president John Ziegler, Chicago Blackhawks owner Bill Wirtz and NHLPA executive-director Alan Eagleson.

The league had traditionally been gate-driven, dominated by shrewd entrepreneurs like Smythe, the Norrises, the Wirtz family and the Molsons, who owned their own arenas and knew how to fill them but had little feel for or interest in marketing the league as a whole.

A series of linked events began to change this. By the summer of 1988, Wayne Gretzky had led the Edmonton Oilers to four Stanley Cups and established himself as the best player in hockey. But to Oilers owner Peter Pocklington he was a depreciating asset whose value had peaked.

Pocklington traded Gretzky to the Los Angeles Kings—sending Edmontonians, and Canadians in general, into mourning, and stunning NHL ownership.

Bruce McNall, then the Kings' owner, promptly raised Gretzky's salary. He reasoned that Gretzky would generate far greater revenues for the Kings, both at the gate and through advertising and he was proved right.

Two years later, the St. Louis Blues used similar logic when they signed Brett Hull, their franchise player, to a three-year contract. Then they signed restricted free agent defenseman Scott Stevens to a four-year deal.

While salaries were rising, there were other parts of the hockey business taking off as well. In the United States more people watched NHL hockey on Fox and ESPN than ever before. In Canada, Saturday became a double dream as *Hockey Night in Canada* began running doubleheaders. And in the US and Canada the NHL found success in five new markets. Anaheim, Ottawa, San Jose, Miami Florida and Tampa Bay all greeted the game with excitement and big crowds. The value of an NHL franchise rose and the level of people wanting to own a team grew.

As the economics of major professional hockey changed, the NHL realized that the old, gate-driven model would not work anymore. Hockey entrepreneurs began to build new, larger arenas, which featured scores of so-called luxury suites, hotel-plush boxes designed to enable corporate executives and guests to enjoy a game in high style.

New forms of advertising

Across the Continental divide: Edmonton GM/coach Glen Sather had his high-flying Oilers play a European style, which led to five Stanley Cups in a seven-year span.

Labor Man: Under executive-director Bob Goodenow, the NHL Players' Association has become more proactive about getting its share of the NHL revenue pie.

opportunities—on scoreboards, rink boards, even on the ice itself—were deployed to generate more money. And the NHL, long a marketing luddite among major professional leagues, got into the merchandising business in a concerted way.

As the hockey business grew more sophisticated, the players became more assertive about their interests, also. Dissatisfaction with the now-disgraced NHLPA executive-director Alan Eagleson's autocratic, company-union style had been growing and, in 1990, the players selected former agent Bob Goodenow, the man who had negotiated Brett Hull's blockbuster contract, as their new director.

At the end of the 1992 season, the players staged an 11-day strike, demanding, among other things, the marketing rights to their own likenesses. They wanted a chunk of the revenue pie, in other words, and were prepared to fight to get it. The players also sought more relaxed free agency guidelines enabling them to sell themselves on the market.

As the league adjusted to a new economic and labor reality, it sought new leadership capable of achieving peace with the players and the league's on-ice officials, and proactively directing its newly ambitious business aspirations.

In 1992, a search committee selected Gary Bettman, a lawyer and former executive with the marketing-slick National Basketball Association to become the league's first commissioner.

Early in his tenure, Bettman made a business statement by recruiting two powerful new partners to set up NHL franchises—the Disney Corporation and Blockbuster Entertainment.

Michael Eisner, the Disney CEO, named his company's team the Mighty Ducks of Anaheim, after a commercially successful movie of the same name. Wayne Huizenga, head of Blockbuster, established a second team in Florida, the Panthers, based in Miami.

It had long been a cliché that pro sports was an entertainment business, but recruiting the likes of Eisner and Huizenga suggested that NHL head office had actually begun to believe this maxim.

One team—the Ottawa Senators—misread the market and grossly overestimated the promotional opportunities available to young stars when they signed untried No. 1 draft pick Alexandre Daigle to a five-year contract in June 1993. The deal included a marketing component that was unrealistically generous for an unproven rookie.

If the Gretzky, Hull and Stevens contracts had lifted the salary ceiling, the Daigle deal significantly raised the entry level and helped cause an ownership backlash. The notion of a rookie salary cap took hold and a second owner-player showdown in three years loomed.

The result was a lockout that cancelled 468 games from October 1, 1994 to January 19, 1995, shrinking the regular season to 48 games with no inter-conference play. The deal finally struck included a rookie salary cap and provided somewhat greater freedom of movement for older players.

The new, five-year deal couldn't help franchises stuck with outmoded arenas, however, and two Canadian teams, the Quebec Nordiques and Winnipeg Jets, moved south to Denver and Phoenix, respectively—Quebec for 1995–96, Winnipeg for the 1996–97 season. The move proved successful for Colorado when they won the Stanley Cup in their first year. A small-market American franchise also packed its bags for the South, as the Hartford Whalers became the Carolina Hurricanes in 1997.

The Next One

Eric Lindros was so dominant as a junior hockey player that he was dubbed 'The Next One'—Wayne Gretzky being 'The Great One'—well before he was drafted No. 1 overall by the Quebec Nordiques in 1991.

He was also supremely confident in his ability and secure in the knowledge that his extraordinary skill and potential as a marketing vehicle gave him unprecedented leverage to negotiate.

He warned Nordiques president Marcel Aubut, with whom he did not get along, not to draft him, saying he would refuse to report if he were selected. Sure enough, Quebec drafted him and Lindros, true to his word, did not report. He played another year of junior and for Canada's Olympic team at the 1992 Olympics in Albertville, France.

In June 1992, Aubut invited a bidding contest for Lindros and thought he had made a blockbuster deal with the New York Rangers. But the Philadelphia Flyers also had an offer on the table that included $15 million US, six players and two first-round draft picks.

An arbitrator was called in and he awarded Lindros to the Flyers in one of the most bizarre transactions in NHL history.

First Commish: On NHL commissioner Gary Bettman's watch, the NHL has expanded into new US markets, and built the fan base.

Going For Gold

The 1997–98 season was an historic one for the NHL, which, for the first time ever, suspended operations to enable the stars from all participating countries to join their respective national teams to compete at the 1998 Winter Olympics in Nagano, Japan. The result was the first-ever best-on-best men's hockey tournament and the Czech Republic won the gold medal, beating Russia 1–0 in the final.

The Olympic Games gave the NHL a great chance to move further away from its pa.rochial Original Six mentality and further establish itself as a major force in the international sporting market.

As the league's vision continues to expand globally, so does its roster of franchises. The Nashville Predators and Atlanta Thrashers launched their franchises in 1998 and 1999, respectively, and the league swelled to 30 teams with the addition of the Minnesota Wild and the Columbus (Ohio) Blue Jackets in 2000. Unlike previous expansion efforts, the NHL, under Bettman, deployed its considerable marketing forces not just to ensure that individual franchises succeeded, but to implant a hockey culture across the United States.

Through its state-of-the-art website, grassroots programs such as the NHL's involvement with in-line and street hockey, as well as its growing involvement with women's hockey, the league is, in fact, raising the profile of the NHL as well as the sport of hockey itself.

Now that the NHL has entered a new millenium, the marketing momentum is building; the league and the sport are growing. Its future has never been more exciting.

Mightiest Duck: Disney Company CEO Michael Eisner transposed cinematic marketing techniques to help sell the sport of hockey in Southern California.

Teams in the NHL

With the growth of the National Hockey League in North America and the influx of bright international stars like Jaromir Jagr, Sergei Fedorov and Peter Forsberg, the NHL is showcasing more individual talent than it ever has. Yet the team concept continues to endure as the bedrock principle of the sport. It's a cliché in hockey that no player—no matter how spectacular his contribution—is bigger than his team.

Consider Eric Lindros, one of the true superstar talents in the NHL. Lindros entered the NHL with Philadelphia in the 1992–93 season, loaded down with achievements. He had helped the Oshawa Generals win the Memorial Cup as Canada's best junior team, helped Canada's National Junior Team win the World Junior Hockey Championship, helped Team Canada win the 1991 Canada Cup (now the World Cup of Hockey) tournament, and helped Canada's Olympic team win a silver medal at the 1992 Winter Olympics in Albertville, France.

He has continued to pile up awards in the NHL, winning the Hart Trophy as the league's most valuable player in 1995. But Lindros and his growing number of followers had to wait while the Flyers surrounded their awesomely talented star with the right supporting cast before seeing their hero lead Philadelphia into the Stanley Cup Finals for the first time in his era in 1997.

The ultimate standard

Successful hockey teams are an amalgam of coaching acumen, solid team defense, great goaltending, timely scoring, leadership, fan support and the most elusive factor of all—team chemistry.

Coaches set the tone for success and none was more successful than Hector (Toe) Blake, the legendary coach of the Montreal Canadiens in the 1950s and 1960s.

In his first meeting with his team, in October 1955, Blake told his players: "There are some guys in this room who play better than I ever did. I have nothing to teach them. But what I can show you all is how to play better as a team."

Blake obviously succeeded. In 13 years as coach of the Canadiens, the team finished first in the regular season nine times and won eight Stanley Cups, including five straight from 1956–60.

Scoring titles and individual awards may be the measure of a player's excellence, but NHL teams are measured by one standard only—their ability to win the Stanley Cup.

Doom Trooper: Big, offensively skilled John LeClair won a Cup with Montreal in 1993, but as a Flyer he has yet to claim the sport's ultimate prize.

An entire generation of Toronto Maple Leafs fans has grown to adulthood without seeing their club win the Cup, yet the legend of an aging Leafs club that did win it in 1967 lives on.

In the early 1970s, the New York Islanders entered the NHL as an expansion club and were carefully crafted into a formidable group by general manager Bill Torrey. The validation of Torrey's genius in drafting Denis Potvin, Mike Bossy, Bryan Trottier, Clark Gillies and others was the four straight Stanley Cups the Islanders won, beginning in 1980.

As great as those stars were, though, the Islanders championship chemistry didn't click until Torrey traded for Butch Goring, a speedy, gritty, centerman. Goring checked the opposing team's top center and, a keen student of the game, designed the Islanders' penalty killing system.

The Edmonton Oilers of the 1980s were loaded with offensive firepower, boasting the likes of Wayne Gretzky, Jari Kurri, Glenn Anderson, Paul Coffey and Mark Messier. But they didn't become champions until coach Glen Sather had taught them to play solid, if not necessarily brilliant, team defense.

Mario Lemieux led Pittsburgh to two straight Stanley Cup triumphs in the early 1990s, but a key member of both teams was Trottier, who brought invaluable playoff experience to those Pittsburgh teams.

New York fans of a certain age have fond memories of stars like Jean Ratelle, Rod Gilbert and Vic Hadfield, the famous GAG (Goal-a-game) line of the 1970s. But none of those players ever won a Stanley Cup.

The Rangers faithful had to wait until 1994, after Messier, who learned how to be a champion with the Oilers, had moved to New York and instilled team values in his new teammates.

Jarome Iginla was one of the many highlights of the 2001-2002 season. His league-best 52 goals and 96 points for Calgary confirmed him as a genuine superstar.

Saving goals

And no team can succeed without great goaltending: the Islanders' Billy Smith; Grant Fuhr of the Oilers; the Rangers' Mike Richter; Tom Barrasso of the Penguins.

No goalie can boast a Stanley Cup performance chart quite like Patrick Roy of the Colorado Avalanche. He led the Canadiens to a Stanley Cup as a rookie in 1986 and backstopped them to another in 1993, when he cooly closed the door on the opposition as Montreal won 10 games in overtime.

In 1996, Roy's stingy netminding was central to Colorado winning the Stanley Cup. In that four-game sweep of the Florida Panthers, Roy gave up just four goals total—one per game. In 1995-96, the talent-rich Red Wings won a record 62 regular-season games, breaking the old record for most victories in a season (60) set in 1976–77 by the Canadiens. But that Montreal team was in the process of winning four straight Stanley Cups.

In 1998–99, the Stanley Cup finally was won by a team from the sunny southern United States. The Dallas Stars had the best regular season record and went on to win the Cup in six games.

The Devils won it all in 1999–00 and just lost out in seven games the following year to the Colorado Avalanche.

In 2001–02, the Detroit Red Wings added to their triumphs in 1997 and 1998, as they again proved to be the NHL's finest.

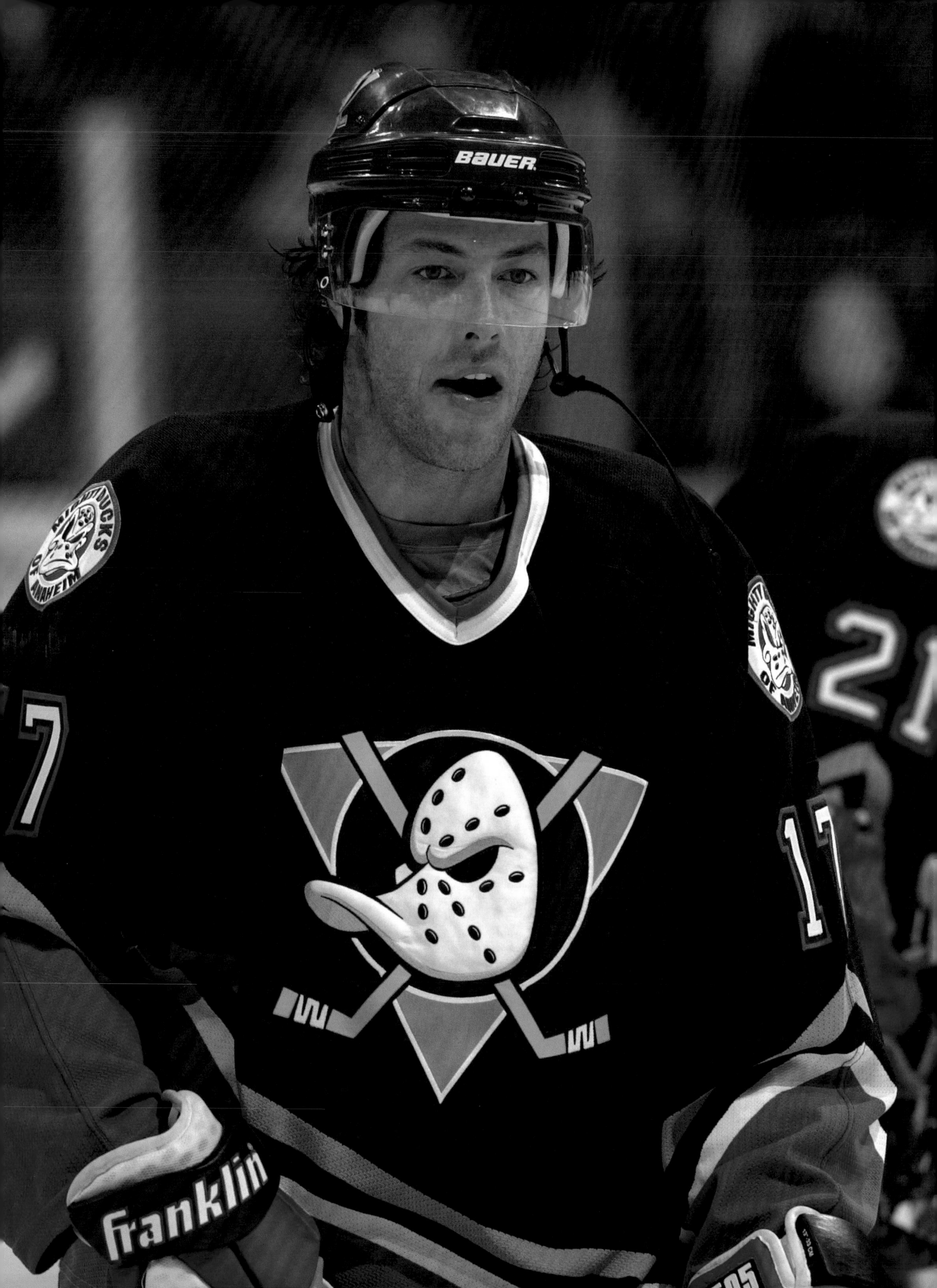
BAUER
Franklin

Mighty Ducks of Anaheim

With the Kariya-Selanne partnership no more, the Ducks are searching for a new formula for success.

It figures that a team based so close to Hollywood would have one of the NHL's most exciting leading men. Paul Kariya is as skilled as they come—blazing speed, shifty moves, rifle shot, soft hands. He's been the cornerstone of the franchise since joining the club in its second year of existence in 1994. For a few years, he had a fellow superstar—Teemu Selanne—on his opposite wing to help shoulder the load. But since Selanne was traded to San Jose in 2000–01, teams have been able to focus on Kariya, and wins have been hard to come by for the Ducks.

In 2001–02, Anaheim struggled, losing 13 more games than it won and finishing with 69 points in the Western Conference. If the Ducks are to return to playoff caliber, some of Kariya's teammates will have to chip in more offense. Anaheim finished 29th out of 30 in the NHL in goals scored last year. Even Kariya struggled with just 32 goals among 57 points.

Babcock takes charge

The task of solving what ails the Ducks falls to new coach Mike Babcock, who was promoted from the bench of minor-league affiliate Cincinnati. Babcock was hired by Bryan Murray, who gave up the team's coaching duties to concentrate on the general manager position he inherited at season's end.

There is good material to work with on the defensive end of the equation. The 198 goals allowed last year was a franchise best. And the Ducks seemed to gel down the stretch, finishing 15–13–2 over the last 30 games. There is a solid corps of defensemen, led by offensive-minded Oleg Tverdovsky and proven veterans Jason York, Keith Carney and Ruslan Salei. The latter practically willed his underdog Belarus team to surprising success at the 2002 Winter Olympics. In net, Jean-Sebastien Giguere is growing into a franchise goalie, finishing last year with a 2.13 goals-against-average.

Babcock has room for optimism up front, too. Speedy Jeff Friesen has been a 30-goal scorer and is capable of returning to that level, especially since he should just be entering his peak years at age 26. Mike Leclerc keeps getting better every year. German Titov is a two-way center who has had three 20-goal seasons, and Matt Cullen is another talented pivot. Plus, the team plays hard every night, which every coach loves to see.

Celluloid birth

The NHL's Mighty Ducks probably wouldn't exist if it hadn't been for Emilio Estevez and a rag-tag bunch of skaters who turned a Disney production into a celluloid success.

"The movie was our market research," recalls Disney chairman Michael Eisner, who approached the NHL about an expansion franchise after the screen version of the Mighty Ducks grossed almost $60 million.

In the fall of 1993, the real-life Mighty Ducks became the NHL's third California-based member, joining the Los Angeles Kings and San Jose Sharks, and were the league's big surprise that first year, tying an NHL first-year team record with 33 victories, including 19 road wins, the most ever by a first-year club.

In the strike-shortened 1994–95 season, they developed their first star players, such as Kariya and Tverdovsky, who was then traded, along with center Chad Kilger, to obtain the high-scoring Selanne from the Winnipeg Jets on February 7, 1996.

The Mighty Ducks are equally powerful at the marketing and merchandising level. Their logo—a goalie mask resembling an angry duck—and team colors of purple, jade, silver, and white are big sellers well beyond the Magic Kingdom.

Matt Cullen finished the year as the Ducks assists leader with 30.

★ ROLL OF HONOR ★

Conference/Division	**Western/Pacific**
First Season	**1993–94**
Honor roll	**Share record for most wins (33) by first-year team**
Home rink/Capacity	**Arrowhead Pond/17,174**
Stanley Cups	**0**

Playing Record

	W	L	T	RT	Pts
Regular Season	269	338	88	11	637
Playoffs	4	11			

Many hockey observers believe that the speedy Paul Kariya is the current version of Wayne Gretzky, combining speed, skill and an uncanny ability to anticipate how plays will develop.

Atlanta Thrashers

With Heatley and Kovalchuk firing, better days are seemingly 'round the corner for the Thrashers.

It hasn't been easy for the Atlanta Thrashers in their first three years as an NHL club. Struggling with growing pains, the club's finishes in the league standings are not unusual for an expansion franchise.

But hope for the future arrived in 2001–02 in a big way. The Thrashers unleashed the two top rookies on the league in forwards Dany Heatley and Ilya Kovalchuk. Heatley led all rookies in points with 67 and Kovalchuk was second with 51, despite playing in just 65 of 82 games. Kovalchuk's 29 goals were tops among newcomers, with Heatley No. 2 with 26. In the YoungStars Game during All-Star Weekend, which featured four-on-four hockey played by the league's best young players, Kovalchuk stole the show, scoring six goals and making a pile of head-turning plays. Heatley and Kovalchuk have the potential to become a dominant combination like Colorado has with Joe Sakic and Peter Forsberg.

Building a foundation

The Thrashers have done a good job in the draft and there is a solid core of young talent besides Heatley and Kovalchuk. But in a quest for immediate improvement, General Manager Don Waddell was committed in the off-season to being active in the free-agent market. The Thrashers can stand to improve most in the defensive aspects of the game. Atlanta allowed a league-high 288 goals last season, 30 more than the next-closest team. The Thrashers would like to see a true No. 1 goalie emerge from the vowel-heavy crew of Milan Hnilicka, Pasi Nurminen and Frederic Cassivi.

Every team needs toughness and leadership and in Atlanta those qualities are packaged together in the form of right wing Jeff Odgers, who missed much of last season with a broken leg. He is a valuable bodyguard to the Thrashers forwards. Journeyman center Tony Hrkac is another veteran presence in the locker room who last year had his best scoring season ever with 18 goals. Lubos Bartecko adds youth and skill to the wing. Coach Curt Fraser has some positive pieces in place as the Thrashers look to improve on their output of 187 goals, which was fifth-lowest in the league.

Atlanta will look for Dany Heatley to build on his impressive rookie season numbers.

Hockey returns

Atlanta was the NHL's original Deep South team when the expansion Flames debuted in 1972 with legendary Bernie "Boom Boom" Geoffrion as coach. The Atlanta Flames toiled in the league for eight years without achieving much success, then bolted in 1980 to become the Calgary Flames.

The NHL's return to the home of the Braves began on June 25, 1997, when Atlanta was awarded an NHL expansion team. Like the baseball Braves and NBA Hawks, the Thrashers are a division of Turner Sports, Inc., an AOL Time Warner Company. Famed head honcho Ted Turner supposedly liked the name Thrashers because the state bird is the Brown Thrasher.

Quite a draw

With so many transplants in the area from traditional hockey hotbeds, the sport is growing rapidly in Georgia and the city was excited to see the NHL return. A billboard hovering above a downtown freeway counted down the days until the Thrashers' first game and the enthusiasm remained throughout year one, despite a tough season on the ice.

Atlanta broke the record for average attendance by a first-year team, drawing 17,205 per game to top the mark of 16,989 set by the 1993–94 Mighty Ducks of Anaheim.

Tony Hrkac finished the season with a valuable 44 points.

★ ROLL OF HONOR ★

Conference/Division	**Eastern/Southeast**
First Season	**1999-2000**
Honor roll	**Set attendance record for an expansion team: 705,398**
Home rink/Capacity	**Philips Arena/18,750**
Stanley Cups	**0**

Playing Record

	W	*L*	*T*	*RT*	*Pts*
Regular Season	**56**	**149**	**30**	**11**	**153**
Playoffs	**0**	**0**			

BOSTON BRUINS

The Bruins' return to form in 2001–2002 looks set to last with Thornton and Guerin at the helm.

Things seem to be back to normal in Beantown. The Bruins are among the NHL's best teams again. A franchise that went 29 straight seasons with a winning record from 1967–68 through 1995–96 hit a bit of a rough patch in recent seasons, finishing out of the playoffs in both 1999–2000 and 2000–01.

But the Bruins bounced back big last season, posting the best record in the Eastern Conference and the second-best record overall with 101 points. Arch-rival Montreal dispatched the Bruins in the first round of the 2002 tournament. That disappointment could not take away from the fact that this is a good team, one poised to be good for several years.

At the heart of the resurgence is Joe Thornton. Boston has a habit of developing franchise players, and since the last one left town a few seasons ago in the personage of Ray Bourque, Thornton has basked in the spotlight. The 23-year-old former No. 1 pick has scored 82 goals in the past three seasons combined. He's missed at least 10 games in each of the past two seasons, so keeping him healthy is a priority. His tough, physical brand of hockey sometimes makes that difficult.

Solid everywhere

The Bruins are equally adept at scoring goals and preventing them. They ranked seventh in the league in goals for last year and 11th in goals against. Besides Thornton, the offensive pyrotechnics are provided by Glen Murray, a prototypical power forward obtained from Los Angeles last season, Sergei Samsonov, the dynamic, young Russian, and speedy Brian Rolston. Murray's 41 goals last year tied for second in the league with teammate Bill Guerin. Guerin, a leader on the ice and off, was one of two major free agents team management would have to make a decision on in the off-season. The other was goalie Byron Dafoe, the team's most important player for several seasons.

The blue line is anchored by aggressive defensemen Sean O'Donnell and Hal Gill. The Bruins feature a tenacious penalty-kill unit that ranked best in the league last season, but to really make the special teams work for them they need to improve on their power play which ranked 26th out of 30 teams. The experienced hand of coach Robbie Ftorek guides this bunch. The former coach of Los Angeles and New Jersey was a 2002 finalist for the Jack Adams Award given to the league's top bench boss.

Awesome Orr

Boston's last Cup triumph was in 1972. That Cup, like the one in 1970, featured the uplifting play of young defenseman Bobby Orr, who first arrived on the scene in 1966–67, after the Bruins had missed the playoffs for seven straight seasons.

On May 10, 1970, Orr, arguably the best defenseman ever until his knees gave out after ten years with Boston, left his personal imprint on the team's first Cup win in 29 years, scoring the winning goal against St. Louis.

Joe Thornton continues to shine in Boston.

Storied franchise

One of the original six NHL teams, the Bruins started play in the 1924–25 season. They were fortunate to have had several glittering performers grace their roster in ensuing years—notably the tough guy defenseman Eddie Shore, right winger Dit Clapper and center Milt Schmidt. But despite these talents they had only three Stanley Cups to their credit before Orr, slick center Phil Esposito and (Chief) Johnny Bucyk combined their talents for the two Cups in the early 1970s.

Orr was the first NHL defenseman to win the scoring title, achieving the feat in 1969-70. Esposito won five scoring titles in just over eight seasons with Boston. In 1968–69, he became the first NHL player to amass more than 100 points in a single season.

Byron Dafoe (right) finished the 2001–2002 season with a 2.13 goals against average.

★ ROLL OF HONOR ★

Conference/Division	**Eastern/Northeast**
First Season	**1924–25**
Honor roll	**29 straight winning seasons**
Home rink/Capacity	**Fleet Center/17,565**
Stanley Cups:	**5 (1929, 1939, 1941, 1970, 1972)**

Playing Record

	W	*L*	*T*	*RT*	*Pts*
Regular Season	**2287**	**1947**	**765**	**23**	**5762**
Playoffs	**238**	**256**	**6**		

Buffalo Sabres

With Hasek now in Detroit, the Sabres missed the playoffs to conclude a disappointing year.

The Buffalo Sabres are still adjusting to life A.H.—After Hasek. For nearly a decade, Dominik Hasek defined the Sabres. The netminder with a "slinky for a spine" earned six Vezina Trophies as the league's top net minder and two Hart Trophies as NHL MVP during his stay with Buffalo. But in the summer of 2001, "The Dominator" got his wish to be traded to a Stanley Cup contender and packed his bags for Detroit. Without him, the Sabres missed the playoffs for just the second time since 1987.

Actually, the Sabres are pretty well stocked at the position Hasek vacated. Goaltender is a traditional strength in Buffalo, and Martin Biron has all the makings of an elite backstopper. Further down the depth chart, Mika Noronen and Ryan Miller are prized goaltending prospects. The play in net isn't what has the Sabres looking for a return to playoff caliber—a lack of consistency is. As a result, Buffalo finished at .500, five points out of the last playoff spot.

Power outage

While the Sabres are strong on the penalty kill, the club is in need of some explosive players on offense to increase their power play percentage. There is one proven sharpshooter on offense—Miroslav Satan. He tied for ninth in the league with 37 goals last year. He has averaged 35 goals per season over the past four. There are several youngsters who have done it in spurts, just not as consistently as Satan. That group includes J.P. Dumont, Maxim Afinogenov and Tim Connolly, whom Buffalo will look to carry a heavy burden of the scoring. As these young stars grow and develop, so too will the club's chances of climbing up the standings and realizing loftier playoff expectations.

Stu Barnes is a great lead-by-example captain. The man Buffalo got in exchange for Hasek, forward Slava Kozlov, was just hitting his stride last year when he suffered a season-ending achilles injury. Kozlov was traded to Atlanta on draft weekend in June. The defense is solid, led by Russian workhorse Alexei Zhitnik.

Lindy Ruff has been coaching Buffalo since 1997, a rare feat of longevity in a profession rife with turnover. He is a stabilizing force on the bench. This was a small-market team which had to rely on smart drafts and quality player development to remain competitive. With more confidence as a team and as young players mature, the Sabres only look to reap the rewards of a more aged and well-developed power play unit.

Tim Connolly contributed 45 points in his sophomore year in Buffalo.

Flashy past

The Sabres were once one of the NHL's flashiest offensive teams. The franchise scored a major coup months before it took to the ice for the first time in the 1970–71 season. Through a stroke of luck—the spin of a numbered wheel—the Sabres got the first draft pick ahead of their expansion cousin, the Vancouver Canucks.

George (Punch) Imlach, the wily former Toronto Maple Leafs coach who was the Sabres' first coach and general manager, plucked a rangy, swift-skating magician named Gilbert Perreault from the junior ranks. The high-scoring center was an anchor for more than a decade, especially when teamed with youngsters Rick Martin and Rene Robert to form the French Connection line. Perreault and Martin still rank 1–2 in club history for goals scored, with 512 and 382, respectively. The trio powered the Sabres to the Stanley Cup final in 1975, where they lost to Philadelphia in six games: a sobering end to their best season—they had a franchise-high 113 points in winning their first Adams Division title. Until 1999, the Sabres had never been closer to a Stanley Cup title, despite the promise of the Scotty Bowman era in the early 1980s.

But Bowman did become the winningest NHL coach while in Buffalo. He passed Dick Irvin's 690 career coaching wins in 1984.

Miroslav Satan continued to find the net for the Sabres in 2001–2002, finishing with 37 goals.

★ ROLL OF HONOR ★

Conference/Division	**Eastern/Northeast**
First Season	**1970–71**
Honor roll	**Stanley Cup Finalists, 1975, 1999**
Home rink/Capacity	**HSBC Arena/18,690**
Stanley Cups	**0**

Playing Record

	W	*L*	*T*	*RT*	*Pts*
Regular Season	**1193**	**951**	**392**	**6**	**2784**
Playoffs	**99**	**110**			

Calgary Flames

Keeping free agent Jarome Iginla in a Calgary jersey is the key to a Flames revival in form.

The Calgary Flames are hoping that seven is their lucky number. The Flames have missed the playoffs six straight seasons. That's the longest current drought in the NHL, equaled by Tampa Bay. Calgary is getting closer to the postseason tournament, however. Its 79 points last year was its most since posting 79 in 1995–96, the last Flames playoff season.

As the Flames build toward contender status, their biggest off-season concern was re-signing restricted free agent Jarome Iginla. The gifted, young winger had a breakout year in 2001–02. He led the league in goals (52) and points (96) and made the jump from rising star to supernova. At 25 years old, he is just entering his athletic prime.

Iginla has given credit to center Craig Conroy for helping elevate his game. Conroy came to Calgary in the spring of 2001 from St. Louis and has been a factor at both ends of the ice. Besides leading the team in assists (49) and finishing second in goals (28) and points (77) last year, he was a finalist for the Selke Award, given to the league's best defensive forward

The exciting Iginla led the NHL with 52 goals in 2001–2002.

Looking for firepower

Calgary will be looking to get more offensive production from the supporting cast this season. The Flames were in the bottom third of NHL teams last year in goals despite having the league's top sniper. More will be expected of the likes of Dean McAmmond and Marc Savard, both of whom have shown flashes.

The defense is anchored by Derek Morris, the power play quarterback. The only thing standing between Morris and elite status in the league is a penchant for injuries. But he is only 24 years old and an anchor of the franchise. Roman Turek provides an established No. 1 goalie in the Flames' net. One area Calgary needs to improve in if it is to become a playoff team is the penalty kill. Special teams win games and the Flames had one of the worst penalty kills in the league last year. The last time Calgary won a playoff series was during its championship spring of 1989. Of course, after six years away from the big dance, fans in Calgary would be happy just to get to the postseason.

Heading South

Exciting was a word used in 1972, when the Flames' franchise got its start—in Atlanta. It was a bold move by the NHL, as it was their first venture into the Deep South of the United States, an experiment that lasted seven years after Georgia businessman Tom Cousins was granted a franchise.

Former Montreal Canadiens star and legend Bernie "Boom Boom" Geoffrion served as coach and showman in the early years, wooing fans by the thousands in an accent every bit as sweet as a Georgia peach. Excited fans would flock to the 15,000-seat rink known as The Omni to watch Geoffrion direct a stunning ice symphony with awesome performers such as dynamic goaltender Daniel Bouchard and flashy forwards Jacques Richard, Eric Vail and Guy Chouinard.

Moving Flames

Alas, the novelty soon wore off. Geoffrion was gone by 1975, and so was the franchise five years later, purchased by Vancouver real-estate magnate Nelson Skalbania, and transferred to Calgary.

It was a humble beginning in the Flames' new abode, the 7,000-seat Stampede Corral, where the club remained until moving into the 20,000-seat Saddledome in 1983.

The Flames would win one Stanley Cup, two Conference titles and two best-overall crowns over the next 15 years. (Badger) Bob Johnson arrived from the University of Wisconsin to coach the Flames in 1982 and took them to the Stanley Cup final in 1985–86.

Three years later, with wisecracking Terry Crisp at the helm, Calgary won its first Cup, becoming the first visiting team to do so against the Canadiens at the Montreal Forum. Fittingly, it was the final bow for Lanny McDonald, the bushy-lipped co-captain who had come to epitomize the heart and soul of the team.

Center Craig Conroy helped his teammates to elevate their game, leading the Flames in assists.

★ ROLL OF HONOR ★

Conference/Division	**Western/Northwest**
First Season	**1972–73 (Atlanta); 1980–81 (Calgary)**
Honor roll:	**First overall in 1987–88, 1988–89**
Home rink/Capacity	**Pengrowth Saddledome/17,158**
Stanley Cups:	**1 (1989)**

Playing Record

	W	*L*	*T*	*RT*	*Pts*
Regular Season	**1071**	**944**	**359**	**12**	**2513**
Playoffs	**69**	**87**			

CAROLINA HURRICANES

The Hurricanes had a fairytale 2001–2002 season that saw them reach the Stanley Cup finals. This year they will look to win it all.

NHL hockey is no longer a novelty in North Carolina. After the former Hartford Whalers moved to Carolina in 1997, the franchise spent a couple of seasons in virtual obscurity in Greensboro before moving to Raleigh.

And after a few seasons in Raleigh, fans got to experience the most exciting event in hockey—the Stanley Cup Finals. Now the Hurricanes are the talk of the town.

Carolina made a Cinderella-like run to the Finals last spring after finishing with just the seventh-best record in the Eastern Conference, but it dropped four straight to powerhouse Detroit in the big series after winning game one in overtime. That gives this young and improving squad major motivation for spring 2003—the players saw first-hand the jubilation of the winning Red Wings in addition to the dedication and teamplay necessary to lift that holy grail You can bet if the Canes get deep in the playoffs again, they won't just be happy to be there.

ROLL OF HONOR

Conference/Division	**Eastern/Southeast**
First seasons	**1979–80 (Hartford); 1997–98 (Carolina)**
Honor roll	**Southeast Division title, 1999, 2002**
Home rink/Capacity	**Raleigh Entertainment & Sports Arena/ 18,730**
Stanley Cups	**0**

Playing Record

	W	L	T	RT	Pts
Regular Season	711	873	238	8	1668
Playoffs	35	49			

Ron Francis is the league's quietest superstar.

Young nucleus

There is a solid core in place in Carolina. There are several proven goals scorers, including franchise legend Ron Francis, who potted that game-one overtime winner. He will be a first-ballot Hall of Famer. Fellow pivot Rod Brind'Amour is another proven veteran with two-way skills. The foundation for the future is Jeff O'Neill. The 26-year-old has scored a combined 72 goals in the last two seasons. Sami Kapanen is a speedy sniper who dates back to the Whaler days, and Bates Battaglia is known for his solid backchecking to complement a nice scoring touch. Erik Cole became a star in the playoffs as a rookie as part of the BBC line with Brind'Amour and Battaglia.

The defense is solid if not flashy. Sean Hill, Glen Wesley, Aaron Ward and the boys stifled opponents in the playoffs, and workhorse Bret Hedican proved to be a nifty midseason trade acquisition. Goaltending is a strength no matter who is between the pipes. Arturs Irbe and Kevin Weekes both had brilliant moments in the playoffs and their teammates showed a lot of confidence in them. Carolina tends to play a close-to-the-vest game that relies on making the most of the other team's mistakes.

Frustrating misses

Hartford was one of four WHA teams to join the NHL in 1979—along with Winnipeg, Quebec and Edmonton. The Whalers fans were loyal to the end, although the lack of a winning tradition was often a source of frustration. The team finished first in its division only once—in 1986–87—and, that season aside, it never ended higher than fourth place. The Whalers missed the playoffs 10 times in their 17 years in Hartford.

Hartford's first NHL season featured the awe-inspiring Howe family, the legendary Gordie—whom the Whalers had signed to a WHA contract in 1977—and sons Mark and Marty. Gordie, a 50-year-old grandfather, played in all 80 games in 1979–80, scoring 15 goals and collecting 41 points, inspiring his young and adoring teammates to the playoffs before retiring at the end of the season.

The player who has most marked the Whalers' history is Francis. He spent all of the 1980s with the club and remains the leader in most of the franchise's offensive categories. Francis collected 821 points and 264 goals in 714 games as a Whaler.

A new beginning

The Compuware group had a successful formula with their youth and junior hockey operations, and they have been trying to adhere to the same blueprint with the Hurricanes. General manager Jim Rutherford and head coach Paul Maurice were both members of that Compuware program.

In fact, it was Maurice who became the youngest head coach in pro sports when he replaced Paul Holmgren behind the Hartford bench in 1995. He had been very successful with the Detroit Junior Red Wings, where he compiled a 86–38–8 record in two years.

Arturs Irbe showed spectacular form during the 2002 playoffs as the Hurricanes made their first Stanley Cup finals appearance.

land
KOHO

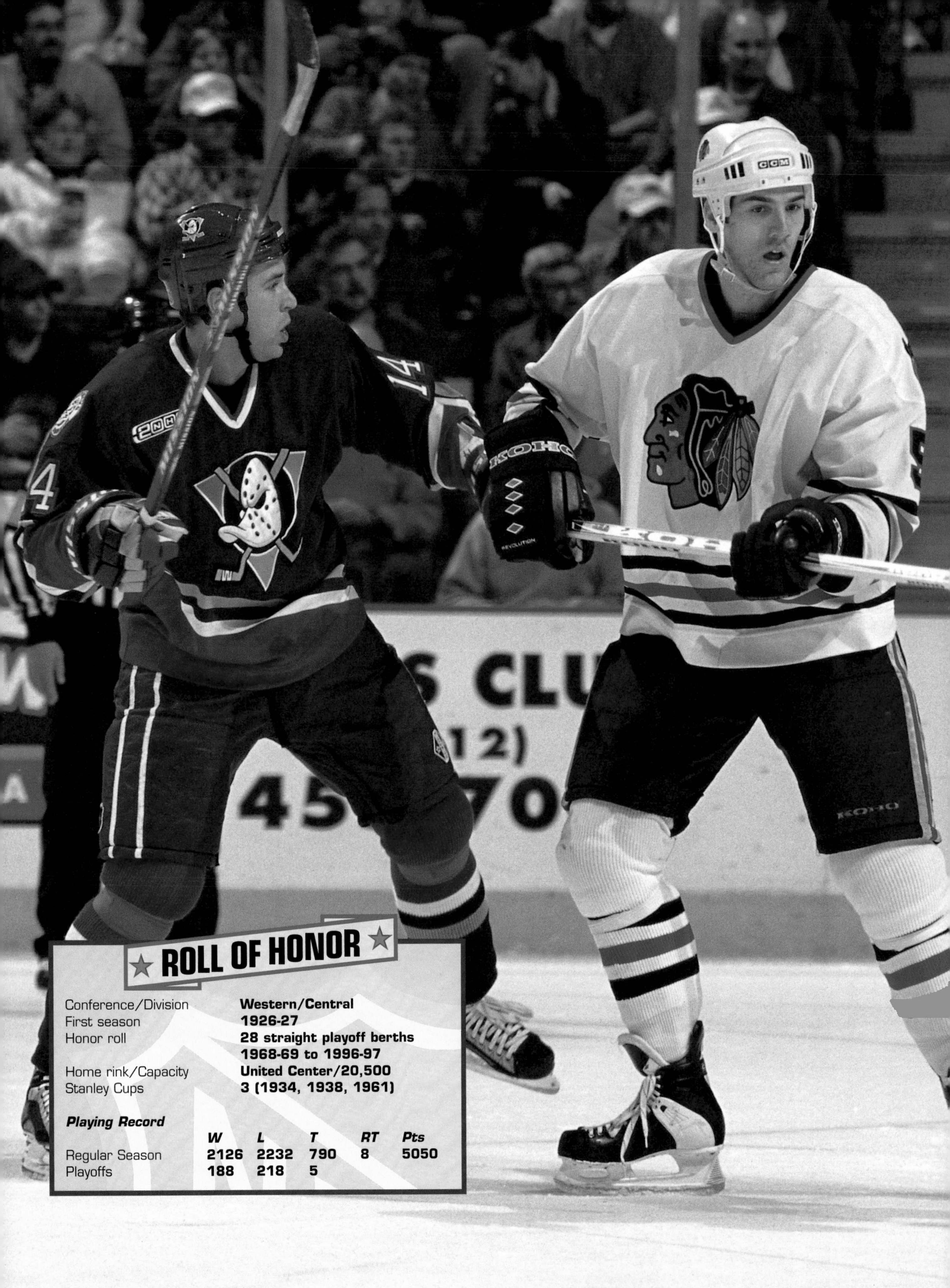

★ ROLL OF HONOR ★

Conference/Division	**Western/Central**
First season	**1926-27**
Honor roll	**28 straight playoff berths 1968-69 to 1996-97**
Home rink/Capacity	**United Center/20,500**
Stanley Cups	**3 (1934, 1938, 1961)**

Playing Record

	W	*L*	*T*	*RT*	*Pts*
Regular Season	**2126**	**2232**	**790**	**8**	**5050**
Playoffs	**188**	**218**	**5**		

CHICAGO BLACKHAWKS

The Blackhawks made a long-awaited return to the playoffs in 2001-2002. This season they are shooting for a repeat.

A streak of 28 straight playoff appearances ended when the Blackhawks missed the postseason in 1998. Then, an unfortunate streak took hold that saw Chicago miss the playoffs four straight years. Now the team is back on track, looking to extend its newest playoff streak.

Chicago is coming off its highest points total (96) since 1992-93. Even so, GM Mike Smith admitted after the season that the team doesn't quite have Stanley Cup talent yet, and he expected a busy off-season. Longtime offensive leader Tony Amonte's imminent departure was greeted with speculation about which free-agent star forward(s) would replace him in the lineup. And they would like to see the regular sellouts of the not-so-distant past return.

One area in which the Hawks need to improve is size and strength up front. In the five-game playoff loss to St. Louis in the first round, Chicago was overmatched by the physical Blues forwards.

Sutter magic

For the first time in what seems like forever, the Hawks are settled on a coach. Brian Sutter worked wonders for Chicago in his first season with the team. The former head man for St. Louis, Boston and Calgary exceeded expectations and was a finalist for the Jack Adams Award as coach of the year.

Jocelyn Thibault has been pretty good in net, but his spot was not safe as the free-agency period approached. Offensively, Eric Daze has been a consistent scoring force. The big winger had 38 goals last year to give him his fourth career 30-goal season. Michael Nylander and Kyle Calder are finesse forwards who can generate scoring chances when given the room.

Muldoon's curse

Despite their playoff streak, actually getting their hands on the Stanley Cup has been a different proposition for Chicago. Victories have been few and far between for the Blackhawks, who joined the NHL way back on September 25, 1926.

Their first head coach was a man named Pete Muldoon, who lost the job after one only season in charge. However, it was a season spiced with intrigue. Muldoon was fired after a woeful display by the Blackhawks. But he didn't go gently. He is alleged to have placed a curse on the team, saying it would never finish first because it had treated him so ignominiously. The Muldoon curse lasted 40 years. Chicago didn't finish first until the 1966–67 season. In Stanley Cup play, they have managed to escape the curse only three times—when they won in 1934, 1938 and 1961.

Eric Daze continued to perform in 2001-2002 finishing with yet another 30-goal season.

Right winger Tony Amonte has been one of Chicago's most reliable players but free-agent status made it likely he would be wearing a new jersey next season.

A history of talent

Yet, it is a franchise which has been blessed with some wonderful talent who, before moving into the spacious United Center in the 1994–95 season, played at raucous Chicago Stadium.

Bobby Hull, the 'Golden Jet' who shellshocked goaltenders with his patented slap shot, became the first NHLer to score more than 50 goals in a season, in 1966. Stan Mikita, the gifted Hockey Hall of Fame center, sparkled for 21 seasons, scoring 541 goals, second to Hull's 604. Both Hull and Mikita are regarded as the unofficial 'inventors' of the curved stick.

Then there was 'Mr. Goalie', Glenn Hall, who introduced the butterfly style of goaltending much in vogue today. After Hall, it was Tony (O) Esposito making some history—his 15 shutouts in 1969–70 are a modern-day single-season NHL record.

COLUMBUS BLUE JACKETS

Ohio now has its very own pro hockey franchise. Fans of the Blue Jackets hope that a winning season will follow soon.

The biggest city in Ohio took a long time to make it to the big time. And, after that long wait, the people of central Ohio are enjoying it big-time, even if their team is struggling with some growing pains.

The Columbus Blue Jackets are entering their third season of NHL play. Despite the fact that Columbus is more populous than longtime major-league Ohio hotbeds Cleveland and Cincinnati, it was noted as just a college sports town until the Blue Jackets took to the ice. Support for the hometown Ohio State University sports teams is legendary. The NHL figured that passion would translate to pro hockey when it was handing out expansion franchises a few years back. The league could not have been more right. Home sellout crowds have become as automatic as the marching band dotting the "i" at an OSU football game.

In the team's inaugural 2000-01 season, there was relative success. The Blue Jackets tied the Chicago Blackhawks, an Original Six team, in the Central Division with 71 points. Seven other teams, including the Montreal Canadiens, finished with fewer points. But in 2001–02, Columbus dropped to 57 points.

More scoring needed

As the Blue Jackets build toward respectability, they'll be looking to increase their offensive capabilities. Columbus scored the fewest goals in the NHL last season. Ray Whitney is the go-to guy. The former Panthers sniper notched a team-high 21 goals and 61 points in 2001–02. Centers Mike Sillinger and Espen Knutsen and wingers Grant Marshall and Geoff Sanderson add some offensive punch to the lineup, but there is a lack of depth up front.

The defensive corps is in need of a depth upgrade, too. Deron Quint anchored the blueline last year, and Jean-Luc Grand-Pierre showed promise as a physical presence. Mattias Timander is a workhorse as a rearguard.

What's the good news? Blue Jackets' fans are rejoicing with the club's selection of Rick Nash with the first overall pick in the 2002 NHL Entry Draft. As a forward with the London Knights of the Ontario Hockey League (OHL), Nash exhibited exceptional skill and Columbus hopes to mold him into an all-star caliber player. Under the proper tutelage, this rookie should make an immediate impact on the club's scoring punch.

In goal, the Blue Jackets have relied on a platoon system with veteran Ron Tugnutt and emerging Marc Denis, who once was the heir apparent to Patrick Roy in Colorado.

Proud local history

While the Blue Jackets elevated the city to the major leagues, minor-league hockey has been around for decades in Columbus. The Columbus Checkers of the defunct International Hockey League played from 1966–70. For a couple seasons in the early 1970s, the Columbus Golden Seals, owned by legendary sports owner Charlie Finley, skated in white skates against their IHL foes. The Seals became the Owls in the mid-1970s. In the 1990s, the Columbus Chill thrilled the local fans.

Forward Espen Knutsen contributed greatly to the Blue Jackets' efforts in the '01-'02 campaign finishing with 31 assists.

The NHL awarded Columbus one of four expansion franchises created in the summer of 1997. The Nashville Predators started play in 1998, the Atlanta Thrashers in 1999, and Columbus and the Minnesota Wild in 2000. Doug MacLean, who had successfully coached the third-year Florida Panthers to the Stanley Cup Finals in 1996, was hired as president and general manager. His experience with guiding a new team to success is invaluable. MacLean hired Dave King, the former coach of the Calgary Flames and the Canadian National and Olympic teams, to be his bench boss. King led Canada to a silver medal at the 1992 Olympics and was an impressive 109–76–31 as head man in Calgary. The present might be a little rough, but the future is in able hands with these two.

Center Mike Sillinger finished last season with 43 points.

★ ROLL OF HONOR ★

Conference/Division **Western/Central**
First Season **2000–01**
Honor roll **Outpointed seven NHL teams in its first season**
Home rink/Capacity **Nationwide Arena/18,136**
Stanley Cups **0**

Playing Record

	W	*L*	*T*	*RT*	*Pts*
Regular Season	**50**	**86**	**17**	**11**	**128**
Playoffs	**0**	**0**			

ROLL OF HONOR

Conference/Division	**Western/Northwest**
First Season	**1979–80 (Quebec); 1995–96 (Colorado)**
Honor roll	**118-point season in 2000–01**
Home rink/Capacity	**Pepsi Center/18,007**
Stanley Cups	**2 (1996, 2001)**

Playing Record

	W	*L*	*T*	*RT*	*Pts*
Regular Season	**815**	**774**	**235**	**6**	**1871**
Playoffs	**113**	**93**			

Colorado Avalanche

The 2001-2002 season was something of a anticlimax for the awesome Avalanche. They only reached the Conference finals!

The Colorado Avalanche might not win the Stanley Cup every season. But you can be sure that they will have a say in which team does. The franchise has known nothing but success since relocating from Quebec in 1995. There were the championships in 1996 and 2001, and an "off" year is when the Avs merely win another division title and get to a Game 7 of the Conference finals, as happened in 2001–02.

There is no shortage of star power in the Rocky Mountains. First and foremost is Patrick Roy. The man who perfected the butterfly style of goaltending is still at the top of his game. Last season, he led the league in shutouts (nine) and goals-against average (1.94) and was a finalist for both the Hart Trophy as NHL MVP and the Vezina Trophy for top goaltender. He has won three Conn Smythe Trophies as playoff MVP.

Dynamic duo

Two men who date back to the Quebec days have helped define Colorado hockey. Joe Sakic, the quiet captain with the lethal wrist shot, and Peter Forsberg, the feisty Swede with the magic stick, are two of the most dominant forwards in the game. Sakic tied for fifth in the league last year with 79 points, which is the kind of production he has consistently provided the franchise with for 14 seasons. Forsberg pulled off the amazing last year, skipping the entire regular season because of injury problems and then returning to be the best player in the NHL for much of the playoffs. A core of talented young forwards complement Sakic/Forsberg, including Chris Drury, who has earned a reputation as a clutch performer, super-skilled Alex Tanguay and speedy Milan Hejduk. Those players help make the Colorado special teams truly special. Whether killing penalties or with the man advantage, the Avs are among the NHL's élite.

The defensive brigade features one of the best in the business: Rob Blake. He is a bruising, physical force but also a premier offensive threat with a booming slapper. Blake was third among league defensemen last year with 56 points. Adam Foote, a former Quebec Nordique, has been clearing the crease with gusto for the franchise since 1991–92.

Checkered history

This is NHL Part 2 in Colorado, and it's been a spectacular sequel thus far. Unlike 1976–77, when Colorado inherited the mediocre Kansas City Scouts, the region managed to entice the Quebec Nordiques, whose owners felt they could no longer financially survive without a revenue-generating new rink in Quebec City.

Nordiques president Marcel Aubut and his ownership group sold the franchise to COMSAT, an entertainment company headed by Charlie Lyons, in the summer of 1995. That returned the NHL to Colorado, without a franchise after the Rockies moved, and they became the New Jersey Devils in 1982.

One of four World Hockey Association teams absorbed by the NHL in 1979, the Nordiques made the playoffs for seven straight years after their initial season. But as star players aged and key draft picks failed to deliver the goods, lean times arrived for the Nordiques. Quebec missed the playoffs for five straight seasons much to the chagrin of the fans.

In 1991, No. 1 draft pick Eric Lindros refused to sign with the Nordiques, setting off a year-long battle that culminated in Quebec trading him to both the Rangers and Philadelphia. An arbitrator had to intervene, awarding him to the Flyers. This trade was a turning point for the franchise. Among the players Quebec acquired was Forsberg, who is becoming as much a part of the Colorado scenery as the Rocky Mountains.

Joe Sakic quietly, unassumingly accumulates his points every season, like clockwork.

Despite a succession of serious injuries that have drastically cut his playing time, Peter Forsberg remains among the NHL elite.

ROLL OF HONOR

Conference/Division	**Western/Pacific**
First season	**1967–68 (Minnesota); 1993–94 (Dallas)**
Honor roll	**Finished with franchise-best 114 points in 1998-99**
Home rink/Capacity	**American Airlines Center/18,532**
Stanley Cups	**1 (1999)**

Playing Record

	W	*L*	*T*	*RT*	*Pts*
Regular Season	**1118**	**1206**	**431**	**13**	**2680**
Playoffs	**133**	**127**			

Dallas Stars

The Stars accomplished the ultimate in 1999, winning their first Stanley Cup; the target for 2003 is to win it all again.

The Ken Hitchcock era is over in Dallas, and a successful one it was. During the demanding coach's stay in Big D, the Stars won a Stanley Cup and made it to the Finals another time, losing to New Jersey. He was let go in January 2002 as the Stars were on their way to missing the playoffs after winning a division title in each of the previous five seasons.

Now the Dave Tippett era dawns for the Stars. Most recently an assistant with the Los Angeles Kings, new head man Tippett caters to a more offensive style than the fiendishly defensive-minded Hitchcock. There certainly are pieces in place to take advantage of a more free-wheeling offense. Exhibit A is Mike Modano, who has evolved from a one-way scoring whiz to one of the best two-way centers in hockey. He tied for ninth in the league in points last year with 77. Pierre Turgeon can also find the back of the net. He has nearly 500 career goals, but last year as a first-year Star he tallied just 15, his lowest total since his rookie season. Although Jere Lehtinen is known primarily as a great defensive forward, he scored a career-high 25 goals last year.

Turco's time to shine

Hitchcock isn't the only familiar face gone in Dallas. Eddie Belfour, the man who backstopped the Stars' recent run, was not re-signed as a free agent. That leaves the No. 1 goaltending job for his former backup, Marty Turco. Turco, the all-time winningest goalie in NCAA history, has done well in two NHL seasons with a limited role. Turco's new goalie coach is a familiar face. Former Stars netminder Andy Moog takes over that position. Another former Dallas player, Guy Carbonneau, joins the management ranks in a front-office position.

The captain sets the physical tone for Dallas. Defenseman Derian Hatcher will make sure no one gets a second crack at goals around Turco's crease. Russian speedster Sergei Zubov runs point on the power play and adds an offensive dimension to the blue line.

Tragic start

The franchise, which has operated in Dallas since 1993, burst on the NHL scene in 1967–68, along with five others: the Seals (with whom the Stars would later merge), Kings, Flyers, Penguins and Blues. They were the Minnesota North Stars then, but an early on-ice tragedy made star-crossed a more appropriate description.

On January 13, 1968, about halfway through the North Stars' inaugural season, a helmetless Bill Masterton struck his head violently on the ice and died in hospital from brain injuries two days later. It was the first and, thankfully, to this day, the only NHL on-ice death.

Bill Goldsworthy was the North Stars' first big goal-scorer. He was the first player from a post-1967 team to score 250 goals, 48 of which came in the 1973–74 season.

Lone Star Star: In center Mike Modano, the Dallas Stars have an outstanding player; now both he and they are Stanley Cup winners.

Defenseman Derian Hatcher provides both leadership and a physical presence for Dallas.

On the move

The North Stars made the Stanley Cup final in both 1981 and 1991, losing to the New York Islanders and Pittsburgh Penguins, respectively. The North Stars' tremendous playoff run in 1991 temporarily revived lagging fan interest in Minneapolis but in 1993 Norm Green, who had become the team owner three years earlier, moved the franchise to Dallas.

Dropping the North from their nickname, the Stars were the first NHL club in Texas and the sixth franchise to be based in the United States 'Sun Belt.' Six years later, the Stars became the first of these teams to have the Stanley Cup shining upon them.

Detroit Red Wings

The Red Wings were the class act of 2001–2002 as they captured the franchise's tenth Stanley Cup championship.

The Detroit Red Wings sit atop the hockey world. For the third time in six seasons they are the defending champions, having capped off a marvelous 2001–02 regular season with 16 wins in the playoffs, the number needed to win the Stanley Cup.

A star-studded roster is chock full of future Hall of Famers. The one major difference this year regards a man who was enshrined in the Hall in 1991. Scotty Bowman retired after earning his record ninth Stanley Cup as a coach—three coming with the Red Wings, one with Pittsburgh and five with Montreal. Everyone associated with the team will have to agree that it won't be the same without him.

Luckily, captain Steve Yzerman isn't going anywhere. Yzerman (658 career goals) has been wearing the "C" in Detroit seemingly longer than they've been making cars there. He played on a badly injured knee and sheer guts during the 2002 Stanley Cup run. His season will start a little late because of off-season knee surgery.

Star power

Red Wings owner Mike Ilitch is the type of owner fans love. His hockey people have assembled a stellar core of homegrown players, and then Ilitch gives the green light to sign expensive finishing pieces to the puzzle. In the summer of 2001, it was two-time league MVP Dominik Hasek in goal and two members of the exclusive 600-goal club, Brett Hull and Luc Robitaille.

The Wings have perhaps the league's most explosive offense. Besides the 600-goal guys, there is 500-goal man Brendan Shanahan and 300-goal man Sergei Fedorov. Fedorov is a joy to watch. He can dominate a game at both ends with his superior skating ability and he has a cannon of a shot. Even role players like Kris Draper pop up with 15-goal seasons, and Tomas Holmstrom parks himself in front of the net and usually gets plenty of garbage goals come playoff time. Super-slick youngster Pavel Datsyuk is the hope of the future.

The Wings have a suffocating defense. The 2002 NHL First All-Star Team defensemen were Detroit teammates Nicklas Lidstrom and Chris Chelios. Lidstrom won his second straight Norris Trophy as the league's best defenseman and he also earned the Conn Smythe Trophy as playoff MVP. He is as smooth and efficient as anyone who ever played the position.

Red hot past

The Red Wings were the NHL powerhouse in the first half of the 1950s, winning four Stanley Cups in six years.

That was the era of the Production Line of (Gordie) Howe, (Ted) Lindsay and (Sid) Abel, defensive stalwarts Red Kelly and Bob Goldham, icy-veined Terry Sawchuk in goal and Jolly Jack Adams at the managerial helm.

Until Wayne Gretzky came along a few decades later, Howe was the NHL's leading career goal-scorer with 801, all but 15 of them coming with Detroit. His linemate Lindsay is regarded by many as the toughest customer of all time. Abel, who went on to coach the Red Wings, was the set-up man on the line.

Sawchuk was impenetrable in goal, recording 85 shutouts with Detroit and an NHL record 103 in his career. The numbers brought Sawchuk an election to the Hockey Hall of Fame, one of dozens of people associated with the Red Wings who have earned such an honor.

The flashiest player on Detroit's roster is undoubtedly Sergei Fedorov, a two-way superstar.

Yzerman may have concentrated more on his defensive role in recent years, but his Red Wings career points total is second only to Gordie Howe.

★ ROLL OF HONOR ★

Conference/Division	**Western/Central**
First season	**1926–27 (Cougars); 1930–31 (Falcons); 1932–33 (Red Wings)**
Honor roll	**Seven straight regular-season titles (1948–49 to 1954–55)**
Home rink/Capacity	**Joe Louis Arena/20,053**
Stanley Cups	**10 (1936, 1937, 1943, 1950, 1952, 1954, 1955, 1997, 1998, 2002)**

Playing Record

	W	*L*	*T*	*RT*	*Pts*
Regular Season	**2263**	**2089**	**794**	**10**	**5330**
Playoffs	**251**	**226**	**1**		

★ ROLL OF HONOR ★

Conference/Division	**Western/Northwest**
First season	**1979–80**
Honor roll	**5 Cups in first 11 seasons**
Home rink/Capacity	**Skyreach Centre/17,099**
Stanley Cups	**5 (1984, 1985, 1987, 1988, 1990)**

Playing Record

	W	*L*	*T*	*RT*	*Pts*
Regular Season	**759**	**626**	**199**	**15**	**1717**
Playoffs	**132**	**78**			

EDMONTON OILERS

The Edmonton Oilers will look to bounce back from a frustrating 2001-2002 season that had promised much.

The Edmonton Oilers may have the financial deck stacked against them as a small-market Canadian club, but they don't let that stop them from being competitive on the ice. While Edmonton is coming off a season in which it did not make the postseason, it did win 10 more games than it lost and finished with 92 points, two points out of the playoffs and a mere seven points behind the No. 2 seed in the Western Conference.

General Manager Kevin Lowe is carrying on the tradition of developing players and making beneficial transactions within a limited budget. Longtime leader and scoring star Doug Weight was dealt prior to the 2001–02 season, yet the Oilers still earned 22 of a possible 28 points down the stretch to make a bid for their sixth straight playoff appearance. The team's strengths are defense and goaltending. Only Colorado allowed fewer goals last season. Goaltender Tommy Salo is impenetrable many nights and he's turned many should-be losses into wins with his stellar play. The defense is anchored by Eric Brewer, a rising star who is just tapping his potential at age 23. Janne Niinimaa is good at moving the puck up ice quickly from the rearguard.

Comrie on the come

Edmonton is perennially a small and speedy team, and the offense was known to sputter last season. The good news is that Mike Comrie looks like the next generation of Oiler sniper. In his first full season with his hometown team, Comrie scored a team-high 33 goals. Mike York is another young player with a developing eye for the net. He came from the Rangers in a trade late last season and compiled 20 goals and 61 points combined for both teams. Ryan Smyth, the master of the ugly goal, is practically a veteran on the NHL's youngest team, joining the Oilers in 1994–95, but he is still just 26.

Craig MacTavish is most famously known as the last player to play without a helmet, but he is quickly earning a new reputation as a fine coach. One of the most popular players in franchise history, he has been behind the bench now for two years, and his teams have averaged 92.5 points.

Camelot on ice

The Edmonton franchise didn't join the NHL until 1979—one of four World Hockey Association franchises to do so—but it surely made up for lost time. In five years, the Oilers built a powerhouse that produced five Stanley Cups in seven years, between 1983–84 and 1989–90. They were successful because a superb nucleus of players came of age together, and former coach/GM Glen Sather displayed a green thumb in developing the vast talent on hand. "In the 1980s it was Camelot," recalls ex-Oilers owner Peter Pocklington. "It was almost surreal. We were always on a roll."

The supporting cast sometimes changed but the main actors did not. There was Wayne Gretzky, arguably the finest player to lace on skates, menacing Mark Messier, crafty Jari Kurri, multi-dimensional Glenn Anderson, the steady Lowe on defense and the unflappable Grant Fuhr in goal.

The shock trade of Gretzky to the Los Angeles Kings in 1988 signalled the impending demise of Camelot, but it wasn't the end of the Oilers' spring skate with the Stanley Cup. Messier, Anderson, Kurri, Fuhr and Lowe were around for one last hurrah, in 1989–90.

Tommy Salo continues to be one of the league's best goalies, adding further strength to Edmonton's water-tight defense.

The Oilers were grateful for Anson Carter's 28 goals and 32 assists in 2001-2002.

★ ROLL OF HONOR ★

Conference/Division: **Eastern/Southeast**
First season: **1993–94**
Honor roll: **Most points (83) by first-year team (1993–94)**
Home rink/Capacity: **National Car Rental Center/19,250**
Stanley Cups: **0**

Playing Record

	W	*L*	*T*	*RT*	*Pts*
Regular Season	270	301	114	21	675
Playoffs	13	18			

FLORIDA PANTHERS

Mike Keenan will hope that his youth movement can help the Panthers rediscover their 1996 form.

Mike Keenan might eventually get around to coaching all 30 NHL teams, but for now he has a major challenge with his current employer, the Florida Panthers. It is the seventh big-league club for the coach. Keenan took over the coaching reins in December 2001 for a team that eventually finished with 60 points.

Under Keenan's leadership, the young squad is expected to flourish and deliver a complete game that is ultimately reflected in the wins column.

Keenan liked what he saw late last season when several young players were given the chance to make their mark. At the head of the class is Kristian Huselius. The young Swedish left winger led the team in goals (23) and was second in points (45). He finished third among all rookies in goals. Marcus Nilson, Olli Jokinen and Ivan Novoseltsev are amongst the most productive members of the youth corps.

Franchise goalie

The Panthers appear to be set between the pipes for a long time to come. Roberto Luongo was the fourth overall pick in the Entry Draft in 1997, the highest-drafted goaltender ever at that time. He is starting to live up to the billing. Although he missed the last month of the 2001–02 season with an ankle injury, he played in 58 games and had a 2.77 goals-against average and .915 save percentage. Sandis Ozolinsh is one of the league's most dynamic offensive defensemen. He came to the Panthers from Carolina midway through last season and proceeded to tally 29 points (10 goals) in just 37 games for his new team.

There are a couple players coming off injury-plagued seasons who will be key to a Florida turnaround. Forwards Victor Kozlov and Valeri Bure have both had 70-point seasons, and Bure averaged 30 goals per game in his last three healthy seasons with Calgary from 1998–2001. His more famous brother Pavel was traded to the Rangers late last season, which left a huge scoring void for the Panthers.

Keenan has a new boss in general manager Rick Dudley, who has had previous GM stints in Tampa Bay and Ottawa.

Early success

Founded by Wayne Huizenga of the Blockbuster Video empire, the Panthers were something of a blockbuster themselves in 1993–94, the season they joined Tampa Bay as the NHL's expansion entries from the Sunshine State. Under renowned hockey tactician Roger Neilson the Panthers became the most successful first-year NHL team, collecting 83 points and narrowly missing a spot in the Stanley Cup playoffs.

Sandis Ozolinsh arrived from Carolina during the 2001-2002 season and compiled 29 points in just 37 games.

Marcus Nilson is one of Keenan's young guns, finishing the year with 33 points.

The Panthers came achingly close to a playoff berth in the strike-shortened 1994–95 season, adhering to the same smothering style and solid goaltending by John Vanbiesbrouck, the first pick in the 1993 expansion draft.

But Panthers management, headed by Bill Torrey, who shaped the New York Islanders' dynasty in the early 1980s, decided a coaching change was required and Neilson was replaced by Doug MacLean, a product of the Detroit Red Wings system.

MacLean modified the neutral-zone trap during the 1995–96 season, favoring a mix of offense and defense, and it vaulted the Panthers to a dramatic seventh-game Conference final triumph over Pittsburgh and a hard-fought six games before succumbing to Colorado in the final.

Los Angeles Kings

After another strong season, the Kings appear closer to achieving their Hollywood dream.

In a town that creates movie magic, the Los Angeles Kings are still looking for their happy ending. While it hasn't happened yet, at least the script appears to be getting better.

The Kings are on the upswing after a mostly forgettable second half of the 1990s. They've made the playoffs three seasons running. In 2001 L.A. defeated heavily favored Detroit in the first round and stretched eventual champion Colorado to seven games in round two, and in 2002 the Kings again took the Avalanche to seven games, this time in round one.

Last year, Los Angeles was as good as any team in the league during the last four months of the season. Despite playing in La-La land, the Kings are known as a hard-working, blue-collar bunch. Only five teams allowed fewer goals than L.A. last year. Felix Potvin is rejuvenated in goal. The 2001–02 season was the first time he spent a full season with the same team since 1997–98, and his 31 wins was the most since he posted 34 way back in 1993–94.

Powerful power play

No team makes its opponents pay for their mistakes like L.A. does. The Kings were a middle-of-the-road team in terms of scoring last year, but with a man advantage they were NHL royalty. L.A.'s 20.6 power-play conversion percentage was tops in the league. Center Jason Allison was second behind Carolina's Ron Francis in power play points (37) and winger Ziggy Palffy and defenseman Jaroslav Modry weren't far behind (27 points each). Palffy is one of the NHL's top snipers. Adam Deadmarsh provides a power forward dimension and a nose for garbage goals.

Defensively, coach Andy Murray relies on a couple of wily veterans. Mathieu Schneider can move the puck with the best of them and Aaron Miller is a stay-at-home type who sets a physical tone. If the Kings can start the way they finished last year, they can stake a claim for being a serious Cup contender.

LA stars

The franchise has had its share of jewels. One of them was Marcel Dionne, a diminutive but Houdini-like center who was acquired in a trade with Detroit after the 1974-75 season. He skated his way into the Hall of Fame, scoring 550 of his 731 career goals—third-best in NHL history—as a member of the Kings. Along the way, Dionne inherited Charlie Simmer and Dave Taylor as linemates, and the Triple Crown Line, as they were dubbed, was the scourge of the league for several seasons.

The Dionne era ended in 1987, when he was dealt to the New York Rangers. But in true Hollywood fashion another superstar arrived on the set just over a year later—Wayne Gretzky. The NHL's marquee player arrived from Edmonton in a blockbuster trade. While Gretzky revived sagging hockey interest in Los Angeles, the Kings got no closer to their first Stanley Cup triumph than the dramatic 1992–93 final against the Montreal Canadiens.

Adam Deadmarsh (below) and Ziggy Palffy (right) were two big reasons why the Kings were the league's best power-play team.

★ ROLL OF HONOR ★

Conference/Division **Western/Pacific**
First season **1967–68**
Honor roll **Reached Stanley Cup final 1992–93**
Home rink/Capacity **Staples Center/18,118**
Stanley Cups **0**

Playing Record

	W	*L*	*T*	*RT*	*Pts*
Regular Season	**1100**	**1255**	**402**	**11**	**2613**
Playoffs	**65**	**105**			

MINNESOTA WILD

The Wild made important strides in 2001–2002. This season progress will again be their goal.

If pedigree counts for anything, the Minnesota Wild are not as far away as they might seem from contending for the Stanley Cup. At the top of the hockey administration ladder are a pair of guys who know how to get it done.

Executive vice president and general manager Doug Risebrough and coach Jacques Lemaire were teammates on the Montreal Canadiens dynasty of the 1970s and they have combined to hoist 16 Stanley Cups during their careers. Lemaire coached the New Jersey Devils to the Cup in 1995.

There are signs that the Wild are headed in the right direction. After an inaugural season in 2000–01 in which Minnesota posted a respectable 25 wins and 68 points—the latter total better than five other NHL teams—the 2001–02 campaign saw an increase of one win and five points. The 73 points bested seven other teams. Minnesota improved from a league-worst 168 goals as a rookie franchise to 195, ranking 25th in the 30-team league.

Slow and steady

Risebrough plans to build the team the right way, through the draft and player development. There will be no drastic forays into free agency. The foundation will be youth. Some of the players needed for such a plan already are in place. Marian Gaborik scored 30 goals despite just turning 20 years old in February. He has speed and a great shot and he is a major building block. Andrew Brunette, a bit of a journeyman who has been solid in stays with Washington, Nashville and Atlanta, stepped up with a career year which included a team-high 48 assists among his team-high 69 points. Brunette is just 29. Sergei Zholtok, another well-traveled 29-year-old, has made himself at home in Minnesota, chipping in 19 goals and 39 points last year.

Impressive young players who will form the core of the team for years to come include defensemen Filip Kuba and Nick Schultz and forward Pascal Dupuis. Dupuis scored 15 goals in his first full season and turned 23 in April.

The situation in goal is a little murky for the Wild. Dwayne Roloson and Manny Fernandez split time last year. The hope has been that Fernandez could become the franchise goaltender, but he hasn't played himself into that role yet.

Hockey hotbed

There is no place in the United States with a greater passion for hockey than Minnesota. The hoopla surrounding the state's high school hockey tournament is akin to that for Indiana's high school basketball tournament. College hockey is also huge. The NHL had a presence in the state previously with the Minnesota North Stars from 1967 to '93, before the club moved to become the Dallas Stars. The NHL returned after a seven-year absence in 2000, when the Wild and Columbus Blue Jackets became the last two of four expansion teams to join the league in a three-year span (Nashville in 1998 and Atlanta in 1999).

The North Stars reached the Stanley Cup Finals twice in their stay in Minnesota, in 1981 and 1991, losing both times. Several native Minnesotans dazzled the home state crowd during the NHL's first go-round there, including star player and Roseau, Minn., native Neal Broten. That tradition has been carried on by center Darby Hendrickson, who is from Richfield, Minn.

Twenty-year-old Marian Gaborik led Minnesota's youth movement with 30 goals.

Andrew Brunette finished the 2001-2002 season with team highs in assists and points.

ROLL OF HONOR

Conference/Division	**Western/Northwest**
First season	**2000–2001**
Honor roll	**Improved by 1 win and 5 points in second NHL season**
Home rink/Capacity	**Xcel Energy Center/18,064**
Stanley Cups	**0**

Playing Record

	W	*L*	*T*	*RT*	*Pts*
Regular Season	**51**	**74**	**25**	**14**	**141**
Playoffs	**0**	**0**			

ROLL OF HONOR

Conference/Division	**Eastern/Northeast**
First season	**1917–18**
Honor Roll	**Record for most consecutive Stanley Cup titles (5)**
Home rink/Capacity	**Molson Centre/21,273**
Stanley Cups	**24 (1916, 1924, 1930, 1931, 1944, 1946, 1953, 1956, 1957, 1958, 1959, 1960, 1965, 1966, 1968, 1969,1971, 1973, 1976, 1977, 1978, 1979, 1986, 1993)**

Playing Record

	W	*L*	*T*	*RT*	*Pts*
Regular Season	2778	1769	822	13	6391
Playoffs	387	255	8		

MONTREAL CANADIENS

Another appearance in the playoffs sees the Canadiens heading into the new season with confidence.

Montreal is back on track. It seems hard to believe, but the Canadiens were absent from the playoffs for three straight seasons from 1998–99 through 2000-01, after having missed the playoffs just six times in the previous 76 years.

Although they barely squeaked into the 2002 postseason field, the Habs made the most of their time in the big dance. First, they knocked off No. 1 seed Boston in round one, then took eventual Stanley Cup Finalist Carolina to six games in round two.

The postseason run was lent some remarkable inspiration by captain Saku Koivu. The nifty Finnish center has been a scoring leader on the team for years, when healthy. His latest medical setback isn't something as relatively mundane as a torn knee ligament. He battled back from abdominal cancer, making it into the lineup for three games at the end of the regular season after being out all year for treatment. In the playoffs, he tied for the team lead with 10 points in 12 games.

Between the posts, Jose Theodore is among the NHL's finest.

Theodore has arrived

Koivu isn't the only feel-good story on the team. Goalie Jose Theodore has emerged as one of the top stoppers in the league. The 26-year-old Quebec native had a breakout season in 2001–02, going 30–24–10 with a 2.11 goals-against average and seven shutouts. He can steal a game all by himself.

Montreal's offense will get a big boost having a healthy Koivu all season. Also in the mix are Yanic Perreault, a steady 25-goal scorer, and Richard Zednik, who suffered an injury in the playoffs. Zednik is usually good for around 20 goals. Quebecers Patrice Brisebois and Karl Dykhuis are steady performers who do yeomen's jobs on the blue line. One of the strengths of the Canadiens, coached by Michel Therrien, is the penalty kill, which ranked sixth in the league last year.

Great expectations

No team has to deal with higher expectations from its loyal followers than the Canadiens—and that's because of the winning tradition of the Club de Hockey Canadien. With 24 Stanley Cups, Montreal has experienced more excellence than any other major North American pro sports franchise except the New York Yankees, who have 26 World Series titles. The Canadiens have 11 more Cup triumphs than their closest pursuer, the Toronto Maple Leafs.

Saku Koivu completed his remarkable comeback from cancer with ten playoff points.

Torch of Glory

Little did J. Ambrose O'Brien realize, when he founded the team on December 4, 1909, that it would gain world-wide renown for its hockey prowess. In fact, he sold the club just one year later. But by 1926 Canadiens players such as Edouard "Newsy" Lalonde, Aurel Joliat, Joe Malone, Georges Vezina and Howie Morenz were stars.

The late 1950s saw an unmatched five consecutive Stanley Cups, as the team responded to an excerpt from the John McCrae poem *In Flanders Fields*—"To you from failing hands we throw the torch. Be Yours to Hold it High" which has been a fixture in the dressing room since 1952. No one grabbed the torch with as much gusto as Maurice Richard, the team's career goal-scoring leader with 544. An icon in Quebec, Richard's suspension for striking a linesman touched off a riot by fans at the Forum on March 17, 1955.

The string of Stanley Cups started the following the year as Jean Beliveau, Dickie Moore, Bernard "Boom Boom" Geoffrion, Doug Harvey, Jacques Plante and Maurice's kid brother Henri led a star-studded cast coached by Toe Blake, who would win eight Cups in 13 seasons behind the bench.

With Scotty Bowman at the helm, the Canadiens added four straight Stanley Cups between 1975–76 and 1978–79.

Nashville Predators

With a promise to their fans to keep, the Predators need to improve in 2002-2003—and quickly!

The Nashville Predators have made an unusual promise to their fans. In a marketing campaign known as the "Playoff Pledge," the team vows it will make the playoffs in 2003 or refund the first season-ticket price increase in franchise history.

That might seem like a pretty strong promise considering the team has never advanced to the postseason in its four seasons of existence. General Manager David Poile, who kept the Washington Capitals at the top of the standings during his GM-ship there, has served notice to players and coaches that the expansion era is over. He has built the team through youth and development and it was expected the team would add some veterans through off-season free agency.

Banking on Legwand

One of the keys to improvement for Nashville is the development of forward David Legwand. The Predators made him the second overall pick in the 1998 Entry Draft, yet Legwand hasn't yet been able to turn enormous skill into consistent production. His top season has resulted in 13 goals and 41 points. Still, he's only 22 and he has three full seasons behind him.

Speedy center Greg Johnson is a catalyst. He has been with the Preds since the first season, and he's good for 40-plus points and solid play at both ends of the ice. Nashville has lacked a go-to guy on offense. Some young players have the potential to become such a player, including Denis Arkhipov and Scott Hartnell. Both are going into their third season and each notched at least 40 points last year.

Coach Barry Trotz, who has helmed the team from the beginning, has an established No. 1 goalie in Mike Dunham, the former backup to Martin Brodeur in New Jersey. In each of his four seasons with the Predators, Dunham has increased his win total. He also was one of the goalies on Team USA in the 2002 Olympics. On the blue line, Nashville is anchored by a pair with contrasting styles. Bill Houlder is a veteran, stay-at-home type who didn't notch a goal last season. Kimmo Timonen is an offensive-minded puckhandling whiz who is just reaching his prime. He tied for ninth among NHL defensemen last year with 13 goals.

Hockey Tonk USA

The team was embraced by the country music industry right from the beginning. Barbara Mandrell had the entire squad over her house for dinner before the 1998–99 season began. Others who bought Predators season tickets included Reba McEntire, Deana Carter and Garth Brooks.

There was a Hockey Tonk Jam in March of 1998 to raise awareness for the Predators, with performances from Faith Hill, Tim McGraw and others. The event included Delbert McClinton's debut performance of "Hockey Tonk (The Predators Song)." McGraw even rewrote one of his hit songs, "I Like It, I Love It," to have a Predators bent and it served as an anthem for the club.

Vince Gill was once spotted banging on the penalty box glass and giving the choke sign to Theo Fleury. The ultimate blending of hockey and country music came when singer Mindy McCready started dating former Panthers defenseman Drake Berehowsky.

(Right) Goalie Mike Dunham's consistency was rewarded with a place on Team USA in the 2002 Olympics.

Center Greg Johnson (Below) is the Predators sparkplug at both ends of the ice.

★ ROLL OF HONOR ★

Conference/Division	**Western/Central**
First season	**1998–1999**
Honor Roll	**Outpointed three NHL teams in its first season**
Home rink/Capacity	**Nashville Arena/17,500**
Stanley Cups	**0**

Playing Record

	W	*L*	*T*	*RT*	*Pts*
Regular Season	**118**	**164**	**36**	**10**	**282**
Playoffs	**0**	**0**			

New Jersey Devils

Stanley Cup champions in 2000, the Devils are looking to once again be the team to beat in the East.

The New Jersey Devils are a model NHL franchise. They draft well, they develop their own star players and they keep payroll reasonable, all while maintaining a perennial spot among the NHL's elite teams.

New Jersey has missed only one postseason tournament since the 1989–90 season. General manager Lou Lamoriello has earned his place as one of the most respected hockey men in the business.

Among the homegrown talent is goaltender Martin Brodeur, a 1990 first-round draft pick. Not only has he backstopped the Devils to two Stanley Cup titles, but in February 2002 he was the man in net when Canada captured gold at the Winter Olympics. He is a world-class player.

Defense, defense

The Devils made their reputation as a defensive stalwart on the way to their first title in 1995. That reputation is still valid. Last year, only Edmonton and Colorado allowed fewer goals than New Jersey. Scott Stevens, the bone-crushing defenseman, sets the physical tone. Defenseman Scott Niedermayer is the fast-break specialist, getting the puck up to his forwards with an accurate outlet pass or skating like the wind through the other team.

The two most important Devils free agents in the off-season were rugged center Bobby Holik, a regular 25-goal scorer, and Patrik Elias, the first Devil to lead the team in scoring three straight years. Scott Gomez won the 2000 Calder Trophy as rookie of the year, but he slumped a bit last year and New Jersey is looking for a return to form from him. Petr Sykora provides the offense with a 30-goal type, and he has a wicked wrister.

From funnies to champs

Few remember that the New Jersey Devils were once the Kansas City Scouts, and only vaguely that they were the Colorado Rockies. John McMullen and his group purchased the team in 1982 and moved to the New Jersey Meadowlands. The Devils were almost as dreadful as the Scouts and Rockies in their early years in New Jersey. In fact, after a 1983 game in which Edmonton routed New Jersey 11–4, Oilers superstar Wayne Gretzky likened the Devils to Mickey Mouse.

Until 1988, the Rockies-Scouts-Devils had qualified for a playoff berth only once in 13 seasons, and had one playoff-game victory—by Colorado in 1977-78.

But the first taste of post-season play as the Devils was memorable as they reached the Wales Conference championship before losing to Boston in seven games. The Devils did not make the conference final again until 1994. That ended in heartbreak, when Stephane Matteau's seventh-game overtime goal sent the New York Rangers, not New Jersey, to the Stanley Cup final.

But under Jacques Lemaire, part of eight Stanley Cup championships as a player with Montreal, the Devils embarked on a 1994–95 playoff run in which it lost only four of 20 games, culminating in a four-game sweep of the favored Detroit Red Wings for the first Stanley Cup in the history of the franchise.

New Jersey be-Deviled the rest of the league again in 2000 when it dethroned defending champion Dallas in the Stanley Cup Finals in six games. The Devils nearly got their third title in 2001. They had a three-games-to-two series lead on Colorado in the Finals heading home for game six, but the Avs took the last two games and the Stanley Cup.

Franchise Defenseman: Scott Stevens anchors a rock-solid defense in New Jersey.

The Devils' goaltender Martin Brodeur remains one of the league's best.

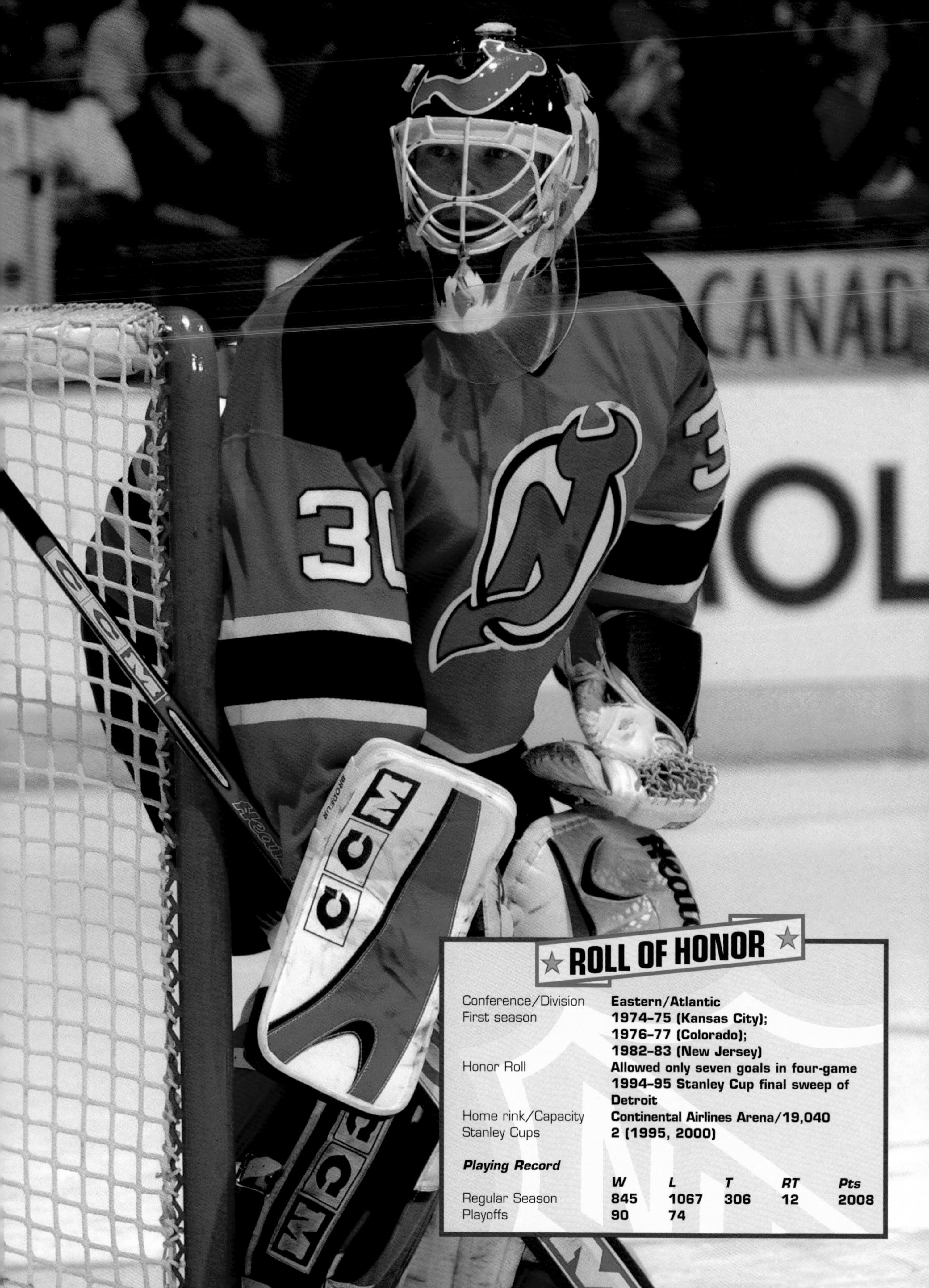

ROLL OF HONOR

Conference/Division **Eastern/Atlantic**

First season **1974–75 (Kansas City); 1976–77 (Colorado); 1982–83 (New Jersey)**

Honor Roll **Allowed only seven goals in four-game 1994–95 Stanley Cup final sweep of Detroit**

Home rink/Capacity **Continental Airlines Arena/19,040**

Stanley Cups **2 (1995, 2000)**

Playing Record

	W	*L*	*T*	*RT*	*Pts*
Regular Season	**845**	**1067**	**306**	**12**	**2008**
Playoffs	**90**	**74**			

★ ROLL OF HONOR ★

Conference/Division **Eastern/Atlantic**
First season **1972–73**
Honor roll **Four straight Stanley Cups, 1979–80 to 1982–83**
Home rink/Capacity **Nassau Veterans Memorial Coliseum/16,297**
Stanley Cups **4 (1980, 1981, 1982, 1983)**

Playing Record

	W	*L*	*T*	*RT*	*Pts*
Regular Season	**1039**	**1014**	**325**	**8**	**2411**
Playoffs	**131**	**94**			

New York Islanders

Long Island saw playoff hockey again in 2002 as the Islanders reversed a seven-year drought.

In the 2001–2002 season, the Islanders enjoyed one of the biggest turnarounds in recent NHL history. After winning four consecutive Stanley Cups in the late 70s and early 80s, the Islanders have been searching for that special magic to keep them on the ice throughout May and, hopefully, early June. For seven straight years, the links season began for Isles players as soon as the NHL regular season ended. In the spring of 2002, they actually had some playoff hockey to play.

And the hope on Long Island is that the players' golf handicaps will continue to rise as the team gets better and deeper into the playoffs than the seven games of round one they experienced against Toronto.

Mike Milbury has been building this team to make a serious run at Lord Stanley's Cup. The general manager now has plenty of keys pieces in place. There is the leadership and gritty play of center Michael Peca, who is coming off summer knee surgery as the result of an injury sustained in the playoffs. There is the superstar stature of sniper Alexei Yashin, who tied for 12th in the league in points (75) in his first season with the Isles. There is Mariusz Czerkawski, who has two 30-goal seasons in the last three years. And the expectation for the off-season was a dip into the big-name free-agent market.

Three on D

There is also a stellar trio of defensemen. Last season, Roman Hamrlik (37 points), Adrian Aucoin (34) and Kenny Jonsson (32) gave the Islanders the distinction of having the only triumvirate of backliners to reach the 30-point plateau. They are not just offensive-minded, as Aucoin's plus-23 and Jonsson's plus-15 were career-high marks in the plus-minus category. Jonsson has been prone to concussions in his career, however, and he was knocked from the playoffs in the spring with another. His health is a key.

Milbury got the team a proven goaltender last year when Chris Osgood left Detroit, where he was part of two Stanley Cup teams. Osgood gives his teammates confidence, and that has led to elevated play from everyone. The improved performance on the ice is drawing more rabid fan support. A once half-empty arena is now sold out many nights.

Torrey magic

The Islanders managed only 12 victories and 30 points in their fledgling season but they improved dramatically from then on, as astute general manager Bill Torrey, who'd been an executive with the expansion California Seals, started weaving his magic. Torrey hired Al Arbour as head coach following the 1972–73 season. One week later, he drafted Denis Potvin, a gifted young junior defenseman. At the draft table the following year, Torrey grabbed a bruising forward named Clark Gillies, and a shifty center named Bryan Trottier.

The combative Billy Smith, a little-known goaltender Torrey had selected in the 1972 expansion draft, became a key component in the building process. In the 1977 draft, Torrey plucked a high-scoring forward named Mike Bossy from the Quebec Major Junior League and the last building block was in place.

By the 1979–80 season, these five players led an Islanders charge that displaced the Montreal Canadiens as the dominant NHL force. The Canadiens were seeking a fifth straight Cup when the upstart Islanders breezed through four series, including a six-game victory over Philadelphia in the final, for the first of four consecutive Stanley Cup championships.

The Islanders narrowly missed matching the Canadiens' record five straight Cups. They reached the final in 1983–84, only to lose to the Edmonton Oilers.

Alexei Yashin confirmed his star status, leading the team in points, goals and assists.

Adrian Aucoin contributed 34 points in 2001–2002.

ROLL OF HONOR

Conference/Division	**Eastern/Atlantic**
First season	**1926–27**
Honor roll	**Ended 54-year Stanley Cup drought in 1993–94**
Home rink/Capacity	**Madison Square Garden/18,200**
Stanley Cups	**4 (1928, 1933, 1940, 1994)**

Playing Record

	W	*L*	*T*	*RT*	*Pts*
Regular Season	**2172**	**2185**	**791**	**8**	**5143**
Playoffs	**183**	**195**	**8**		

New York Rangers

An open checkbook and superstar players weren't enough to see the Rangers back in the playoffs.

With an influx of future Hall of Famers and the addition of one of the deadliest snipers in hockey history, by way of Pavel Bure, the Rangers set their sights on proving that they are a force to be reckoned with, just as much in the post-season as the regular-season.

The last time the Rangers made the playoffs was 1997. General manager Glen Sather is as accomplished a hockey man as there ever was, having lorded over the Edmonton dynasty of the 1980s, so if anyone can figure out how to change the Rangers' fortunes, he can.

There is no shortage of star power in the Big Apple. Likely Hall of Famers from the 2001–02 roster included Mark Messier, Eric Lindros, Pavel Bure, Theo Fleury, Brian Leetch and Mike Richter. As usual, New York was expected to have a busy summer of 2002 with free agent comings and goings. The checkbook seems to never run dry in New York, and big-name players love the bright lights of Broadway.

Shoring up the defense

Only Atlanta gave up more goals last year than the Rangers, so defensive play is a huge priority for the team this season. Leetch is as good as they come on the blue line. Young Tom Poti, obtained from Edmonton last season, has some flair as an offensive defenseman. Big Vladimir Malakhov tied for third on the team with a plus-10 rating last year.

Any offense that contains the explosive Bure and the powerful Lindros is not going to be denied for long. The good news for Rangers fans is that Lindros is coming of a relatively healthy season in which he missed just 10 games, and down the stretch the concussion-prone centerman was back to his usual body-knocking style.

Teenager Dan Blackburn, who backed up Richter last year, is the goalie of the future. The Ranger netminders don't get much help when the team is down a man.

Goaltender Mike Richter played behind a New York Rangers defense that allowed too many shots on goal.

From Cup to Cup

Success in the playoffs hasn't been a Rangers hallmark. No NHL team has won a Stanley Cup one year after joining the league, as the Rangers did in 1928, but no team has gone without a Stanley Cup for 54 years, as the Rangers did before making up for lost time and striking paydirt in 1993–94.

In the early years, Madison Square Garden echoed with exhortations for scoring star Frank Boucher, brothers Bill and Bun Cook and Lester Patrick, the club's first coach and general manager. In the second game of the 1928 Stanley Cup finals, the 44-year-old Patrick was pressed into service as the team's goaltender. He allowed only one goal, the Rangers won in overtime, and Patrick was forever etched in the club's history as a Rangers hero.

Another brother combination—Mac and Alex Shibicky—joined with future Hall of Famer Neil Colville to lead the Rangers to their 1940 Cup triumph. While the Rangers' Cup drought continued, the club made the playoffs nine straight years, starting in 1966–67.

The Rangers, who lost to Montreal in the 1978 final, wouldn't get another chance for nearly 20 years until 1994 in the final against Vancouver. The Cup-clinching goal in Game 7 of the final came from Messier, a five-time Cup winner with Edmonton and one of several acquisitions made by Rangers former general manager Neil Smith in building his championship squad

Despite the speed and skill of Pavel Bure, the Rangers struggled in 2001–2002.

OTTAWA SENATORS

After six straight years in the playoffs, the Senators are looking to keep the run alive in 2002–2003.

Ottawa has mastered the regular season. Now the Senators are looking to take that next step and make a serious run at the Stanley Cup. The 2001–02 season was the team's fifth straight winning campaign and the sixth consecutive playoff season.

The Senators beat the second-seeded Flyers in round one and went to seven games with provincial rival Toronto in round two. The seven playoff wins is a franchise record.

The most important position on any hockey team is goaltender, and the Senators seem to have found a reliable No. 1 in Patrick Lalime. He was the big question mark for Ottawa entering the 2002 postseason, but he ended up as one of the stars of the first couple rounds. In 12 games, Lalime recorded four shutouts and had a 1.39 goals-against average and an amazing .946 save percentage.

Explosive offense

Ottawa can score with the best of them. Last year, the Sens finished fifth in the league in goals thanks in part to a productive power play. The core of the offense is formed by some nifty Europeans: Daniel Alfredsson, Radek Bonk, Marian Hossa and Martin Havlat. Alfredsson is coming off his career-best season for goals, 37, and he provides leadership and desire as the captain. Speedy veteran Shawn McEachern continues to spark the offense at age 33.

Jacques Martin has been coaching the Sens since 1996, which is impressive longevity for an NHL boss. He has a good corps of defensemen in Ottawa. Wade Redden is a terrific all-around player and Zdeno Chara, the tallest player in NHL history, manages to make 6"9" look graceful. Chris Phillips and Sami Salo are also solid on the blue line.

Walking the plank

While the past several seasons have been filled with regular season success, there have been plenty of stormy moments in their brief history. Mel Bridgman, the club's first general manager was fired immediately after the Senators' maiden season of 24 points. The first-year Senators also tied an NHL record with only one road victory.

The record gave Ottawa the first draft choice in 1993, and the Senators grabbed Quebec Junior League scoring whiz Alexandre Daigle. Signed to a five-year contract, Daigle never lived up to expectations and became a journeyman before disappearing from the NHL altogether.

With young talent that has proven to be among the best in the league, Ottawa is destined to reach new heights. The players are younger, more competitive and highly skilled, more than enough intangibles to make a serious run at the fabled Cup in any of the upcoming NHL seasons.

Ottawa is on its sixth general manager, but with a more secure future, things now look brighter.

Patrick Lalime recorded four shutouts in the 2002 playoffs.

Daniel Alfredsson (right) has had some injury setbacks, but when healthy he sets an example for his teammates with a strong work ethic.

★ ROLL OF HONOR ★

Conference/Division	**Eastern/Northeast**
First season	**1992–93**
Honor roll	**Northeast Division title, 1999, 2001**
Home rink/Capacity	**Corel Center/18,500**
Stanley Cups	**0**

Playing Record

	W	L	T	RT	Pts
Regular Season	288	392	97	13	686
Playoffs	17	27			

JOFA

ROLL OF HONOR

Conference/Division	**Eastern/Atlantic**
First season	**1967–68**
Honor roll	**Consecutive Stanley Cups, 1974–75**
Home rink/Capacity	**First Union Center/19,523**
Stanley Cups	**2 (1974, 1975)**

Playing Record

	W	*L*	*T*	*RT*	*Pts*
Regular Season	**1383**	**947**	**429**	**9**	**3204**
Playoffs	**161**	**148**			

Philadelphia Flyers

The Flyers hope that the new Hitchcock era will translate to greater success in the playoffs.

The Flyers know how to cruise at a high altitude during the regular season. It's the playoffs that keep causing turbulence. With a first-round exit courtesy of Ottawa in the 2002 playoffs, that makes four first-round ousters in five years. Enter Ken Hitchcock, the newest pilot invited to the Flyers' cockpit.

Hitchcock is Philadelphia's ninth coach in 10 years. He boasts an impressive résumé, most notably a Stanley Cup and a near-repeat as head man in Dallas. The style of play he favors is defense, defense, defense. Hitchcock's success in the playoffs will be a welcome asset for a team that scored a mere two goals in its five-game playoff stint last spring.

Tenacious D

Playing to the new coach's liking, Philly is already a good defensive team. Last season, the Flyers ranked seventh in the league in goals against, riding the tandem of Roman Cechmanek and Brian Boucher in net. Hitchcock likes having an entrenched No. 1 goalie. The off-season was expected to add a new mask to the mix.

The defensive corps is led by longtime workhorse Eric Desjardins, a gifted two-way player who usually is good for a double-digit-goal season. Fourth-year NHLer Kim Johnsson impresses at the point. He had 11 goals and 41 points last year. Veteran Eric Weinrich is a steadying influence on the blue line.

Philly's also a pretty good offensive team, ranking eighth in the league in goals-for during the regular season before the power outage in the playoffs. Simon Gagne is one of the bright, young stars of the sport. Just 22 years old, he already has 80 career goals in three NHL seasons. Another youngster the organization is high on is Justin Williams, who scored 17 times last season. There are plenty of decorated veterans up front, including captain Keith Primeau, sniper John LeClair, shifty Mark Recchi and feisty Jeremy Roenick. That group combined has over 1,400 career goals. The Flyers are good on the penalty kill with so many big names on the roster.

Intimidating force

There's always been something special about the Flyers, one of the six expansion teams to join the NHL for the 1967–68 season. Six years later, they became the first expansion team to win the Stanley Cup, an exploit repeated in 1974–75. The Flyers of that era were tough and talented, attributes exemplified by acknowledged on-ice leader Bobby Clarke, who today is the Flyers' president and general manager.

Enforcers Dave (The Hammer) Schultz, Bob (Hound Dog) Kelly and Don Saleski did plenty of body-thumping. The Flyers' bruising defense corps of Andre (Moose) Dupont, the Watson brothers—Joe and Jim—and Ed Van Impe dished out more bitter medicine.

But the Flyers, under coach Fred Shero, were much more than brawn. They had a 50-goal man in Rick MacLeish, another in Reggie Leach, who in 1975–76 notched 61 goals, only the second NHLer to reach that mark. And they had Bill Barber, whose 420 goals in 903 games as a Flyer remain the career best on the club.

In goal, Bernie Parent, traded to Toronto in 1971 and re-acquired two years later, won the Conn Smythe Trophy as the most valuable performer in the Stanley Cup playoffs in both 1974 and 1975, the first player to accomplish the feat. Amid the triumphs, there was also tragedy. Barry Ashbee, one of the Flyers' best defensemen, had his career ended in 1974 after being struck in the eye by a puck, and Vezina Trophy winner Pelle Lindberg was killed in an automobile accident at the height of his goaltending career in 1985.

Jeremy Roenick brings experience, leadership and tenacity to the Philadelphia offense.

Savvy veteran John LeClair shows no signs of slowing down.

Phoenix Coyotes

The Phoenix Coyotes will be hoping that Gretzky's Midas touch will soon pay dividends in the desert.

Wayne Gretzky assembled a championship team for the 2002 Winter Olympics. Now he hopes to oversee a similar success story with the Phoenix Coyotes. Gretzky, arguably the greatest player ever and the captain of four Stanley Cup-winning teams in Edmonton, was in charge of Canada's gold-medal-winning team last winter.

As managing partner of the Coyotes, he doesn't have the luxury of enlisting the top players in the game with a simple invitation to compete for free.

The centerpiece for a contending team is in place. Goaltender Sean Burke has had a good career, but last year he took it to the next level. The big backstop was a finalist for both the Vezina Trophy as the league's best goalie and the Pearson Award as the player-voted MVP. He set career highs in wins (33), goals-against average (2.29) and shutouts (five). There was no better proof of his value than Phoenix's 33–16–6–4 record in games he started and its 7–11–3–2 record in those he did not.

Daymond Langkow led the Coyotes with 62 points.

No-name bunch

The post-Keith Tkachuk/Jeremy Roenick era is short on star power but not short on talent. There are a host of guys in their mid-20s who seem to be hitting their stride or closing in it: center Daymond Langkow had a bust-out season last year with 27 goals and 62 points, fellow center Daniel Briere almost tripled his previous career high with 32 goals, Shane Doan is a solid power forward, Ladislav Nagy is a pure goal scorer who deposited 23 in his first full season, and Michal Handzus is best known for his defensive play but he can also bury the puck. Veteran Brian Savage, a five-time 20-goal scorer who came to Phoenix midway through last season, strengthens one of the league's best offenses.

Teppo Numinen has been a defensive ace for the franchise so long he actually has played two more seasons as a Winnipeg Jet than as a Phoenix Coyote. The two-way player seems to be defying father time, evidenced by his 13 goals last year, a career high. Danny Markov and Paul Mara also get a lot of ice time on the blue line.

Shaping influence

The Coyotes' NHL roots are in Winnipeg, where the Jets entered the league in 1979. While not very proficient in the NHL, the club was instrumental in the evolution of European players and, so, had much to do with shaping the style and substance of the game.

While Swedish stars Ulf and Kent Nilsson, and Anders Hedberg from Winnipeg's WHA years didn't accompany the Jets to the NHL, European stars such as Willy Lindstrom and Lars-Erik Sjoberg carried the torch successfully. The Jets also had NHL scoring great Bobby Hull for 18 games that first season, before trading him to Hartford.

As the 1980s unfolded, two players emerged to become the cornerstones of the Jets franchise. Dale Hawerchuk, a rangy center who was the No. 1 overall pick in the 1981 NHL draft, was the team's leading scorer for the next nine years, a remarkable stretch of form that catapulted him to the team's all-time leader in goals (379) and points (929).

Thomas Steen, of Sweden, wasn't a prolific scorer. But he combined toughness, speed and grace for 14 seasons with the Jets, making him the club's longest-serving player. There wasn't a dry eye in the Winnipeg Arena when the Jets retired Steen's No. 25 in a ceremony following the 1995 season.

Daniel Briere (right) scored a team-high 32 goals in 2001–2002.

★ ROLL OF HONOR ★

Conference/Division	**Western/Pacific**
First season	**1979–80 (Winnipeg); 1996–97 (Phoenix)**
Honor roll	**Club record 43 wins and 96 points in 1984–85**
Home rink/Capacity	**America West Arena/16,210**
Stanley Cups	**0**

Playing Record

	W	***L***	***T***	***RT***	***Pts***
Regular Season	**762**	**848**	**237**	**13**	**1714**
Playoffs	**29**	**63**			

PITTSBURGH PENGUINS

Super Mario and his Penguins will hope for an injury-free 2002--2003 season and a return to the playoffs.

There is no more hands-on owner in the NHL than Mario Lemieux. Of course, he's not hands-on in a meddlesome way. He's hands-on in a scoring-a-clutch-goal way. Lemieux, already a member of the Hockey Hall of Fame, took over ownership of the Penguins during his retirement of the late 1990s. Since he unretired a couple years ago, the only thing that has slowed him down is injury.

In fact, injuries have been a problem for many of Lemieux's teammates/employees. The departure of superstar Jaromir Jagr last season created a huge hole in the lineup, but health problems affecting key personnel contributed greatly to the fall from Eastern Conference playoff finalist in 2001. The Penguins lost 330 man-games to injury, second most in the NHL. Besides Lemieux, top-line-caliber forwards Martin Straka, Robert Lang and Alexei Kovalev all missed significant time. Straka, in fact, played in just 13 games courtesy of a broken leg. Lemieux gutted out a chronic hip problem enough to help Canada win a gold medal in the February Olympics, but he got in just 24 games for the Penguins. He was expected to be at 100 percent by the start of this season and he has stated a goal to play until age 40.

Need for defensive upgrade

The Penguins gave up more goals last year than all but four teams, so defense is a position that could stand some improvement. Pittsburgh is not particularly big or tough in this area. Michal Rozsival is developing nicely, although defensemen take longer to hit their peak than forwards and he will be just 24 this season. Andrew Ference is another youngster with much upside potential.

Johan Hedberg is the No. 1 goalie in Pittsburgh. He splashed onto the scene in the 2001 playoffs. GM Craig Patrick made Rick Kehoe, a member of the Pittsburgh franchise for nearly three decades, head coach last October. Kehoe and his players had all summer to shake off the disappointment of an 0–8–1–1 finish. A reversal of health fortune would be a first step to getting back in the playoffs. Last year's early spring was the first for Pittsburgh since 1990.

Bolstering a center

The history of the Penguins did not start on June 9, 1984, the day they selected Lemieux as the top pick in the NHL entry draft — but the fortunes of the franchise improved dramatically as of that date. Gradually, general manager Patrick assembled strong support for Lemieux. Jagr, a gifted Czechoslovakian, was grabbed in the 1990 entry draft, two-way center Ron Francis was obtained in a trade with Hartford, and rangy Larry Murphy was added to the defense corps to clear the goal crease for netminder Tom Barrasso.

Two great hockey minds joined the Penguins for the 1990–91 season — (Badger) Bob Johnson as coach and Scotty Bowman as director of player development. Together, the former Stanley Cup-winning duo made the Penguins, out of the playoffs in seven of the previous eight seasons, into sudden Stanley Cup champions.

Bowman made it two straight Cups in 1992 when he relieved Johnson as coach at the start of that season. Johnson died of cancer several weeks later and fans honored his memory in a candlelight ceremony at the Civic Arena.

Alexei Kovalev led Pittsburgh in points, goals and assists in 2001–2002 despite missing 15 games through injury.

The Penguins hope that Martin Straka makes a successful return to form after a broken leg ended his 2001–2002 campaign.

ROLL OF HONOR

Conference/Division	**Eastern/Atlantic**
First season	**1967–68**
Honor roll	**Five division titles, two Stanley Cups in last 10 years.**
Home rink/Capacity	**Mellon Arena/16,958**
Stanley Cups	**2 (1991, 1992)**

Playing Record

	W	***L***	***T***	***RT***	***Pts***
Regular Season	**1149**	**1236**	**369**	**14**	**2681**
Playoffs	**109**	**99**			

ROLL OF HONOR

Conference/Division	**Western/Pacific**
First season	**1991–92**
Honor roll	**Upset first-round playoff opponent 1994, 1995, 2000**
Home rink/Capacity	**Compaq Center/17,483**
Stanley Cups	**0**

Playing Record

	W	*L*	*T*	*RT*	*Pts*
Regular Season	**311**	**446**	**100**	**13**	**735**
Playoffs	**29**	**38**			

San Jose Sharks

The Sharks continued their progression by winning the Pacific Division in 2002. Next stop the Stanley Cup?

The San Jose Sharks seem to be on the verge of something great. The franchise has been steadily gaining momentum for five years, and last year it almost made the jump to the big time. In making the playoffs every season during the last half-decade, San Jose has steadily increased its point total from 78 to 80 to 87 to 95 to a Pacific Division championship with 99 points last season. Not only that, but the Sharks nearly eliminated defending Stanley Cup champion Colorado from the second round of the 2002 playoffs. San Jose pushed the Avalanche to a seventh game, having led the series three games to two before coming up short in a pair of one-goal games.

The heart and soul of the team is Owen Nolan, one of the game's premier power forwards. Nolan has been with the club since 1995, and he has posted as many as 44 goals in a season. He also likes to stir things up with a physical brand of hockey. The balanced scoring attack also includes center Vincent Damphousse, who has a well-deserved reputation as one of the savviest veterans in the league. And when it comes to pure grit, there is no one who out-grinds center Mike Ricci, whose wild, untamed hair seems suited to the all-out style he plays. Scott Thornton, a checking-line player much of his career, busted out as a scoring threat last year. His 26 goals were a career high. Teemu Selanne, one of the most gifted players of his era, has provided the superstar aura the last season-plus, but he entered the off-season as an unrestricted free agent.

Nabokov the real deal

In just two full NHL seasons, Evgeni Nabokov has developed into one of the finest young goalies in the NHL. He was phenomenal in game 7 against the Avalanche, so he already has proven that playoff pressure doesn't get to him.

The busiest men in San Jose are defensemen Marcus Ragnarsson and Brad Stuart. Both are products of an excellent scouting system which finds good players in the early rounds (Stuart) and the late rounds (Ragnarsson).

Killer sharks

San Jose joined the NHL for the 1991–92 season, 17 months after the league granted permission to George and Gordon Gund to sell the Minnesota North Stars in return for the rights to an expansion team in San Jose.

A first order of business was to come up with a suitable nickname for the new club that would appeal to the fans. A competition was held and the Sharks emerged as the favorite.

The nickname is fitting for a franchise that has frequently struck without warning and shattered the Stanley Cup aspirations of the old guard. Ask the Detroit Red Wings, a strong Cup contender in 1993–94 who were ripped apart by the Sharks in the first round, losing in an emotion-charged seventh game. San Jose was in only its third season at the time, and had managed only 11 victories in an 84-game schedule the previous year.

The Sharks, whose team colors of Pacific teal, gray, black and white were an instant merchandising hit with the fans, pulled another major surprise in 1994–95, eliminating the second-seeded Calgary Flames in seven games in the opening round of the Western Conference playoffs.

San Jose center Mike Ricci doesn't need the letter "C" on his uniform to provide veteran leadership for the Sharks.

Teemu Selanne is an unrestricted free agent and could start the 2002–2003 season wearing new colors.

St. Louis Blues

Buoyed by their awesome defense, the Blues had a superb season that ended, predictably, with a playoff berth.

The Blues are the model of consistency. For 23 straight years, they have capped their regular season with a playoff run. That's even more impressive when one considers that because of expansion, only about half the teams in the NHL now make the postseason, as opposed to the majority of teams making it back when the streak started. Their playoff streak is the longest one going in major pro sports.

At the heart of the St. Louis roster is a pair of dominating defensemen, Al MacInnis and Chris Pronger, who play monster minutes. The seemingly ageless MacInnis first played in the NHL way back in 1981–82, before some current players in the league were even born. He is best known as the perennial winner of the hardest shot competition during All-Star Weekend, but his all-around excellence has been a long-standing fact of NHL life. Pronger is the big, tough guy who can clear the crease as well as anyone and then start the break. The former Hart Trophy winner as league MVP (2000) is coming off knee surgery.

St. Louis' All-Star defenseman Al McInnis continues to produce for the Blues despite having played 20 years in the NHL.

Star forwards

The Blues are not only loaded with star players on defense. There are also forwards such as Keith Tkachuk, Doug Weight and Pavol Demitra. Tkachuk is the ultimate power forward. He can muck it up in the corners but he can also pop the puck in the net with alarming regularity, as he's done nearly 400 times in his career. Demitra is a speedy goal scorer. Both Tkachuk (38 goals, 75 points) and Demitra (35 goals, 78 points) were among league leaders in scoring last year. Weight is a crafty center with a deft passing touch. The Blues have a pretty good power play with such manpower.

Despite the fact that St. Louis allowed the fifth-fewest goals in the league during the regular season, the big question mark entering the 2002 playoffs was goaltending. Then young Brent Johnson went out and put on a show in the first round against Chicago. The big backstop threw three shutouts at the Blackhawks. He looks like a keeper of a keeper for Joel Quenneville, the man who has coached the Blues since 1997.

Sentimental favorites

In their early years, the Blues, a product of the NHL's 1967 expansion, provided every hockey fan with a trip down memory lane, drafting or signing many of the heroes of their youth—Glenn Hall and Jacques Plante in goal, Doug Harvey, Al Arbour and Jean-Guy Talbot on defense, center Phil Goyette and diminutive forward Camille Henry. The first year, the Blues even managed to coax the former Montreal Canadiens great Dickie Moore out of retirement.

Teaming up with young snipers such as Red Berenson, Gary Sabourin and Frank St. Marseille, the old-timers were sprightly enough to get the Blues into the Stanley Cup final in each of the club's first three seasons, winning the West Division regular-season title in two. They were sentimental favorites in all the Stanley Cup finals but, despite a gritty effort, they were swept two straight years by Montreal and by Boston in 1969–70. Scotty Bowman, launching a Hall-of-Fame coaching career, was behind the Blues' bench those last two seasons.

The Blues haven't returned to the Stanley Cup final since those halcyon days, despite a number of talented performers passing through their ranks. Brett Hull, acquired in a 1988 trade, emerged from virtual obscurity to become the Blues' career goal-scoring leader, including 86 goals in 1990–91, a single-season output topped only by the great Wayne Gretzky. The latter became Hull's teammate for the last few weeks of the 1995–96 season, after the Blues obtained his services in an unsuccessful bid to reach the Stanley Cup final.

Chris Pronger is among the league's biggest and best defensemen.

★ ROLL OF HONOR ★

Conference/Division	**Western/Central**
First season	**1967–68**
Honor roll	**Made Stanley Cup final first three years in NHL**
Home rink/Capacity	**Savvis Center/19,022**
Stanley Cups	**0**

Playing Record

	W	*L*	*T*	*RT*	*Pts*
Regular Season	**1208**	**1140**	**410**	**10**	**2836**
Playoffs	**134**	**157**			

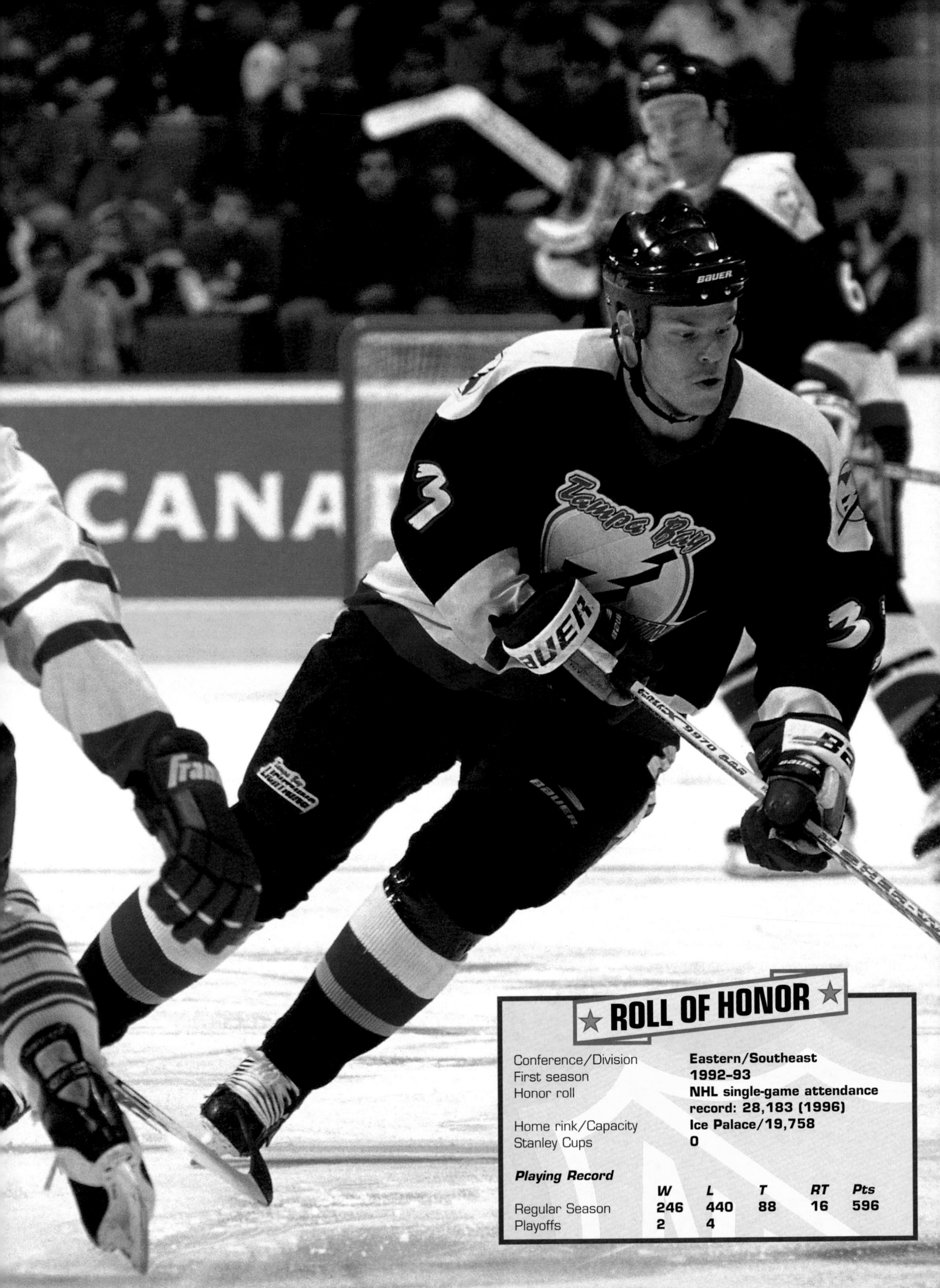

ROLL OF HONOR

Conference/Division	**Eastern/Southeast**
First season	**1992–93**
Honor roll	**NHL single-game attendance record: 28,183 (1996)**
Home rink/Capacity	**Ice Palace/19,758**
Stanley Cups	**0**

Playing Record

	W	*L*	*T*	*RT*	*Pts*
Regular Season	**246**	**440**	**88**	**16**	**596**
Playoffs	**2**	**4**			

Tampa Bay Lightning

Things are finally starting to look up in Tampa Bay after several barren seasons.

As the 1998 NHL Entry Draft approached, prospect Vincent Lecavalier was getting the kind of advanced notice that had been previously reserved for players such as Mario Lemieux and Eric Lindros. With Tampa Bay selecting first in '98, the Lightning took the teenage phenom and made him the cornerstone of what they hoped was an up-and-coming franchise.

Now more than four years later, the team and the player appear ready to finally fulfill such promise.

The Lightning have made the playoffs just once in their relatively short history. That came in 1996, after the team's only winning season (88 points). But there were signs of improvement in 2001–02. Tampa had its best record since 1996–97, and it improved a full 10 points from the 59 it had in 2000–01. The Lightning have upped their point total four straight seasons now. Lecavalier is showing signs of impending greatness, too. The big, shifty centerman, who is still just 22 years old, scored six goals in the last eight games of the season to make it to 20 for the third straight year. He is the only Lightning player ever to record three consecutive 20-goal seasons. If he can carry that momentum to the start of the 2002–03 season, the sky could be the limit.

Vincent Lecavalier, the first overall pick of the 1998 draft, is a superstar in the making, finishing last season with another 20 goals.

The Bulin Wall

They don't come any better in goal than Tampa goalie Nikolai Khabibulin. Nicknamed "The Bulin Wall," Khabibulin gives the Lightning a chance to win every night, whether the rest of the team is playing well or not. He backstopped Team Russia to a bronze at the 2002 Olympics. Young defenseman Pavel Kubina logs the most ice time in front of Khabibulin and he has shown good offensive skills. Fellow Czech Stan Neckar is a stay-at-home type.

A weakness Tampa is trying to overcome is a lack of offensive production. Only Anaheim and Columbus had fewer goals than Tampa's 178 last year. Besides Lecavalier, the Lightning are looking to players such as Vaclav Prospal, the versatile former Ottawa Senator who had a comeback season last year (55 points); hard-shooting Fredrik Modin, a pillar of the organization who was beset by injuries in 2001–02; and baby-faced Brad Richards, the 22-year-old who has already posted two 20-goal seasons.

Big box office

The Lightning came into the league in 1992 along with the Ottawa Senators. Because the team moved in its second season into the ThunderDome, with the largest seating capacity in the league, the team drew large crowds, including an NHL record 27,227 for its 1993–94 home opener against state-rival Florida Panthers, an expansion team that year. The Lightning left the Dome after the 1995–96 season, but not before establishing a new attendance record of 28,183 which still stands.

Former Maple Leaf Fredrik Modin is known for his lethal wrister.

Goaltender Manon Rheaume made history with the Lightning in 1992. She became the first woman to play in any of the four major sports leagues when she started a preseason game for Tampa. In her one appearance, she made seven saves in 20 minutes of action. Afterward, she joined a Tampa minor league affiliate.

Phil Esposito, the Hall of Fame forward, was the driving force behind getting an expansion team for Tampa. Esposito served as general manager and alternate governor until being replaced by Jacques Demers in that role after the Lightning started the 1998–99 season 0–1–1.

★ ROLL OF HONOR ★

Conference/Division	**Eastern/Northeast**
First season	**1917–18 (Arenas); 1919–20 (St. Patricks); 1926–27 (Maple Leafs)**
Honor roll	**Only NHL team to rally from a 3–0 games deficit in Stanley Cup final to win (1942)**
Home rink/Capacity	**Air Canada Centre/18,800**
Stanley Cups	**13 (1918, 1922, 1932, 1942, 1945, 1947, 1948, 1949, 1951, 1962, 1963, 1964, 1967)**

Playing Record

	W	*L*	*T*	*RT*	*Pts*
Regular Season	**2329**	**2275**	**766**	**12**	**5436**
Playoffs	**242**	**258**	**4**		

★ ROLL OF HONOR ★

Conference/Division **Western/Northwest**
First season **1970–71**
Honor roll **Reached Stanley Cup final, 1982, 1994**
Home rink/Capacity **General Motors Place/18,422**
Stanley Cups **0**

Playing Record

	W	*L*	*T*	*RT*	*Pts*
Regular Season	**936**	**1220**	**368**	**18**	**2258**
Playoffs	**56**	**78**			

Washington Capitals

The Capitals will hope that Jaromir Jagr's second season in D.C. is more successful than his first.

The Jaromir Jagr era in Washington isn't off to as flying a start as Capitals fans would have hoped, but with arguably the best one-on-one player in the league wearing a Capitals uniform, that is bound to change. Jagr came to D.C. last year from Pittsburgh with expectations being that the Caps would be a serious contender. But Washington finished out of the playoffs by two points and Jagr had an ordinary season by his high standards. Sure he tied for fifth in the league with 79 points, but he's used to winning the scoring title. Don't expect a second straight "down" season from the human stickhandling machine.

Jagr isn't the only Washington winger with a Hall of Fame résumé. Peter Bondra continues his excellent play. He still has speed to burn and his 39 goals last year was the fifth-best total in the league. He now has more than 400 career goals, all for the Caps. Andrei Nikolishin is a gifted centerman, although that position is one Capitals GM George McPhee has been working to shore up. One of the main areas in which Washington hopes to improve over last year is in the training room. Key players, including Jagr, Steve Konowalchuk, Jeff Halpern and Calle Johansson were sidelined with injuries. That was a big factor in not making the playoffs.

Gonzo Gonchar

There are offensive defensemen and then there is Sergei Gonchar. The rushin' Russian's 26 goals last year was the most in his position. No other NHL blueliner had more than 17. He has great skating ability and he quarterbacks one of the most deadly power plays in the league. The defense overall is looking to bounce back from the NHL's sixth-highest goals-against total.

Olie the Goalie, aka Olaf Kolzig, has been a fixture in the D.C. pipes for many seasons. In fact, the big backstop played his first games for the Caps way back in the 1989–90 season. He led the team to the heights of the 1998 Stanley Cup Finals and he is looking to regain that magic. Washington got a good look at young Sebastien Charpentier late last year, and he is a promising goaltender of the future. A coach of the past is Ron Wilson, the bench boss since 1997 who was let go in May.

Rough start

Right from the start of its NHL existence, the only way was up for the Capitals. It could not have gotten any lower for a team that joined the NHL as an expansion franchise in 1974–75 and proceeded to set all kinds of modern-day league records for futility. Most of the records are still in the book, more than two decades later.

But that first year? The 1974–75 Capitals established a record for the fewest points—21 in a 70-game season. They managed only one victory on the road.

Out of the pit

But climb the Capitals did—incrementally at first as Guy Charron arrived as a bonafide scorer and, finally, beyond the .500 mark and into the playoffs for the first time in 1982–83. That coincided with the arrival of the inspirational David Poile. Under Poile the Capitals had only two seasons under .500, and captured one Patrick Division title, in 1988–89.

Olaf Kolzig had a reasonable season for the Capitals in 2001–2002, finishing the year with a .903 save percentage.

Key draft picks such as sparkplugs Mike Gartner, Bobby Carpenter and Ryan Walter joined with defensemen Scott Stevens, Larry Murphy and Rod Langway—the latter pair coming after big trades with Los Angeles and Montreal—to continue Washington's rise from rags to respectability in the competitive cauldron of the NHL.

The Capitals finally made it to hockey's zenith by appearing in the Stanley Cup Finals during the 1997–98 season for the first time in club history. Currently, with the likes of Jagr, Bondra, Gonchar and Olie the Goalie, the Caps hope to regain that magic. Leading the Caps to the next level will be this talented group's ultimate responsibility, not just putting up gaudy statistics.

Peter Bondra scored a team-high 39 goals in 2001–2002.

ROLL OF HONOR

Conference/Division	**Eastern/Southeast**
First season	**1974–75**
Honor roll	**Lost out to Detroit Red Wings in the 1998 Stanley Cup Final.**
Home rink/Capacity	**MCI Center/18,672**
Stanley Cups	**0**

Playing Record

	W	*L*	*T*	*RT*	*Pts*
Regular Season	**949**	**988**	**285**	**8**	**2191**
Playoffs	**67**	**81**			

Hockey Heroes

It's a truism in professional team sports that collective play wins championships. It's no less true that fans come out to watch the stars of the game, to marvel at their virtuosity, as much as to root for a winner.

Across its long history the National Hockey League has produced and continues to produce as richly varied a cast of sporting legends as any professional league in the world.

Each generation of fans, it turns out, has its Golden Age; each new wave of player talent leaves behind indelible memories of sporting brilliance that resonate forever in the collective imagination.

Some of the memories are passed down, like the legend of One-Eyed Frank McGee, who once scored 14 goals—eight of them consecutively—in a Stanley Cup game, a 23–2 drubbing of Dawson City by the Ottawa Silver Seven. McGee's nickname was no joke—he lost an eye when he was struck there by the butt end of a hockey stick.

Keen hockey fans, even the young ones, know of Frank Nighbor, who perfected the poke check, of Fred (Cyclone) Taylor, said to have scored a key Stanley Cup goal while skating full speed backwards, of Joe Malone, who once scored 44 goals in a 20-game season.

They certainly know the story of Lester Patrick, the coach of the New York Rangers, who in a 1928 Stanley Cup game, shed his jacket, shirt and tie and put on the goalie pads, and replaced the injured Lorne Chabot. The Rangers won the game and, later, the Cup.

Patrick was surely one of many stars of his era. The NHL of the 1920s and 1930s boasted names like Syl Apps, Ace Bailey, King Clancy, Clint Benedict, the first goalie to wear a mask, and Howie Morenz, known as the Stratford Streak, and the most electrifying player of his time.

What's my line?

The 1930s, 1940s and 1950s were famous for the marvelous forward lines that made hockey magic. The Toronto Maple Leafs had the Kid Line, with Gentleman Joe Primeau flanked by Harvey (Busher) Jackson and Charlie Conacher. The Boston Bruins featured the Kraut Line—Milt Schmidt, Bobby Bauer and Woody Dumart.

The Avalanche have boasted a strong lineup of star players since arriving in Colorado in 1995, resulting in two Stanley Cups and four additional trips to the conference finals.

Rangers' Rocket man

PAVEL BURE

The explosive "Russian Rocket" brings fans out of their seats like no other player in hockey.

After Pavel Bure's first game with the Vancouver Canucks, the media nicknamed him the "Russian Rocket" and his brilliant rookie season touched off Pavelmania among the long-suffering Canucks fans.

In Bure, the Canucks finally had landed a superstar to build a true contender around. The 5-foot-10, 189-pound right winger certainly arrived in Vancouver with pedigree. He first dazzled North American hockey people at the 1989–90 World Junior Championships in Anchorage, Alaska. Playing on a line with Sergei Fedorov and Alexander Mogilny, Bure scored eight goals and totaled 14 points to help the USSR win the gold medal in that tournament. He was named the tournament's top forward.

The following year, he helped the Soviets win gold at the World Hockey Championships. He starred for both the junior and senior men's teams in 1990–91 also, helping the juniors win a silver medal and the senior men win the bronze.

Bure frenzy

The Canucks had drafted Bure in the sixth round of the 1989 entry draft, only to have then-NHL president John Ziegler rule him ineligible. The decision was reversed more than a year later, clearing the way for Bure to join the Canucks.

Three years after Bure was named rookie-of-the-year in the Soviet National League, he scored 34 goals for the Canucks and won the Calder Trophy as the top freshman in the NHL—and created a frenzy among Vancouver hockey supporters. In 1992–93, Bure scored 60 goals and added 50 assists for 110 points, becoming the first Canuck ever to score as many as 50 goals and reach 100 points in a season.

Pavel Bure's knack for goals has enabled him to win back-to-back Maurice Richard Trophies.

CAREER RECORD

Personal					
Birthplace/Date	**Moscow, USSR/3-31-71**				
Height/Weight	**5-10/189**				
Awards					
Calder Memorial Trophy	**1992**				
First All-Star Team	**1994**				
Maurice Richard Trophy	**2000, 2001**				
NHL Career	**7 seasons Vancouver Canucks**				
	3½ seasons Florida Panthers				
	½ season New York Rangers				
Playing Record					
	Games	***Goals***	***Assists***	***Points***	***PIM***
Regular Season	**663**	**418**	**331**	**749**	**468**
Playoffs	**64**	**35**	**35**	**70**	**74**

Bure snapped off another 60-goal season in 1993–94, slipping to 47 assists and 107 points. He then led all playoff goalscorers with 16, leading the Canucks to the Stanley Cup final, which they lost in a seven-game thriller to the New York Rangers.

He negotiated a rich new contract in the midst of the playoff run. Bure obviously had learned that leverage matters in the free enterprise system, another indicator that he was a quick study in adapting to North American life and the NHL.

Leaving Vancouver

In the mid-1990s, Bure was affected by injuries. But he gritted his teeth at the start of the 1997–98 season, determined to prove he was not past his best. He scored 51 goals in what turned out to be his last season in Vancouver and carried that goal-scoring touch to the 1998 Olympics, where he netted a tournament-high nine goals for silver medalists Russia. Russia President Boris Yeltsin presented Bure with the prestigious Order of Honor during a ceremony at The Kremlin shortly after the Olympics.

For "personal reasons," he demanded a trade and eventually got one—to the Florida Panthers in January 1999. He made an immediate impact, scoring 13 goals in 11 games. But then he blew out his right knee.

Bure came back strong from that setback, scoring 58 goals in just 74 games in 1999–2000 and winning the Maurice "Rocket" Richard Trophy for top scorer by a wide margin—14 goals. He won the Richard Trophy again in 2000–01 with a league-high 59 goals.

The Big Apple came calling in March of 2002, when a trade landed Bure with the New York Rangers. After scoring 12 goals in just 12 games after the trade, it's safe to say the Russian Rocket is a hit on Broadway.

Detroit's All-around Star

SERGEI FEDOROV

This three-time Stanley Cup champion and former league MVP is the total hockey package.

"FEDOROV IS AS GOOD AS ANYBODY IN ANY ERA SKILLWISE. FEDOROV IS ONE OF A KIND."

AN NHL SCOUT

When Sergei Fedorov arrived in Detroit, the Red Wings already had a No. 1 center—veteran Steve Yzerman. So Fedorov, brilliantly talented offensively, was asked to handle a big part of the defensive load. That would seem a waste. Except Fedorov applied himself to the task and, in his second season in the NHL, he was named runner-up to Guy Carbonneau for the Frank J. Selke Trophy as the league's best defensive forward.

Two years later, in 1994, he won the trophy.

He also won the Hart Trophy that year as the league's most valuable player, was named to the first all-star team and won the Lester B. Pearson Award, voted on by his peers and awarded to the league's outstanding player.

Fedorov's skills are widely acknowledged as amongst the best in the NHL. Keeping him motivated has always been the challenge.

Russian might

He came to the league with impeccable credentials. As a junior in Russia, he centered a line with wingers Pavel Bure and Alexander Mogilny—one of the most electrifying trios ever assembled.

Fedorov played four years with Central Red Army, and helped the Soviet National team win gold medals at the World Championships in 1989 and 1990.

With his speed, improvisational moves executed at full speed, and all-around game, Fedorov made an immediate impact on the NHL, leading all rookies in goals (31), assists (48) and points (79) in 1990–91. He finished runner-up to Ed Belfour in the voting for the Calder Trophy.

As exciting as his skills are, Fedorov always has understood that even star players perform best as part of an ensemble.

Luckily, his Detroit coach, Scotty Bowman, understood this also. It was Bowman who acquired veteran Russian Igor Larionov and assembled a five-man unit with Fedorov, Vyacheslav Kozlov, Vlyacheslav Fetisov and Vladimir Konstantinov.

The unit, used selectively by Bowman, a master strategist, performed brilliantly for the Red Wings in 1995–96. Fedorov, ever the team man, moved to right wing on the unit, ceding the center position on the line to Larionov, who centered the famous KLM (Vladimir Krutov, Larionov and Sergei Makarov) for the Soviet National team in the 1980s.

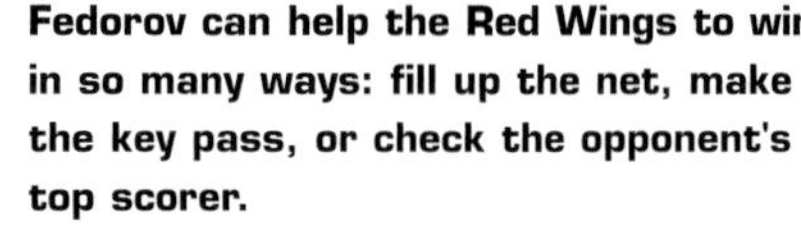

Fedorov can help the Red Wings to win in so many ways: fill up the net, make the key pass, or check the opponent's top scorer.

Like the five-man units in the Russian national teams, Detroit's unit stressed puck control and patience, preferring to circle back in the neutral zone, and to hold on to the puck in the offensive zone rather than try a low percentage play.

Russian light

Fedorov's spectacular play, sly sense of humor and good looks convinced Nike to make him their poster boy for their hockey equipment. He showcased Nike's new line of skates and is considered very worthy of attention by the newspapers.

The 1997–98 season threw up highs and lows for Fedorov. A free agent following Detroit's 1997 Stanley Cup victory, he sat out the first half of the year over terms and played his first hockey of the season for Russia at the Olympic Games in Nagano. Just after Fedorov had returned, with a silver medal, Carolina made a huge offer, which Detroit matched, so he returned to the Red Wings.

Fedorov was a key part of the Red Wings' Stanley Cup championships in 1998 and 2002. Now in his 30s, the Russian speedster is in his prime.

CAREER RECORD

Personal

Birthplace/Date	**Pskov, USSR/ 12-13-69**
Height/Weight	**6-2/200**

Awards

All-Rookie Team	**1991**
First All-Star Team	**1994**
Frank J. Selke Trophy	**1994, 1996**
Lester B. Pearson Award	**1994**
Hart Trophy	**1994**

NHL Career **12 seasons Detroit Red Wings**

Playing Record

	Games	Goals	Assists	Points	PIM
Regular season	828	364	507	871	535
Playoffs	158	49	111	160	113

Big talent in a little package

Fleury has proved to the size conscious NHL that small is not only beautiful, but powerful too.

THEOREN FLEURY

In the hyper-macho world of the NHL, size is said to matter above all. Theoren Fleury's entire career has been a refutation of that cliché. Not outlandishly larger than the average thoroughbred jockey, Fleury—swift, skilled, creative and combative—has been a star at every level of hockey. He has forced hockey people, who don't let go of their stereotypes easily, to see past his stature and recognize the dazzling things he can do with the gifts he possesses, to forget about the things he cannot do.

As a junior star with the Moose Jaw Warriors, Fleury was an offensive machine, racking up 472 points in four seasons. In his final year as a junior, he produced 160 points, including 68 goals—and 235 minutes in penalties in the rough and tumble Western Hockey League. He was a member of Canada's National Junior Team in 1987 and 1988, when the team won a gold medal.

Rarely has a junior player achieved more than Fleury did. Yet he was taken 166th in the NHL Entry Draft in 1987, his low selection an obvious result of his size.

CAREER RECORD

Personal

Birthplace/Date	**Oxbow, Saskatchewan/6–29–68**
Height/Weight	**5-6/180**

Awards

NHL 2nd All-Star Team	**1995**
Co-winner Alka Seltzer Plus Award (league plus-minus leader) —with Marty McSorley	**1991**

NHL Career

10½ seasons Calgary Flames
½ season Colorado Avalanche
3 seasons New York Rangers

Playing Record

	Games	*Goals*	*Assists*	*Points*	*PIM*
Regular season	**1030**	**443**	**612**	**1055**	**1763**
Playoffs	**77**	**34**	**45**	**79**	**116**

Playing big

He began his pro career in the minors playing for Calgary's Salt Lake City farm club, but by season's end that year—1988–89—he was playing for the NHL Flames in Calgary, helping them win their first Stanley Cup championship by beating the fabled Montreal Canadiens, and in the legendary Forum, to boot.

In his first full season with the Flames, he scored 31 goals, 30 being a benchmark of excellence. The following season—1990–91—he bagged 51 goals, establishing himself as a star. He has delivered big scoring numbers every season he has played in the NHL. And playing on a team that has featured bigger, stronger players like Gary Roberts, Joe Nieuwendyk and Doug Gilmour, Fleury topped the Flames' scoring list six times from 1991 through 1998.

Dream on

Small-market Calgary faced reality in 1998–99. Fleury was due to become an unrestricted free agent, and the team wouldn't likely be able to pay what he could earn in the open market. So the Flames traded Fleury to Colorado during the season, but not before he became the team's all-time leader in points. After the trade, Fleury was once again with a contender and he was a big part of the Avs pushing Dallas to seven games in the Western Conference Finals.

In 1999, free-agent Fleury signed with the New York Rangers, taking his show to North America's biggest stage. He has been among the Rangers top-three point producers in each of his three seasons with the team. For a guy considered too small early in his career, Fleury certainly scaled impressive heights in hockey.

The modestly sized winger is a dangerous man with the puck on his stick, scoring 443 career goals.

The Simmering Swede
PETER FORSBERG

Colorado Avalanche's fiery Peter Forsberg breaks the mold of the traditionally timid European player.

The stereotype of the European player has been that of a player with great skill but no grit and determination. Colorado Avalanche center Peter Forsberg lays waste to that notion. He's got the skilled part—few players in the league can match him in that department—but he's also got a mean streak that seems hewn right out of the Canadian plains.

Forsberg is that rare combination of athlete—he is very creatively offensively, but he also has a defensive conscience. He skates back hard and is not afraid of blocking a shot. He's an intelligent player, but he also likes to get in people's faces and stir up a bit of trouble.

No retreat

"I'll tell you what sticks out in my mind isn't so much his talent level, but his toughness," said former Avalanche goaltender Craig Billington, whose role as Colorado's back-up goaltender gave him the best seat in the house on many nights to watch the gifted Swede. "He's tough," continued Billington. "When you watch him play, he's gritty and tough and he doesn't back down; and he gives it back. You get a lot of people who are skilled in this game, but who perhaps don't have the grittiness."

New Jersey Devils goaltender Martin Brodeur, two-time winner of the Jennings Trophy for lowest goals-against average, has written of Forsberg: "To me, Forsberg is the most complete hockey player in the game today. There are so many ways he can hurt you—a clutch pass, a precise slap shot or wrist shot upstairs, he does it all!"

Forsberg is an awesome combination of skill and grit. His GM wouldn't be surprised to see him win the scoring championship and the award for best defensive forward in the same season

Peer respect

Many hockey people agree with Brodeur's assessment. In a *Toronto Sun* poll of hockey experts a few years ago, Forsberg was deemed top performer in hockey. Said an ESPN analyst: "Forsberg can do so many things. But what impresses me most is the way his peers talk about him. They just shake their heads in awe at Forsberg's play, game in and game out."

Forsberg is not only a great player, he is a winner—and passionate about it. He hates losing, he can't stand it. In 1994, he scored the gold medal-winning goal for Sweden in the Olympic final versus Canada. It was in a shootout, and the unorthodox deke he used has been immortalized on a Swedish Postage stamp. Two years later, he helped lead the former Quebec Nordiques to the Stanley Cup in their first season as the Colorado Avalanche.

He was on the sidelines for much of the Avs run to the 2001 Cup after having his spleen removed. That and foot surgeries kept him out of the entire 2001–02 regular season. He returned for the 2002 playoffs in incredible fashion, dominating games as if he had never left. And playing that same gritty, two-way style.

Forsberg's GM, Pierre Lacroix, has said: "He could win the scoring championship and at the same time win the Selke Award (as best defensive forward)." Don't be surprised if the Swede one day pulls off that feat.

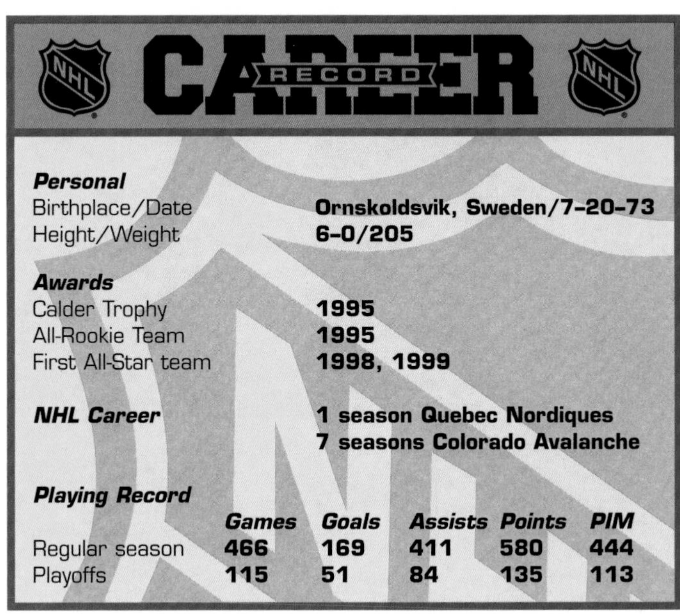

CAREER RECORD

Personal

Birthplace/Date	**Ornskoldsvik, Sweden/7-20-73**
Height/Weight	**6-0/205**

Awards

Calder Trophy	**1995**
All-Rookie Team	**1995**
First All-Star team	**1998, 1999**

NHL Career **1 season Quebec Nordiques**
7 seasons Colorado Avalanche

Playing Record

	Games	*Goals*	*Assists*	*Points*	*PIM*
Regular season	466	169	411	580	444
Playoffs	115	51	84	135	113

A hockey legend hangs them up
DOMINIK HASEK

No one had a bigger effect on a game than Detroit's former superstar netminder.

Around the time of the 1998 Olympics, Wayne Gretzky, recognized as the best player of all time in a comprehensive poll of hockey experts by the *Hockey News*, had this to say about Dominik Hasek: "I think he is the best player in the game. He's just at a level that nobody else is at right now. He's simply sensational."

In June 2002, Hasek finally got the one trophy that had eluded him—the Stanley Cup.

That's a pretty ringing endorsement, considering the source. Hasek has earned such an accolade, and the awards are stacking up as proof. In 1997, he became the first goalie in 35 years to win the Hart Trophy as league MVP. He repeated his "Hart" trick in 1998, joining immortals Wayne Gretzky, Guy Lafleur, Bobby Clarke, Bobby Orr, Stan Mikita, Bobby Hull, Gordie Howe, Eddie Shore and Howie Morenz as the only players to win consecutive Hart trophies. He is the only netminder to win the award more than once

Vezina monopoly

As for the award designed for goaltenders, the Vezina Trophy, Hasek has won that more times than he can count on one hand. In 1997–98, Hasek endured early boos from the home crowd. Popular Sabres coach Ted Nolan was not brought back for the season after winning the 1997 Jack Adams Award as coach of the year. It was no secret that Hasek was not a Nolan supporter, and fans in Buffalo made Hasek into one of the villians at the start of the year.

Hasek was not the "Dominator" until December, when he recorded six shutouts and got himself back on track. He eventually went on to lead the league in save percentage (.932) for the fifth straight season and his 13 shutouts were the most since Tony Esposito's 15 in 1970. Along the way Hasek took the time to lead his underdog Czech Republic to a gold medal in the 1998 Winter Olympics in Nagano, Japan, in dramatic fashion. He stoned Canada in a shootout in the semi-finals, stopping all five attempts by Canadian players in the shootout while the Czechs scored once, then shut out Russia in the gold-medal game to win 1–0.

The acrobat

In the 1998 playoffs, Hasek led the Sabres to the conference final for the first time since 1980. In 1999, he was the driving force behind Buffalo making its first Stanley Cup Finals appearance in 24 years, where the Sabres took the Dallas Stars to six games.

When it comes to style, there is none like Hasek. He flops, he does splits, he makes sprawling saves that no one expects. One of his most famous moves is to drop his stick and grab the puck with his blocker hand—unorthodox to say the least.

One NHL scout says: "He has one of the most unorthodox styles I think I've ever seen in a goalie, but he gets the job done. The man is amazing. I've never seen anyone like him in goal."

In the summer of 2001, Hasek wanted to be traded to a contender and he got what he asked for, going to the star-laden Detroit Red Wings. Everything went according to script for him after that. The Wings were the best regular-season team, then they went on to capture the one trophy—the Stanley Cup—which had eluded Hasek in his NHL career. Now the Dominator, has truly accomplished it all and subsequently, decided to go out on top. The Red Wings goaltender made it official on June 25th when he announced his retirement at a press conference at Joe Louis Arena, appropriately the site of his greatest triumph.

CAREER RECORD

Personal

Birthplace/Date	**Pardubice, Czech/1-29-65**
Height/Weight	**5-11/168**

Awards

NHL First All-Star Team	**1994-95, 1997-99, 2001**
Vezina Trophy	**1994-95, 1997-99, 2001**
Hart Trophy	**1997, 1998**
Jennings Trophy	**1994, 2001**

NHL Career

2 seasons Chicago Blackhawks
9 seasons Buffalo Sabres
1 season Detroit Red Wings

Playing Record

	Games	Wins	Losses	Ties	GAA
Regular Season	581	288	189	80	2.23
Playoffs	97	53	39	0	2.03

The ultimate sniper BRETT HULL

The son of a star was a legend in St. Louis but, more importantly a Stanley Cup-winner in Dallas and Detroit.

When Bobby Hull was on the ice, all eyes were on him. Brett Hull plays a different game from his dad. A methodical skater, the younger Hull moves quietly around the ice, particularly in the offensive zone, circling into spaces others have left, positioning himself to accept a setup pass. He tries to draw as little attention to himself as possible, laying in the weeds, as the hockey players say. Until, that is, he unleashes The Shot.

By the time the defenders realize it is Hull who is shooting, it often is too late. Possessing one of the fastest, hardest slap shots in hockey, Hull is a prolific but mostly unflashy scorer. He has been called the NHL's Stealth Bomber.

Quietly to the top

Similarly, Hull insinuated himself into the NHL élite quietly. Because of his name, the NHL saw Hull coming up through the junior and college ranks, but he was not regarded as a rising star.

The Calgary Flames selected Hull in the sixth round of the 1984 entry draft, an unheralded 117th overall out of the University of Minnesota-Duluth. In his full first NHL season—1987–88—Hull scored 26 goals in 52 games for the Flames, who traded him before season's end to St. Louis.

With the Blues, Hull was paired with Adam Oates, one of the league's top playmakers. Hull and Oates quickly became a hit.

Hull scored 41 goals and added 43 assists for 84 points in his first full season with the Blues, but that was merely the warm-up.

In 1989–90, Hull scored 72 goals to lead the NHL in goal-scoring for the first of three straight seasons. The following year his quick-release shot found the net 86 times and another 70 times in 1991–92.

Along with the goal-scoring blitz came official recognition. Hull was a first-team all-star three straight times, won the Lady Byng as the league's most sportsmanlike player and the Hart Trophy as the most valuable player.

The Golden Brett scored the Stanley Cup-winning goal for Dallas in 1999 and had several key goals during Detroit's 2002 Cup run.

CAREER RECORD

Personal

Birthplace/Date	**Belleville, Ontario/8-9-64**
Height/Weight	**5-10/201**

Awards

NHL First All-Star Team	**1990-92**
Lady Byng Trophy	**1990**
Hart Memorial Trophy	**1991**
Lester B. Pearson Award	**1991**

NHL Career

1/2 season Calgary Flames
10 1/2 seasons St. Louis Blues
3 seasons Dallas Stars
1 season Detroit Red Wings

Playing record

	Games	Goals	Assists	Points	PIM
Regular season	1101	679	567	1246	424
Playoffs	186	100	84	184	69

Ups and downs

He was named captain of the Blues, but he had made himself something more important to St. Louis—its franchise player.

The Blues traded Oates, the set-up man, to the Bruins in February 1992, but replaced him with Craig Janney, another able playmaker. Still, some of his fans were disappointed when Hull "slumped" to 54 goals in 1992–93 and managed "only" 57 goals in 1993–94. In the lockout-shortened 1994–95 season, Hull delivered 29 goals in 48 games, which pro-rates to 49 goals over an 82-game schedule. Strictly routine for the Golden Brett, some would say.

Head coach Mike Keenan stripped Hull of the captaincy in 1995–96. Nothing personal, he assured people.

Gone, too, was the playmaking Janney, who had been traded to San Jose during the 1994–95 season. In March 1996, Keenan traded for Wayne Gretzky, the ultimate playmaker, but the Hull-Gretzky duo was shortlived. Gretzky left for New York as a free agent at season's end. Partway through the 1996–97 season, yet another playmaking center was brought in—Pierre Turgeon.

Then, in the summer of 1998, it was the Golden Brett himself who was involved in a move. Hull had St. Louis hockey fans singing the blues when he signed as a free agent for the Dallas Stars.

It turned out to be a great move for the Golden Brett. A man who has had his share of individual honors bought into the Stars' team-first defensive style and found himself in the Stanley Cup Finals in June. With a flair for the dramatic, he scored the championship-winning goal in the third overtime of game six. Last year, he got his name on the Cup a second time as one of the future Hall of Famers on the Detroit Red Wings roster. That gives the Golden Brett one more title than his famous father.

The Edmonton native could well dominate the Art Ross Trophy for many years to come.

The Scoring Machine
JAROME IGINLA

Over the decades of the 1980s and 1990s, and even early into the 2000s, the Art Ross Trophy—given to the player who leads the league in scoring points—was handed out to just a trio of players.

Wayne Gretzky, Mario Lemieux and Jaromir Jagr had a monopoly on the award from 1981 through 2001. But in 2002, there was a new kid in town. And Jarome Iginla looks like he may start a new Art Ross dynasty.

Iginla dominated the NHL in 2001–02, scoring a league-high 52 goals (11 more than the next-closest player) and recording an NHL-best 96 points (six more than the runner-up). His goal-scoring feat earned him the Maurice Richard Trophy. He did it on a team without a lot of supporting firepower.

The Flames were 11th out of 15 teams in the Western Conference in goals, and the No. 2 goal scorer on the team had just 28. Iginla's offense fueled wins.

While the team finished three games under .500, it was 23–10–5–2 when Iginla potted a goal and 20–3–5–2 when he had a multiple-point game.

An Edmonton man in Calgary

Such heights always have been envisioned for the Edmonton native. He was selected 11th overall in the 1995 Entry Draft by Dallas and he was a prized prospect. But the Stars were on the verge of something great and they needed immediate help, so while he was still playing junior Iginla was shipped to Calgary in a deal that netted Flames star Joe Nieuwendyk for Dallas.

It was strange for someone from Oiler country to don the flaming "C" jersey of Alberta's rival team. Iginla says that his family was happy he would be playing closer to home, but he jokes that it took friends a long time to convert from being Oilers fans to being Flames fans—and that he's still working one some of them.

Iginla experienced immediate success in the NHL, making the All-Rookie team in 1996–97 and finishing second behind Bryan Berard in voting for the Calder Trophy, given to the league's top newcomer. The future Art Ross Trophy winner scored 21 goals and had 50 points as a rookie.

Getting better all the time

There has been steady improvement on those stellar rookie numbers. After a bit of a sophomore slump when Iginla missed 12 games and finished with 13 goals and 32 points, he's gotten better every year. He had 28 goals and 51 points in 1998-99, 29 goals and 63 points in 1999–2000 and 31 goals and 71 points in 2000–01. He got a confidence boost going into the 2001–02 season by participating with Canada's best players in a pre-Olympic camp, and that helped him get off to a scorching start on the regular season. Iginla also credits playing with center Craig Conroy, a multiple Selke Award nominee (best defensive forward) who came to Calgary from St. Louis in March 2001, with elevating his own game.

As the first black player to lead the league in scoring, Iginla says he would consider it a tremendous honor if he is considered a role model for black kids. He looked up to Oilers star goalie Grant Fuhr, among other black players, when he was young. They were important to him and he tries to live up to that image. Iginla promotes hockey as a great game for everyone.

The most important color for him in the past year has been gold. As a member of the gold-medal-winning Olympic team at the 2002 Salt Lake Games, he helped bring a great sense of pride to all Canadians after a 50-year gold-medal drought in their native sport. Score another one for the kid from Edmonton.

Jarome Iginla led the NHL in scoring 2001-2002 to capture the Art Ross Trophy.

CAREER RECORD

Personal

Birthplace/Date	**Edmonton, Alberta/ 7-1-77**
Height/Weight	**6-1/205**

Awards

All-Rookie Team	**1997**
Maurice Richard Trophy	**2002**
Art Ross Trophy	**2002**

NHL Career **6 seasons Calgary Flames**

Playing record

	Games	Goals	Assists	Points	PIM
Regular Season	470	174	189	363	289
Playoffs	2	1	1	2	0

Washington's Artist On Ice

He's flashy, he's strong, he scores goals like no one else—and he picks up the odd trophy now and again

JAROMIR JAGR

Jaromir Jagr is the closest thing the NHL has to a rock star. He's flashy, good looking and, for many years, he had long, unruly hair, too long for his helmet to contain. Jagr loves to laugh, too, and who can blame him? There seems little the 6-foot-2, 230-pound forward cannot do.

He's the most potent force in the NHL. He's been a force from the get-go. As a rookie in 1990–91, he made the all-rookie team by scoring 27 goals and adding 30 assists. He added 13 points in the Pittsburgh Cup-winning playoff run. Jagr is a fixture as one of the top offensive players in the league. Indeed, in 1994–95, Jagr won the scoring title with 70 points, including 32 goals in the lockout-shortened, 48-game regular season.

More important, he arrived as a mature player, having to step up and shoulder the burden of being the go-to guy for Pittsburgh. Teammate Mario Lemieux took the season off to recover from his bout with Hodgkin's Disease and chronic back problems.

Record breaker

Playing the star comes effortlessly for Jagr, who has a long, fluid, deceptively swift skating stride, and he's equally fluid handling the puck. He truly creates art on ice.

"He is a master of deception," said New York Rangers goaltender Mike Richter. "If you try to anticipate with him, you'll often guess wrong. And if you just try to react, he's too fast and you get beat."

In 1995–96, Jagr lifted his artistry to new heights. He and Lemieux each scored 60-plus goals that season. But the two were friendly, complementary talents, not rivals. Jagr says he never has felt overlooked, never worried that he was playing in Lemieux's shadow.

"No, I never looked at it that way when we were winning the Stanley Cup," said Jagr. "As long as we were winning, nothing else mattered."

CAREER RECORD

Personal

Birthplace/Date	**Kladno, Czechoslovakia/2-15-72**
Height/Weight	**6-2/230**

Awards

Art Ross Trophy	**1995, 1998, 1999, 2000, 2001**
Hart Memorial Trophy	**1999**
All-Rookie Team	**1991**
First All-Star Team	**1995, 1996, 1998, 1999, 2000, 2001**

NHL Career	**11 seasons Pittsburgh Penguins** **1 season Washington Capitals**

Playing Record

	Games	Goals	Assists	Points	PIM
Regular Season	**875**	**470**	**688**	**1158**	**623**
Playoffs	**140**	**65**	**82**	**147**	**121**

Jaromir Jagr has taken his skills to the nation's capital.

Center Stage

He potted 47 goals and added 48 assists for 95 points in 1996–97, but improved on that in 1997–98 by becoming the only man to top the century mark (102 points—35 goals and 67 assists). The subsequent Art Ross Trophy was the second of his career and rounded off a spectacular season for Jagr that also brought him his third First All-Star appearance and a chunk of gold that was pretty unexpected.

In February 1998, Jagr was a member of the Czech Republic squad which won the gold medal at the Winter Olympics in Nagano, Japan, beating Russia 1–0 in the final.

In 1998–99, Jagr became the leader. Lemieux was busy buying the team and Ron Francis was in Carolina, so Jagr became the captain in name and substance. He was not only the best skater in the league, winning his third Art Ross Trophy by outscoring his closest competitor by 20 points, he also took an active leadership role.

Jagr won his third straight Art Ross Trophy in 1999–2000, tallying 96 points on 42 goals and 54 assists even though he missed 19 games. He was briefly reunited with Lemieux when Super Mario unretired in 2000–01, but in July 2001 a new era dawned. Jagr was traded to the Washington Capitals. Now in a town known mainly for politics, Jagr is making hockey a hot topic of conversation.

The Net Magician

CURTIS JOSEPH

A master of the angles, Cujo brings both excitement and a unique style to his position.

Curtis Joseph came late to hockey. He didn't join a team until he was 10 or 11 years old, and did so then only because his cousin had paid for a spot on a team but was moving. Joseph took the place of his cousin, who happened to be goalie, which worked out great since Joseph says he couldn't skate.

NHLers who have to face him on a nightly basis wish that his cousin never would have moved. Then Joseph wouldn't have gotten into the sport and he wouldn't be making their lives so difficult now.

Joseph made up for lost time quickly after his late start in hockey. He was never drafted by an NHL team, but after a stellar freshman season at the University of Wisconsin in 1988–89 in which he was named to the conference's first all-star team, he was signed as a free agent by the St. Louis Blues. "Cujo," as Joseph is known, played only 23 games in the minors before becoming a fixture with the Blues.

Curtis Joseph takes a gambler's approach to goaltending, but it is controlled chaos.

The acrobat

In the early 1990s, Joseph was an indefatigable force in the St. Louis net. He had consecutive seasons of 60, 68 and 71 games played. In St. Louis he honed his style. Or, as some observers might suggest, his lack of style.

Joseph takes a gambler's approach to the position. He is unpredictable and his acrobatic saves fill up the highlight reels. He also wanders out of net on a regular basis to play the puck. But it is controlled chaos. Joseph has great balance and he knows the percentages. His knack for starting the breakout resulted in nine assists in 1991–92, the second-highest total ever for a goaltender.

In 1995, Joseph was dealt to the Edmonton Oilers, where his reputation as a giant-killer in the playoffs soared. On the strength of Cujo's brilliant netminding, the small-market Oilers toppled heavily favored Dallas in 1997 and Colorado in 1998. He was also Canada's starting goalie in the 1996 World Cup of Hockey and also on the roster for the 1998 and 2002 Olympic teams.

Coming home

Cujo grew up just north of Toronto, so it was a homecoming when he signed with the Leafs as a free agent in the summer of 1998. The Leafs were in need of a star netminder when he arrived, having missed the playoffs two straight seasons. But with the goaltending position shored up, Toronto became an instant contender.

Over the past four seasons, the Leafs posted two 100-point seasons and two seasons in the 90s, while winning six playoff series. Joseph was runner-up for 1999 Vezina Trophy, given to the league's best goaltender, and he was a finalist for the 2000 award. His numbers are not gaudy, but his effect on the game is certainly profound.

With Dominik Hasek's retirement as star netminder of the 2002 Stanley Cup Champions, the Detroit Red Wings were looking for an elite goalie to fill the void. Like Hasek, the fabled Cup has eluded Cujo and unrestricted free agency presented an opportunity to remedy the situation. On July 2, the Red Wings quickly decided that Cujo was the perfect fit for the veteran club with signing Joseph to a three year deal. With Cujo in front of the net, the Red Wings clearly plan to defend their title in the 2002–2003 season.

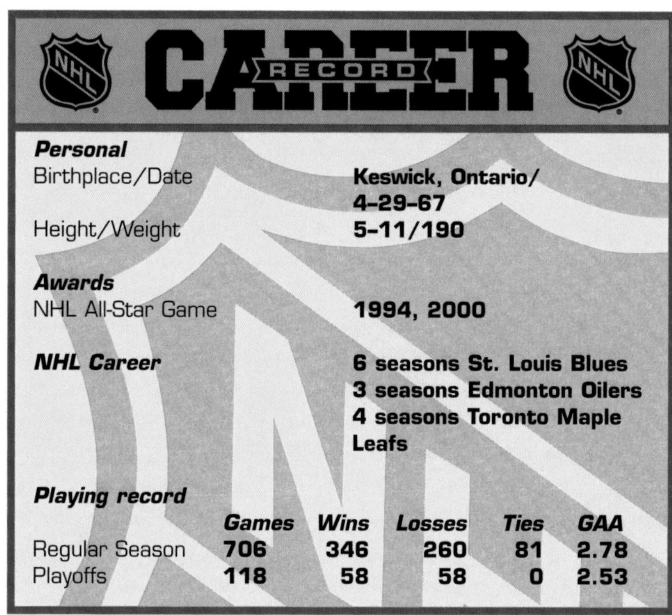

CAREER RECORD

Personal

Birthplace/Date	**Keswick, Ontario/ 4-29-67**
Height/Weight	**5-11/190**

Awards

NHL All-Star Game	**1994, 2000**

NHL Career

6 seasons St. Louis Blues
3 seasons Edmonton Oilers
4 seasons Toronto Maple Leafs

Playing record

	Games	Wins	Losses	Ties	GAA
Regular Season	706	346	260	81	2.78
Playoffs	118	58	58	0	2.53

The Mighty Duck

PAUL KARIYA

Anaheim's Paul Kariya is rated as one of the fastest men on the ice in the NHL.

When he gets his motor running, nobody in the NHL is more dangerous than Paul Kariya. At top speed, he is a blur rushing down the ice, with enough moves in his arsenal to reduce even the best defensemen in the league into pylons.

Left-winger Kariya sets the excitement meter on atomic and he proves just how entertaining the game of hockey can be to watch. Before the 1997–98 season, Kariya was rated as the league's best player by *The Hockey News*. It pointed to his breathtaking skating, speed and quickness, puck skills, ability to raise his own play and that of his teammates and his work ethic. It also praised his hockey smarts, which is no surprise coming from a former dean's list student at the University of Maine.

The Mighty Ducks' Kariya has demonstrated that if a player has the right amount of self-confidence he can live with the big boys of the NHL.

Small is beautiful

The only thing Kariya doesn't have going for him is size. He is 5-10 tall and weighs 172 pounds. Too small? Scotty Bowman, the NHL's all-time winningest coach said of him: "They said the same thing about Gretzky."

Kariya hasn't always been able to showcase that speed as much as he would like because he hasn't been able to stay in the lineup. He missed parts of 1996–97 and 1997–98 and two big international competitions—the 1996 World Cup of Hockey and the 1998 Olympics in Japan (from where his father's side of the family descends)—because of a succession of injuries. A concussion kept him out of the 1998 Olympics and the end of that season, but he came back well.

Entering 1998–99, Kariya vowed to be aggressive and not stand for opponents taking cheap shots at his head. He played all 82 games that season and was his usual sparkling self, finishing third in the league in points with 101 (then teammate Selanne was second with 107). He missed 24 combined games in the 1999–2000 and 2000–01 seasons, but last year he once again made it through the entire 82-game marathon. With health on his side, Kariya will continue to go warp speed ahead.

ICE TALK

"Kariya is so good because he can carry the puck at top speed."

Scotty Bowman

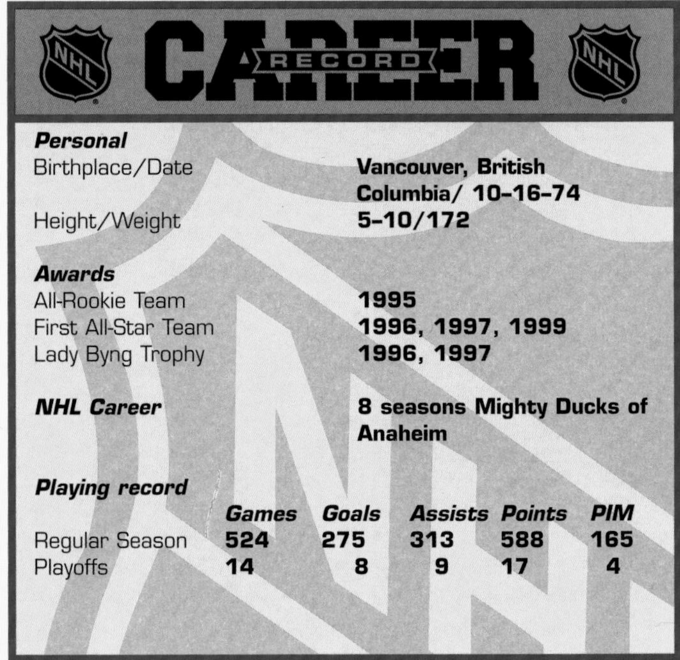

CAREER RECORD

Personal

Birthplace/Date	**Vancouver, British Columbia/ 10-16-74**
Height/Weight	**5-10/172**

Awards

All-Rookie Team	**1995**
First All-Star Team	**1996, 1997, 1999**
Lady Byng Trophy	**1996, 1997**
NHL Career	**8 seasons Mighty Ducks of Anaheim**

Playing record

	Games	Goals	Assists	Points	PIM
Regular Season	524	275	313	588	165
Playoffs	14	8	9	17	4

Flyer Sharp-Shooter
JOHN LÉCLAIR

Hungry for hockey and tough on ice, this rock-loving powerhouse excels at golf, works for good causes, and is a superb role model.

In his days with the Montreal Canadiens, strapping left winger John LeClair had the nickname of Marmaduke, after the playful but uncoordinated comic-strip canine. "John used to fall down a lot," recalled defenseman Kevin Haller, a teammate of LeClair's both in Montreal and in Philadelphia.

"He didn't have real good balance and he wasn't strong on his skates. Now, he's totally the opposite."

Indeed, LeClair, is solid as a rock in every facet of the game. He sends opposing players scattering like bowling pins with his 6-foot-3, 226-pound frame. He has developed into one of the NHL's finest two-way forwards, while at the same time being one of its top sharpshooters, following up on a 51-goal season in 1995–96 with a 50-goal performance the following season and then, in 1997–98, he became the first American in NHL history to record three straight 50-goal seasons as he netted 51 goals.

"He is a great two-way player," said former teammate Mikael Renberg. "He's strong in our zone, and along the boards. He's also a great role model for our younger players."

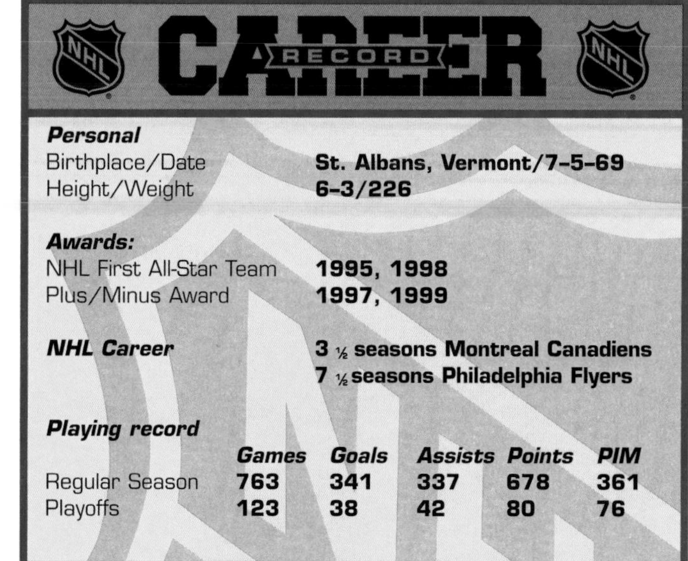

CAREER RECORD

Personal					
Birthplace/Date	**St. Albans, Vermont/7-5-69**				
Height/Weight	**6-3/226**				
Awards:					
NHL First All-Star Team	**1995, 1998**				
Plus/Minus Award	**1997, 1999**				
NHL Career	**3 ½ seasons Montreal Canadiens**				
	7 ½ seasons Philadelphia Flyers				
Playing record	***Games***	***Goals***	***Assists***	***Points***	***PIM***
Regular Season	**763**	**341**	**337**	**678**	**361**
Playoffs	**123**	**38**	**42**	**80**	**76**

Rockin' and scorin'

LeClair, the first player from the U.S. state of Vermont to make the NHL, emerged from obscurity with the Canadiens in the 1992–93 playoffs, in which Montreal surprisingly won the Stanley Cup. LeClair scored an overtime goal in both the third and fourth games of the series, which Montreal won in five games. He became the first player to score consecutive overtime game-winners in the Stanley Cup finals since Don Raleigh of the Rangers in 1950.

But LeClair could do no better than a 19-goal output the following season—matching his total of the previous year. Early in the 1994–95 season, with both LeClair and the Canadiens struggling, he was dealt to the Flyers, along with defenseman Eric Desjardins and forward Gilbert Dionne, for the high-scoring Mark Recchi.

The change in scenery had an immediate effect on LeClair. "It was a situation where I wasn't expected to score in Montreal," said LeClair, attempting to account for the transformation. "Here, they put me with Eric Lindros and Mikael right away, and it was an entirely different philosophy."

LeClair started to rock, which is an appropriate term for someone who is a huge fan of U2 and 1980s rock music, with hundreds of CDs in his collection. A tireless worker, LeClair improved his skating, refined his already booming shot, and used his imposing frame to create havoc around the net.

"My shot is hard, but a lot of times it's not how hard you shoot it, it's how quick you get it away," explained LeClair. "I think that's one of the things I've really worked on."

Hungry Flyer

Even as a youngster, growing up in St. Albans, Vermont, which is only a one-hour drive from Montreal, LeClair would spend hour after hour whacking a tennis ball against a shed. That's when he wasn't racing to be the first person in the bathroom each morning, since there were seven in the family.

Whether it is golf, a sport at which he also excels—according to Lindros, LeClair has Babe Ruthian drives off a golf tee—or the many charitable causes in which he is involved, LeClair has a hunger to succeed. That passion is evident even at Flyers practices.

"John is the hungriest guy on the ice, even in practice," said former Flyers goaltender Ron Hextall.

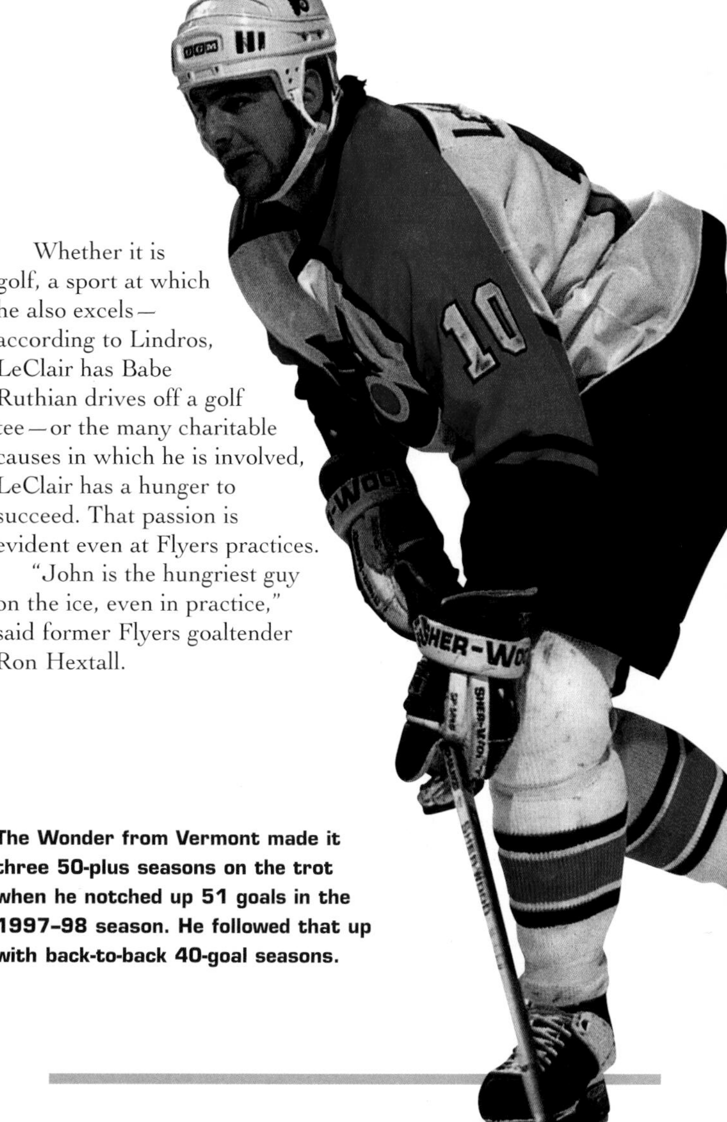

The Wonder from Vermont made it three 50-plus seasons on the trot when he notched up 51 goals in the 1997-98 season. He followed that up with back-to-back 40-goal seasons.

New York's Prime Mover

The Rangers rely heavily upon their captain and he takes care of business at both ends of the rink.

BRIAN LEETCH

A compact package combining quick acceleration and excellent straightahead speed, playmaking brilliance, a hard accurate shot and sound defensive ability, Brian Leetch is a Renaissance player—a defenseman who can do it all.

It was Leetch, lifting his game to new heights of virtuosity, who led the New York Rangers to a Stanley Cup championship in 1994, the club's first in 54 years. He led all playoff scorers with 34 points, including 11 goals. He scored five times in the seven-game final series against the Vancouver Canucks and fully earned the Conn Smythe Trophy as the most valuable performer in the post-season.

Texas hockey

He was the first American-born player—born in Texas, but raised in Connecticut—to capture the Conn Smythe.

He joined the Rangers in 1988–89, after a year with the U.S. National team, and an Olympic appearance as captain of the U.S. team. The international experience, coupled with one year with the Boston College Eagles, had fine-tuned his explosive raw talent—Leetch was named rookie-of-the-year in his first NHL season.

His numbers dropped off the next season, scoring 11 times and adding 45 assists, before being knocked out of action by a fractured left ankle.

But in 1990–91, Leetch re-asserted his claim to being a franchise defenseman by scoring 16 goals and adding 72 assists for 88 points, breaking Hall of Famer Brad Park's team record for most points (82) in a season by a defenseman.

In 1991–92, Leetch totaled 102 points, including 22 goals and won the James Norris Memorial Trophy as the best defenseman in the league. He won the award again in 1996-97.

Leetch's acceleration launches him on rinklength dashes that often result in goals—by the speedy defenseman or one of his teammates.

Undeterred by injury

Injuries hit Leetch in 1992–93, when he missed 34 games with a neck and shoulder problem. Then he slipped on some ice on a Manhattan street, fracturing his right ankle, and he missed the final 13 games of that season.

Since the 1993–94 season, however, Leetch had missed six games—all in 1997–98, a down year for him and the Rangers too—until a broken right arm sidelined him for 11 weeks in 1999–2000. His reliability has been a huge asset for the Rangers. New York demands a lot of its sports heroes and Leetch grew into the role of captain after the 1997 departure of Mark Messier (who subsequently returned).

Leetch was strong in the 1994–95 playoffs, generating 14 points (6 goals) in 10 games as the Rangers failed to advance beyond the second round. He was also one of the main reasons that Wayne Gretzky signed with the Rangers as a free agent in 1996.

"As much as I've done offensively, I know that to win championships, you need defense," said Gretzky, who retired in 1999 without a title in the Big Apple.

"The Rangers have great defense. Playing with Brian Leetch was obviously part of the attraction. He reminds me of Paul Coffey."

Leetch's claim to greatness couldn't possibly be stamped with more authenticity than that.

ICE TALK

"Playing with Brian Leetch was obviously part of the attraction."

Former teammate Wayne Gretzky on one of the reasons he joined the Rangers in 1996.

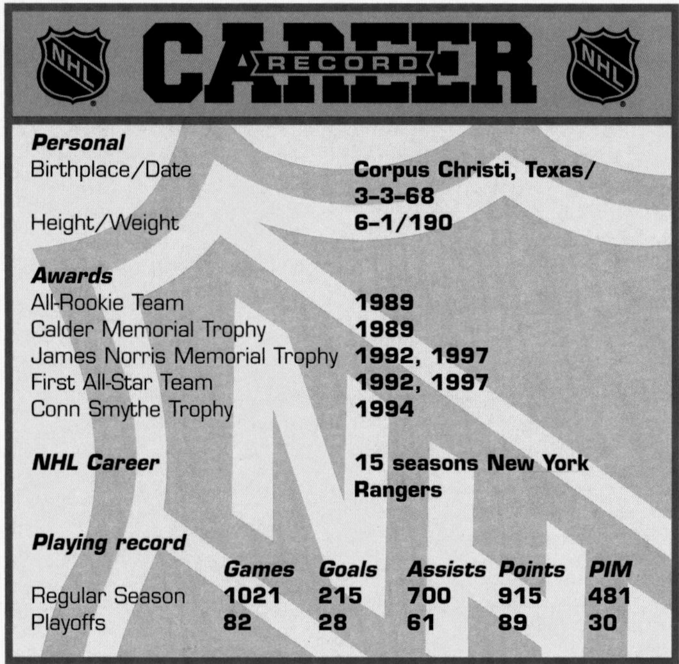

CAREER RECORD

Personal

Birthplace/Date	**Corpus Christi, Texas/ 3-3-68**
Height/Weight	**6-1/190**

Awards

All-Rookie Team	**1989**
Calder Memorial Trophy	**1989**
James Norris Memorial Trophy	**1992, 1997**
First All-Star Team	**1992, 1997**
Conn Smythe Trophy	**1994**

NHL Career — **15 seasons New York Rangers**

Playing record

	Games	Goals	Assists	Points	PIM
Regular Season	1021	215	700	915	481
Playoffs	82	28	61	89	30

New York's Power Source

He combines the finesse of Gretzky, the size of Lemieux and the presence of Messier.

ERIC LINDROS

An astonishing blend of fearsome physical strength, speed, skill, rink savvy and unquenchable competitive desire, 6-foot-4, 236-pound center Eric Lindros moved with ridiculous ease up the hockey ladder—junior to international competition to the NHL.

Lindros is the most imposing star player in the league—he can make an impact with his size, strength, speed, rink savvy and his considerable skill.

ICE TALK

"His sole focus is getting his team to the Stanley Cup."

Former teammate Craig MacTavish

Before he had played an NHL game he had served notice that he was going to be a force. While still junior age, Lindros helped Canada win the gold medal at the Canada Cup. During that tournament, he knocked rugged Ulf Samuelsson out of action with a devastating check that appeared easy for him.

The Legion of Doom

Injuries reduced his effectiveness in his first two seasons—yet he still scored 85 goals and chipped in 87 assists in 126 games. Much of that production came while playing on a line with Mark Recchi and Brent Fedyk. The line, called the Crazy Eights, was an instant hit in Philadelphia, where fans quickly warmed to Lindros. But he really hit his NHL stride in 1995 when Flyers coach Terry Murray grouped him with big wingers John LeClair and Mikael Renberg.

As talented as any trio in the league and certainly the best combination of skill and sheer physical power, the line was christened The Legion of Doom. Lindros totaled 70 points, including 29 goals, in 46 games in 1994–95, tying Pittsburgh's Jaromir Jagr for the points lead, but losing the scoring title, on the final day of the season, because Jagr scored three more goals.

Lindros and the Legion led the Flyers to the club's first division title since 1987 and first playoff berth since 1989. The Flyers lost in the conference final to the New Jersey Devils, the eventual Stanley Cup champions. The strong performance by Lindros earned him the Hart Trophy as the most valuable player in the NHL.

The whole package

Few have come into the NHL with a greater potential than Lindros, whose leadership abilities were quickly recognized by the Flyers, who named him captain at age 21. In 1995–96, both Lindros and LeClair took serious runs at 50-goal seasons—Lindros finished with 47, LeClair with 51. The Flyers challenged the Penguins and the New York Rangers for first place overall in the Eastern Conference all season long.

Lindros has grown comfortable with the dominant role foreseen for him when the Quebec Nordiques drafted him first overall in 1991. With a strong interest in acquiring the intimidating forward, the Flyers offered the Nordiques a considerable trade, sending eight players to Quebec in exchange for Lindros.

The 1997–98 season was not his best. A concussion kept Lindros out of action for a while, but it was especially poignant for him, because his younger brother's career was curtailed by such an injury.

He had a strong 1998–99, netting 93 points despite missing 11 games, but the nightmare returned the following season. He suffered more concussions and finally made his playoff debut in Game 6 of the Conference Finals, only to go down in a heap with his third concussion of the season.

Lindros did not play in the 2000–01 season, and he was traded to the New York Rangers. In his first campaign, Lindros played in 72 games and led the team with 37 goals and 73 points. He did suffer another minor concussion in December, but by the end of the season, he was back to his trademark physical play. And when Lindros is healthy and playing his style, no one in the league can stop him.

At least, that's what the Rangers are counting on from this six time All-Star.

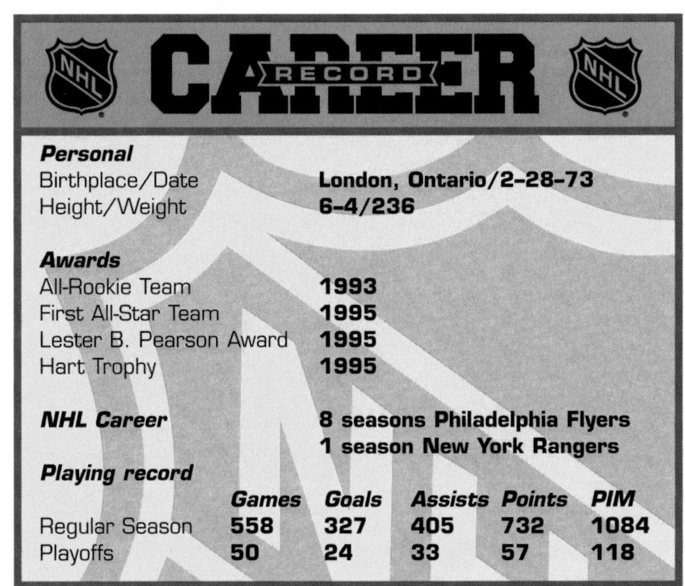

CAREER RECORD

Personal

Birthplace/Date	**London, Ontario/2-28-73**
Height/Weight	**6-4/236**

Awards

All-Rookie Team	**1993**
First All-Star Team	**1995**
Lester B. Pearson Award	**1995**
Hart Trophy	**1995**

NHL Career

8 seasons Philadelphia Flyers
1 season New York Rangers

Playing record

	Games	Goals	Assists	Points	PIM
Regular Season	558	327	405	732	1084
Playoffs	50	24	33	57	118

Mr. Intensity

MARK MESSIER

This six-time winner of the Stanley Cup is a legend who just wants to keep winning.

Speed defines some hockey players, strength others, still others personify skill. Mark Messier displays ample amounts of all three qualities, but to understand his essence, you start with the glare.

When Messier gets that look, his teammates get into formation behind him and opponents blanch just a little. The glare could translate into a game-breaking goal, a skillful passing play, a bone-rattling body check or even a well-timed, lethal elbow to an opponent's jaw.

Messier is the ultimate hockey player: big, fast, strong, skillful and junkyard-dog mean.

The Edmonton native is above all an incomparable on-ice leader, the capstone player on any team he has played for. He was a central player on five Edmonton Oilers teams that won the Stanley Cup, a leader on three Canadian teams that won the Canada Cup and indisputably the central force that carried the Rangers to the Stanley Cup in 1994, their first championship in 54 years.

Some consider him the fiercest, most inspirational leader in all of North American pro sports. He certainly has the portfolio.

Trail of a giant

He has won two Hart Trophies as the league's most valuable player, one Conn Smythe Trophy as the best individual performer in the playoffs and two Lester B. Pearson Awards as the most outstanding player in the league, as voted on by his peers.

His individual performance chart reveals impressive statistics: one 50-goal season; six seasons of 100 points or more; more than 100 playoff goals and almost 300 post-season points; a record 14 playoff shorthanded goals. But the true measure of Messier seems to be how teams he plays for perform. In 1990–91, Edmonton was 29–20–4 (won-lost-tied) with Messier in the lineup, just 8–17–2 without him. In the 1991 Canada Cup, Team Canada coach Mike Keenan extended an eligibility deadline to make room on the team for Messier. Canada won the tournament that year.

In 1984, even with the Wayne Gretzky Oilers, it was Messier who won the Conn Smythe Trophy as the most valuable player in the Stanley Cup playoffs as Edmonton won its first Cup in franchise history.

Messier is known as one of the most inspirational leaders in hockey, a man who never suffers a lapse in determination and demands the most from his teammates.

CAREER RECORD

Personal					
Birthplace/Date	**Edmonton, Alberta/1-18-61**				
Height/Weight	**6-1/205**				
Awards					
First All-Star Team	**1982-83, 1990, 1992**				
Conn Smythe Trophy	**1984**				
Hart Trophy	**1990, 1992**				
Lester B. Pearson Award	**1990, 1992**				
NHL Career	**12 seasons Edmonton Oilers**				
	8 seasons New York Rangers				
	3 seasons Vancouver Canucks				
Playing record	***Games***	***Goals***	***Assists***	***Points***	***PIM***
Regular Season	**1602**	**658**	**1146**	**1804**	**1838**
Playoffs	**236**	**109**	**186**	**295**	**244**

No rash promise

The most celebrated illustration of Messier's leadership abilities came before Game 6 of the 1994 Stanley Cup semifinals against the New Jersey Devils.

The Devils held a 3–2 series lead, but Messier told a TV audience he guaranteed a victory by the Rangers in Game 6. He backed it up by scoring the hat trick as the Rangers won the game 4–2, sending the series to a seventh game in Madison Square which the Rangers won in double overtime, the third of three games decided in a second overtime period.

Not since New York Jets quarterback Joe Namath guaranteed a Super Bowl victory over the Baltimore Colts in 1969 had a New York sporting hero been so brash, then backed up his boast. Messier's guarantee had profound resonance for New York hockey fans.

In 1997, free-agent Messier left the Big Apple for Vancouver. He returned to the Rangers as a free agent in 2000. He entered the 2002 off-season as an unrestricted free agent once again, intent either to re-sign with the Rangers or take a well-deserved break and retire after a long and distinguished career that has been best measured in wins and championships.

Stars Scorer

MIKE MODANO

Modano has become a complete player in recent seasons, adding a defensive conscience to his array of offensive gifts.

As a kid growing up in Livonia, Michigan, Mike Modano would spend plenty of hours in the family basement honing his hockey skills. Often, he would beg his mother to serve as a goaltender and hold up the top part of a garbage can, which Mike used as a target to develop pinpoint precision in his shooting.

The hours certainly weren't wasted. After a brilliant junior career, the then-Minnesota North Stars made Modano the No. 1 pick overall in the 1988 draft.

Excluding the 1994–95 strike season and an injury-hit 1997–98 campaign, Modano has led the team—which moved to Dallas prior to the 1993 season and became the Stars—in every season since 1991–92,when he collected 77 points. His biggest goal-scoring season, however, came in 1993-94 when he became the first center in the history of the franchise to score 50 goals.

"I started to improve on my ability to go to the net that season," recalled Modano. "That obviously wasn't a part of my game the first few years, but the more you do it, the more you get used to it."

Michigan Mike's career reached its zenith with a Stanley Cup win in 1999.

Sharpshooting leader

On the ice, Modano has blossomed into one of the NHL's swiftest skaters and most feared sharpshooters. He's also changed his game from that of pure offense to one of two-way dominance. He bought into former Dallas coach Ken Hitchcock's disciplined style, and now he makes just as big an impact in his own zone as he does in the opponent's end.

The Stars have become a powerhouse the last few years, capped by their first-ever Stanley Cup in 1999. Modano has proven his toughness in the postseason.

Modano badly injured his wrist in the 1999 Stanley Cup Finals, and was expected to miss some games. But he fought through the pain and didn't miss a game, while giving his usual stellar performance.

He assisted on all five of the Stars' goals in the last three games of the Finals vs. Buffalo, including the series winner in triple overtime of Game 6.

The former pretty boy has become a complete player—complete with a Stanley Cup ring.

Matinee idol

Modano was under a great deal of pressure to produce in the early years. The North Stars had missed the playoffs for two straight seasons prior to drafting Modano, who at the time was only the second American-born player to be selected No. 1. One year after that draft, Modano was a bona fide member of the North Stars, amassing 75 points as a rookie, including 20 points in the Stanley Cup playoffs, as the upstart North Stars went all the way to the final.

Still, Modano was a long ways from refinement. The concern for Bob Gainey, who at the time had the dual role of coach and general manager, was Modano's play in the offensive zone when he didn't have the puck. Gradually, Modano learned to let other players work the puck to him, rather than vacate a good offensive position because of his own impatience and frustration.

Modano's star continued to rise when the North Stars relocated in Dallas. More than a hockey star, he became a matinée idol, especially when his handsome features found their way into some of the top women's magazines, and Giorgio Armani used him as a runway model.

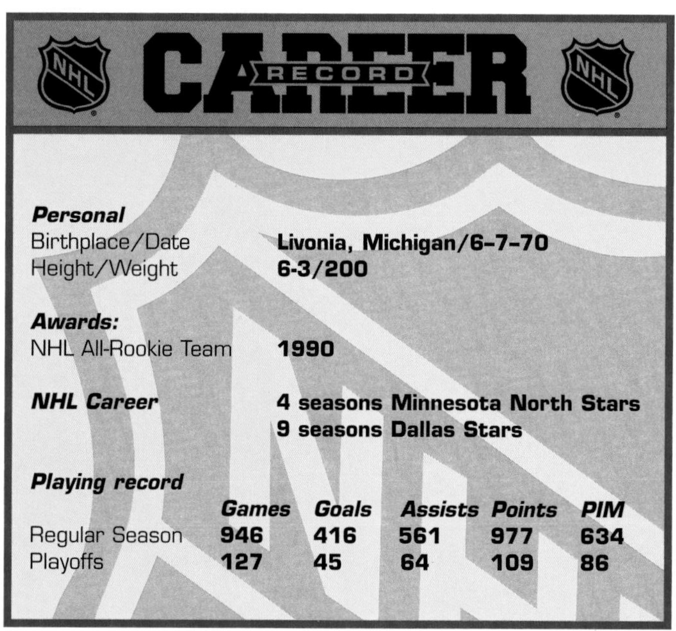

CAREER RECORD

Personal

Birthplace/Date	**Livonia, Michigan/6-7-70**
Height/Weight	**6-3/200**

Awards:

NHL All-Rookie Team	**1990**

NHL Career

4 seasons Minnesota North Stars
9 seasons Dallas Stars

Playing record

	Games	Goals	Assists	Points	PIM
Regular Season	946	416	561	977	634
Playoffs	127	45	64	109	86

Heavy-hitting blueliner
CHRIS PRONGER

The Blues defenseman has progressed from simple banger to franchise MVP.

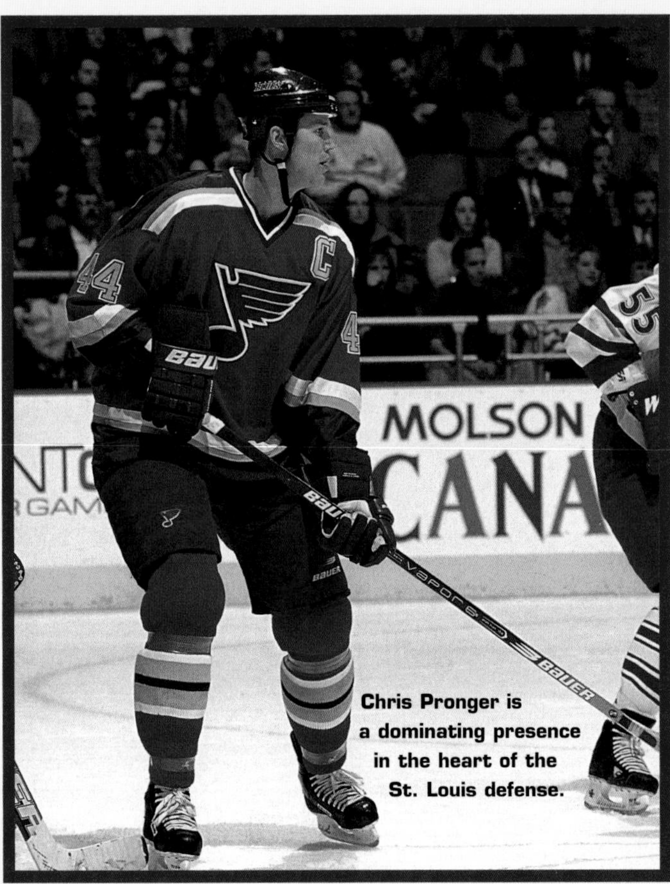

Chris Pronger is a dominating presence in the heart of the St. Louis defense.

There isn't a more dominating physical presence in the NHL these days than Chris Pronger. The 6' 6" defenseman clears the slot the way former St. Louis baseball slugger Mark McGwire smacked a fastball—with brute force.

But Pronger is no longer just the banger he was when he arrived in the NHL as teenager in 1993. He has evolved into what many consider one of the best all-around blueliners in the game. He can mix it up physically, has one of the best outlet passes in the game, boasts a long reach which makes it nearly impossible to get around him, and has offensive skills to rival those of just about any other backliner in the league. Most of all, though, he is a workhorse who can average 30 minutes per game and play the 30th minute just as effectively as the first.

Early impact

Pronger made an immediate impact in the NHL. He was drafted second overall in the 1993 Entry Draft by Hartford and he played 81 of a possible 84 games for the Whalers as a rookie in 1993–94, notching five goals and 25 assists to be voted the team's most valuable defenseman. The Ottawa Senators would undoubtedly love to redo that 1993 draft. They picked speedy forward Alexandre Daigle with the top overall pick but he never lived up to expectations and traveled around the league before exiting the NHL in 2000.

In 1995, Pronger was half of a big trade which sent star forward Brendan Shanahan to Hartford and Pronger to St. Louis. At the time it was a swap of a proven commodity (Shanahan) for potential (Pronger). Seven years later, both are among the NHL's élite, a rarity in a one-for-one deal.

Pronger became a cornerstone in St. Louis, but he didn't have the pressure in his early years of carrying the load. Future Hall of Famers such as Brett Hull, Grant Fuhr and Al MacInnis and, briefly, current Hall of Famer Wayne Gretzky, were the headliners. But the Blues eventually became Pronger's team. In 1997, he was named captain, the franchise's youngest-ever.

Joining the élite

With Pronger's selection to the 1998 Canadian Olympic team, he had arrived as a premier player. He led the league in plus-minus that season (plus-47) and he's only gotten better since. He and MacInnis combine to form one of the most lethal one-two defensive punches in the league. The Blues allowed the fewest goals in 1999–2000 on the way to the Presidents' Trophy for most points in the regular season.

Pronger's many individual accomplishments that season included leading the league in minutes per game (30:14), finishing second among defensemen in scoring (14 goals, 48 assists, 62 points), and another plus-minus title (plus-52). He won the Hart Trophy (MVP as voted by the media) and the Norris Trophy (best defenseman), and also was a finalist for the Pearson Award (MVP as voted by players).

The summer of 2002 was spent rehabbing a knee injury suffered in the playoffs while delivering a body check. Once a frequent target of the referees, Pronger has kept his penalty minutes below 100 in two of the past three seasons. He has toned down his feistiness, but he still plays with a chip on shoulder. That's not surprising for a guy whose nickname growing up was "Chaos," which his dad says fit him perfectly because he was hell on wheels. These days, he's hell on skates.

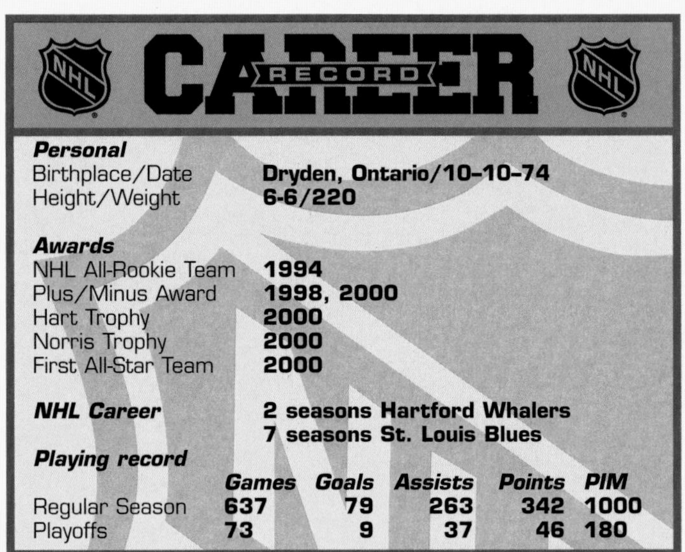

CAREER RECORD

Personal

Birthplace/Date	**Dryden, Ontario/10-10-74**
Height/Weight	**6-6/220**

Awards

NHL All-Rookie Team	**1994**
Plus/Minus Award	**1998, 2000**
Hart Trophy	**2000**
Norris Trophy	**2000**
First All-Star Team	**2000**

NHL Career **2 seasons Hartford Whalers**
7 seasons St. Louis Blues

Playing record

	Games	*Goals*	*Assists*	*Points*	*PIM*
Regular Season	637	79	263	342	1000
Playoffs	73	9	37	46	180

A Stand-Up Guy
MIKE RICHTER

A steady force between the pipes, this goalie's goaltender always keeps his cool and always gives his best.

Take it from one of his goaltending brethren: Mike Richter is one of the best around when it comes to winning a big game or series. "There are not many goalies who can win games by themselves, but Mike is capable of doing it," said Martin Brodeur, the New Jersey Devils No. 1 backstop. "He did it in the World Cup, and he did it against us."

In the first instance, Brodeur was referring to Richter's stellar play in the fall of 1996, which spearheaded the United States squad to a 2–1 triumph over Canada in the best-of-three series at the first-ever World Cup hockey tournament. The second allusion was to Richter's performance against the Devils in the 1997 Eastern Conference semifinal, in which Richter stopped 178 of 182 shots, recorded two shutouts and led the Rangers to a five-game upset of the Devils in the best-of-seven series.

Richter wasn't able to lead an injury-decimated Rangers lineup past the Philadelphia Flyers in the Eastern Conference final, but that didn't detract from the accomplishments of the nimble netminder who grew up a Flyers' fan in Flourtown, Pennsylvania. The Rangers would likely not have got as far as they did without a vintage Richter, who compiled a 2.68 regular-season goals-against average.

Notorious success

Before the elimination by the Flyers, Richter revived memories of 1994, when he was an instrumental force in the Rangers ending a 54-year Stanley Cup drought. Richter started all 23 of the Rangers' playoff games that year, leading the NHL with 16 wins, posting a 2.07 goals-against average and recording four shutouts, which tied a league record for shutouts in post-season play.

Perhaps Richter's finest moment in that year's playoffs was his 31-save effort in the Rangers' seventh-game double-overtime triumph over New Jersey to win the Eastern Conference finals.

Richter's notoriety earned him guest spots—along with teammates Mark Messier and Brian Leetch—on the *David Letterman Show* following the Stanley Cup win. Articulate and comfortable as a communicator, Richter, a past winner of the Rangers' "Good Guy Award" for cooperation with the media, was in his element on the popular U.S. late-night television program.

Two years later, Richter was in the spotlight again, when he won the Most Valuable Player Award at the World Cup. With the U.S. team trailing Canada 1–0 in the best-of-three series, Richter made 35 saves in Game 2 as the Americans tied the series and, in Game 3, he kept the U.S. in the game—the team was outshot 22–9 through two periods—enabling it to go on to a 5–2 win in the decisive third game.

Cool courage

When he's not throwing his body in front of pucks, Richter is deeply involved in social causes. He has won awards for "Excellence and Humanitarian Concern", and an "Award of Courage" for his work with hospitals. He has also served as honorary hockey chairman of the Children's Health Fund.

Placid and cool under the constant pressures of trying to stifle some of the game's finest sharpshooters, Richter is equally collected in his approach to his craft. "You have to realize you are probably as good or as bad as the team in front of you," he once explained. "But one of the attractions of being a goaltender is that you are the guy on the spot. There's pressure on everybody, but that's a lot easier to bear than not having the opportunity to deliver under pressure."

Mike Richter has backstopped both the New York Rangers and Team USA to championship glory.

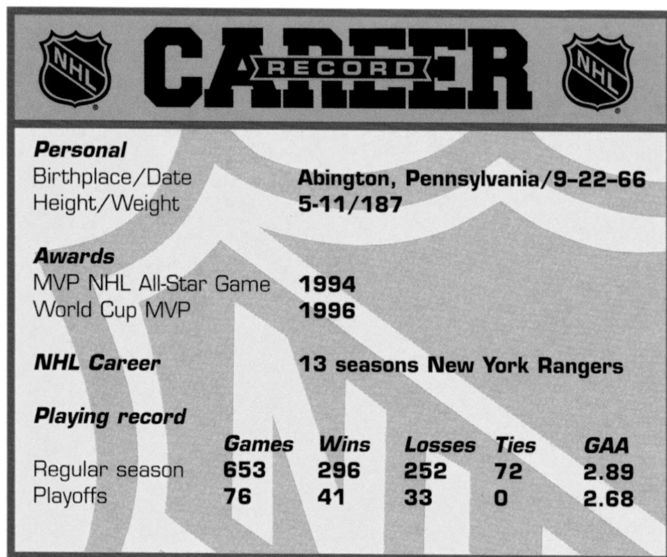

CAREER RECORD

Personal

Birthplace/Date	**Abington, Pennsylvania/9-22-66**
Height/Weight	**5-11/187**

Awards

MVP NHL All-Star Game	**1994**
World Cup MVP	**1996**

NHL Career **13 seasons New York Rangers**

Playing record

	Games	Wins	Losses	Ties	GAA
Regular season	653	296	252	72	2.89
Playoffs	76	41	33	0	2.68

Mile-High Goaltender PATRICK ROY

Miraculous and often unbeatable, the man who made the butterfly style famous shines on.

Patrick Roy is known for his postseason successes. He has been playoff MVP three times and in 1999 became the first goalie to win 100 career playoff games.

During games, the rookie goaltender talked to his goalposts, and before each game started, he skated 40 feet in front of his net, turned and stared intently at his workplace, skated hard right at the crease, veered away at the last second, then settled into his work station for another night of brilliance.

Even among goaltenders, who are known for their eccentricity, Patrick Roy was a classic from his first NHL season in 1986.

Roy was magnificent during the playoffs as the Canadiens, with a rookie-laden club, won the Stanley Cup, surprising the hockey world, and he won the Conn Smythe Trophy, winning 15 and losing just five playoff games and posting a goals-against average of 1.92. He had staked his claim to the title of the best goalie in the NHL.

The next three seasons, he won the William Jennings Trophy, for the goalie whose team allows the fewest goals against. Three times (1989–90, 1992) Roy also won the Vezina Trophy, awarded to the league's best goalie, as voted on by the general managers.

Roy refined his goaltending technique the hard way. As a junior goalie, playing for the sad sack Granby Bisons of the Quebec Major Junior Hockey League, it was not uncommon for Roy to face 60- or 70-shot barrages.

Stellar start

When he arrived in the NHL as a regular, Roy was only 20, and had played one single, solitary game in minor pro hockey, but he was seasoned, which he quickly proved. Roy has been at his best in pressure situations. His stellar play led the Canadiens to three Stanley Cup finals (1986, 1989, 1993), and two championships.

Both those years, he won the Conn Smythe Trophy as the most valuable player in the playoffs. His performance in the 1993 Stanley Cup playoffs, when the Canadiens won ten of 11 overtime games, was just this side of miraculous. It's not for nothing the Forum came to be known as St. Patrick's Cathedral during his glory years there.

In 1994, Roy was stricken with appendicitis after two games of the opening-round series against the Boston Bruins and had to be hospitalized. Antibiotics forestalled the need for surgery and Roy rose from his hospital bed to record two straight victories over the Bruins, one a 2–1 overtime thriller at the old Boston Garden in which he made 60 saves.

At his best, Roy is technically flawless, using a butterfly style in which he goes to his knees and splays his leg pads to cover the lower portion of the net, protecting the upper portion with his body and his cat-quick left hand.

Superstar shock

Roy was Montreal's franchise player so it was stunning when the goaltender requested a trade after a loss on December 2, 1995, his last game with the Montreal Canadiens. Three days later, he was sent to Colorado. Roy would make his new home his shrine. In his first season with the Avalanche, he backstopped Colorado to the Stanley Cup. Roy also managed a small feat on October 17, 2000 when he became the NHL's all-time winningest goaltender with his 448th career win against the Washington Capitals.

Roy has continued to show excellent form. In 2001, he led the Colorado Avalanche to their second Stanley Cup title, winning his third Conn Smythe Trophy in the process. St. Patrick keeps producing miracles.

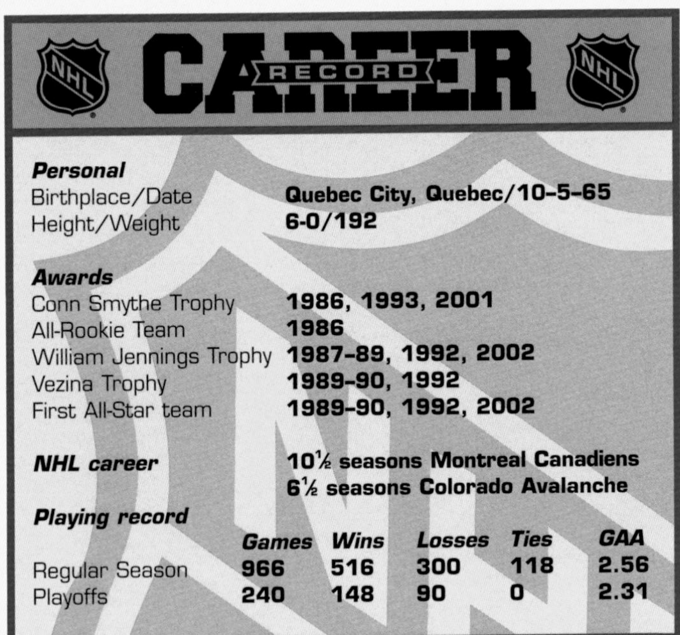

CAREER RECORD

Personal

Birthplace/Date	**Quebec City, Quebec/10-5-65**
Height/Weight	**6-0/192**

Awards

Conn Smythe Trophy	**1986, 1993, 2001**
All-Rookie Team	**1986**
William Jennings Trophy	**1987-89, 1992, 2002**
Vezina Trophy	**1989-90, 1992**
First All-Star team	**1989-90, 1992, 2002**

NHL career **10½ seasons Montreal Canadiens**
6½ seasons Colorado Avalanche

Playing record

	Games	Wins	Losses	Ties	GAA
Regular Season	966	516	300	118	2.56
Playoffs	240	148	90	0	2.31

Colorado's Sharpshooter

JOE SAKIC

A deadly, stealth-like force on the ice, this sniper has perhaps the most lethal wrister in the game.

He's not big, in fact, he's almost small by National Hockey League standards, but Joe Sakic is elusive, a slick, clever passer, an accurate shooter and perhaps the most unassuming superstar in hockey.

Sakic was a first-round draft pick by the then-Quebec Nordiques in 1987. He was taken 15th overall after a monster season (60 goals, 133 points) with the Swift Current Broncos of the Western Hockey League.

When he joined the once-mighty Nordiques, for the 1988–89 season, they had just finished last in the Adams Division. For the next three years, the club struggled to move up in the standings to no avail. It would take some time time before Quebec turned things around for the better. Sakic's NHL apprenticeship did not come easy.

Nordique blues

Sakic was fortunate enough to have Nordiques' star center Peter Stastny around for most of his first two seasons as a role model. Sakic, it turned out, didn't need that much guidance.

He scored 23 goals and added 39 assists for 62 points in his first season, then recorded the first of five 100-plus point seasons the very next year, when he led the Nordiques with 39 goals and 63 assists.

When the Nordiques traded Stastny, their first real superstar, to the New Jersey Devils in 1990, the torch had been passed to the smallish, shifty Sakic. The Nordiques would soon surround Sakic with some of the best young talent in the game. As the club improved, adding players like Owen Nolan, Mats Sundin, Curtis Leschyshyn, Stephane Fiset, Valeri Kamensky etc, expectations also began to soar.

In 1992–93, the Nordiques made the playoffs for the first time in five years and drew provincial rival Montreal Canadiens as their first-round opponent. The talent-rich Nordiques won the first two games.

But Montreal goalie Patrick Roy stiffened and the Canadiens stunned the Nordiques, winning the next four games in a row. The critics howled, many of them at Sakic, but the quiet-spoken Sakic took the loss as a learning experience. In the lockout-shortened 1994–95 season, Sakic's 19 goals and 43 assists put him fourth in league scoring and the Nordiques finished first overall in the Eastern Conference, but lost to the Rangers in the first round of the playoffs.

Colorado dawn

In Colorado's first season in Denver, Sakic collected 120 points, finishing third in the regular-season scoring race. Then he guided the Avalanche to the Stanley Cup, winning the Conn Smythe Trophy as the most valuable player in the playoffs.

In the 1997–98 season, things didn't go so well as Sakic picked up an injury while playing for Team Canada in the Nagano Olympics. A collision with teammate Rob Blake during the quarter-final win against Kazakhstan left Sakic with a sprained knee that sidelined him for several weeks. But Sakic, whom many consider to have the best wrist shot in the league, was back in form in 1998–99. He tallied 96 points, the fifth-best total in the league.

Perhaps Sakic's most impressive season came in 2000–01, which ended with Colorado's second Stanley Cup. He had 54 goals, 118 points and won the Hart Trophy, Pearson Award and Lady Byng Trophy. The quiet superstar isn't able to keep too quiet anymore.

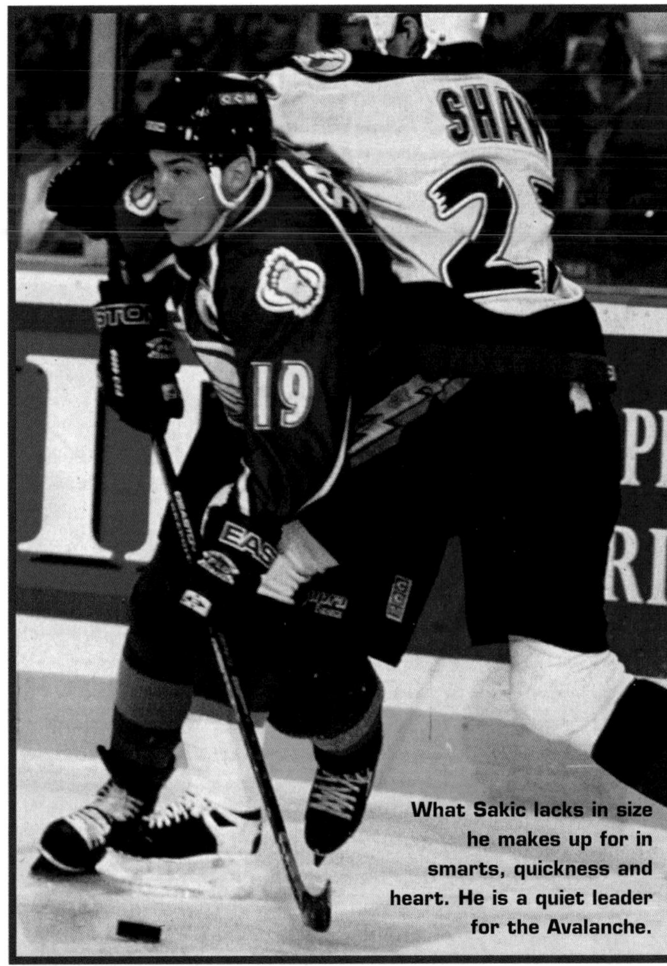

What Sakic lacks in size he makes up for in smarts, quickness and heart. He is a quiet leader for the Avalanche.

CAREER RECORD

Personal

Birthplace/Date	**Burnaby, British Columbia/ 7-7-69**
Height/Weight	**5-11/185**

Awards

First All-Star Team	**2001, 2002**
Conn Smythe Trophy	**1996**
Hart Trophy	**2001**
Lady Byng Trophy	**2001**
Pearson Award	**2001**

NHL Career — **7 seasons Quebec Nordiques**; **7 seasons Colorado Avalanche**

Playing record

	Games	Goals	Assists	Points	PIM
Regular season	1016	483	774	1257	416
Playoffs	135	65	83	148	62

A Nose for the Net

TEEMU SELANNE

The Finnish Flash is a potent combination of blazing speed and scoring smarts.

When you blend world-class skill and offensive creativity with eye-popping speed, you really discombobulate a defense. That description fits Teemu Selanne perfectly.

The Finnish Flash blazed through the National Hockey League in his first season with the Winnipeg Jets, scoring 76 goals and adding 56 assists. His goal total shattered the NHL's rookie record.

Fully-grown rookie

The 6-foot, 200-pound Finnish speedster zoomed into the NHL in 1992. To say he adjusted from Jokerit in the Finnish Elite League with ease is to understate the magnitude of his achievement.

Selanne recorded his first three-goal hat trick in his fifth NHL game. In late February that season, Selanne scored four goals in a defeat of Minnesota, and produced a string of scoring streaks that left Jets fans dizzy: a 17-game streak that produced 20 goals and 14 assists, nine games (14 goals), eight games (nine goals and 11 assists) and five games (11 goals). In the Jets' final six games, Selanne blasted 13 goals and added two assists.

In his first NHL playoff game, against the Vancouver Canucks, he not only scored a goal, he recorded another three-goal hat trick.

His Calder Memorial Trophy award as the top rookie in the league was expected. Astonishing was his arrival as a fully formed superstar, competing with both rookies *and* the best players.

His 76 goals tied for the league lead with Alexander Mogilny and he was selected as the right winger on the first All-Star team.

Kid start

Selanne was a mature player upon arrival in North America because he had not hurried his development in his native Finland.

He grew up in the minor hockey system in Helsinki, playing for KalPa-Espoo from the age of five. By nine, he was competing against players two years his senior, and at 16 he joined Jokerit, one of the most successful of the teams in the Finnish Elite League, for five seasons before he made the jump to the NHL.

"It is good to play there and get better and then come (to the NHL) later, when you are ready," he has said. "I had dreams to play in the World Championship and the Olympic Games before I came here and when I came here, I had done all that. I left with a clear conscience."

It was clear that Selanne found a kindred spirit when he was traded to Anaheim in 1996. Paul Kariya operated on his opposite wing, and the two formed what many considered the most dangerous duo in hockey. In 1998–99, they finished two-three in the NHL scoring race with 107 points for Selanne and 101 for Kariya. A year later they were fourth (Kariya with 86 points) and fifth (Selanne, 85).

Near the end of the 2000–01 season, Selanne was shipped to San Jose. He helped the Sharks win the 2002 Pacific Division title and the team pushed defending champion Colorado to a game 7 in the second round of the playoffs.

CAREER RECORD

Personal

Birthplace/date	**Helsinki, Finland/7-3-70**
Height/Weight	**6-0/200**

Awards

Calder Memorial Trophy	**1993**
Maurice Richard Trophy	**1999**
All-Rookie Team	**1993**
First All-Star Team	**1993, 1997**

NHL Career

3 1/2 seasons Winnipeg Jets
5 1/2 seasons Mighty Ducks of Anaheim
1 1/2 seasons San Jose Sharks

Playing record

	Games	Goals	Assists	Points	PIM
Regular Season	719	408	447	855	273
Playoffs	39	18	12	30	12

Selanne, who led Team Finland to an unlikely bronze medal in the 1998 Olympics, never shies from the spotlight. And when he gets his motor revving, there is no slowing him down.

Selanne scored 47 goals in 1998–99 to capture the inaugural Maurice Richard Trophy and has continued to impress ever since.

Detroit's Fighting Forward

Wicked one-timers and bodychecks are equal parts of his arsenal.

BRENDAN SHANAHAN

The Detroit Red Wings were so eager to welcome rugged left winger Brendan Shanahan into the fold that the team delayed a morning practice so that Shanahan, who was on a flight from Hartford following his trade from the Whalers in October 1996, could join them.

There were definitely great expectations for Shanahan—and with good reason. While Detroit was the fourth stop for the quintessential power forward, Shanahan had established a reputation as one of the NHL's premier players. Selected No. 2 overall by New Jersey in the 1987 entry draft, Shanahan scored 81 goals in his last three seasons with the Devils prior to being dealt to St. Louis, where he topped 50 goals in two of his four seasons, and then it was on to Hartford, where he had 78 points in 74 games in 1995–96.

Disgruntled in Hartford, Shanahan pressed for a trade because the club wasn't a contender, and the small market franchise really couldn't afford to keep him. Enter the Red Wings, a team that had both the money and contending status, and needed a productive, strapping forward to put it over the top.

Fighting start

The October 9 trade saw Shanahan and defenseman Brian Glynn head to Detroit for Keith Primeau, Paul Coffey, and a 1997 first-round draft pick. "I don't look at this as the end of something," Shanahan said when he learned of the trade. "I look at it as the beginning. The Red Wings' game is to win the Stanley Cup, and that's my game, too."

They were prophetic words indeed. Shanahan fit into the Red Wings lineup like a glove, blending strong physical play—he got into his first fight four minutes into his first game with Detroit—along with a knack around the net to score 46 goals and collect 87 points in 79 regular-season games. He also racked up 131 minutes in penalties.

Shanahan contributed nine goals and eight assists in 20 post-season games, helping the Red Wings end a 42-year Stanley Cup drought. It was mission accomplished, both for Shanahan and the Red Wings, who were still smarting from a four-game sweep by the New Jersey Devils in the Stanley Cup final two years earlier.

Missing link

Shanahan said watching the Devils, his former team, win the Cup, only increased his yearning to join a contender. "I saw friends and fans I know celebrate that Cup win, and it hit pretty close to home," said Shanahan, who had left New Jersey when St. Louis signed him as a free agent in July, 1991. The Devils were awarded defenseman Scott Stevens as compensation for signing Shanahan. "I really thought I was going to get a Cup win in St. Louis," added Shanahan. But in July, 1995, he was on the move again—to Hartford for defenseman Chris Pronger. To some, the Blues made the trade for economic reasons. Shanahan believes it was because Blues coach Mike Keenan "wanted to bring in his own guys."

In his only full season with the Whalers, Shanahan was named the team captain, a testimony to his leadership abilities. When he arrived in Detroit, he was immediately made an assistant captain to captain Steve Yzerman.

In 1998, the Wings repeated their Cup championship. Detroit won it all again four springs later, in 2002. Shanny has been an integral part of all three championship teams, averaging 35 goals per season during his stay in Detroit. He also won a gold medal for Canada at the 2002 Winter Olympics. You could say Shanahan was doubly blessed with the luck of the Irish in 2002.

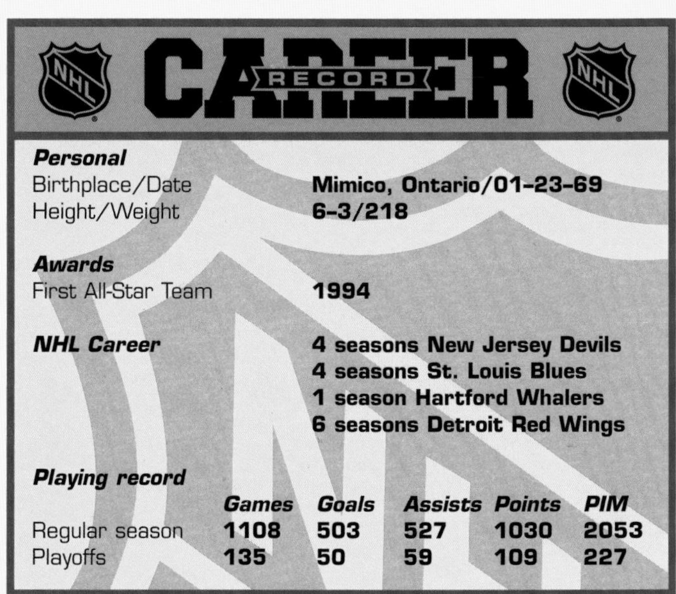

CAREER RECORD

Personal

Birthplace/Date	**Mimico, Ontario/01-23-69**
Height/Weight	**6-3/218**

Awards

First All-Star Team	**1994**

NHL Career

4 seasons New Jersey Devils
4 seasons St. Louis Blues
1 season Hartford Whalers
6 seasons Detroit Red Wings

Playing record

	Games	Goals	Assists	Points	PIM
Regular season	1108	503	527	1030	2053
Playoffs	135	50	59	109	227

Power forward Brendan Shanahan provides grit, drive, leadership and offense for the Red Wings.

The Maple Leafs' Leader

MATS SUNDIN

With his seemingly effortless offensive prowess, Sundin is the engine that drives the Leafs.

Mats Sundin had franchise player written all over him when he was drafted first overall in the 1989 Entry Draft. As things have unfolded, Sundin has filled that office for not one franchise, but two.

Big, strong, a swift, powerful skater with a hard, accurate shot and an impressive bag of creative offensive tricks, Sundin certainly has the requisite tools to be the key player wherever he earns his pay check.

For four years, Sundin was one of the building blocks around whom the Quebec Nordiques were going to surge from the ashes to contend for a Stanley Cup. But Sundin only had one shot at Stanley Cup playoff action with Quebec (now the Colorado Avalanche). That was in 1992–93, the year Sundin scored 47 goals and totalled 114 points in all, tops on the talent-rich Nordiques, whose lineup boasted Joe Sakic and Valeri Kamensky.

Tall hustler

The Nordiques won the first two games of their only playoff series that spring against the Montreal Canadiens, but that was it. The Canadiens would ride the goaltending brilliance of Patrick Roy to the Stanley Cup championship that season, while the Nordiques would take a year to recover from the shock. The following season, they missed the playoffs altogether.

"Sometimes it doesn't look like bigger guys hustle as much as the little guy who has to take maybe three strides while the bigger guy takes one," Sundin says. "I'm known to have been criticized sometimes, when people say that I'm kind of cruising around or pacing myself. I'm 6-foot-4 ½, almost 6-foot-5, and I know that when I'm on the ice, I'm always working hard."

Toronto hope

Sundin was traded to Toronto in a blockbuster trade that sent popular Maple Leafs winger Wendel Clark to Quebec. If there was pressure in replacing the fan idol Clark, it has not been evident. Sundin has led the Maple Leafs in scoring all eight seasons he has played there—the first Leaf to achieve such a level

... scoring all eight seasons he ... achieve such a level of

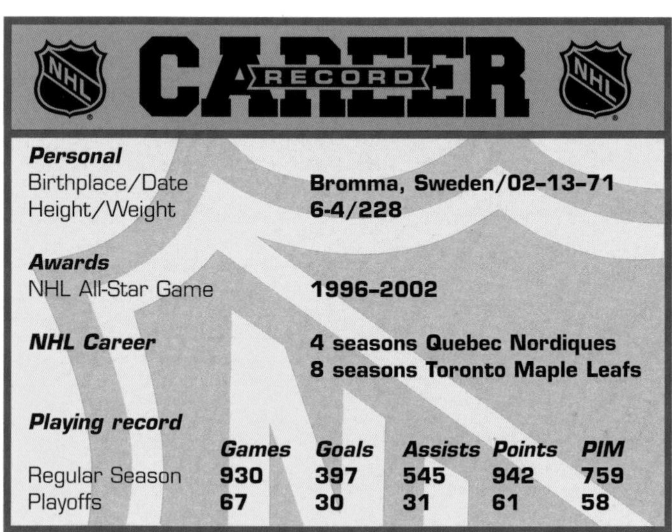

CAREER RECORD

Personal					
Birthplace/Date	**Bromma, Sweden/02-13-71**				
Height/Weight	**6-4/228**				
Awards					
NHL All-Star Game	**1996-2002**				
NHL Career	**4 seasons Quebec Nordiques**				
	8 seasons Toronto Maple Leafs				
Playing record					
	Games	***Goals***	***Assists***	***Points***	***PIM***
Regular Season	**930**	**397**	**545**	**942**	**759**
Playoffs	**67**	**30**	**31**	**61**	**58**

The Tough Blue
KEITH TKACHUK

The prototype power forward can crash and bang or shoot and score with equal effectiveness.

In his first full season as a Blue, Tkachuk tied for seventh in the league with 38 goals.

him when he was named captain by scoring 41 goals and adding 40 assists and staking a solid claim to being one of the best young power forwards in hockey. But it was in 1995–96 and 1996–97 that Tkachuk really blossomed. He scored 50 goals in 1995–96 and 52 in 1996–97, the franchise's first in its new home in Phoenix as the Coyotes, not the Jets.

Smile for the hitman

The 1996–97 preseason was when Tkachuk established himself on the international hockey stage by helping lead Team USA to the gold medal in the inaugural World Cup of Hockey in September.

He scored five goals in seven games and managed to find an outlet for his renowned toughness, too, breaking the nose of Claude Lemieux in a fight.

"There were a lot of toothless smiles around the league," said former Coyotes teammate Jim McKenzie.

Tkachuk's style always has involved blending physical toughness with offensive skill, and he managed it again during the 1997–98 season as he racked up 40 goals in 69 games.

He managed 36 goals in just 68 games the following season. Late in the 2000–01 season, Tkachuk was traded to the St. Louis Blues, where he has been a force, scoring 44 goals in 85 regular-season games since the trade. He has played in 25 playoff games over the past two seasons after never having played in more than seven in any previous season. Post-season success is all that's left for Tkachuk to conquer. This three-time Olympian (1992, 1998, 2002) has a silver medal from his latest Olympics, and he's won a World Cup. Now he's hungry for a Stanley Cup. With a talented supporting cast including Chris Pronger, Pavol Demitra, and Doug Weight, St. Louis fans are expecting their beloved Blues to follow the lead of their superstar forward deep into the postseason.

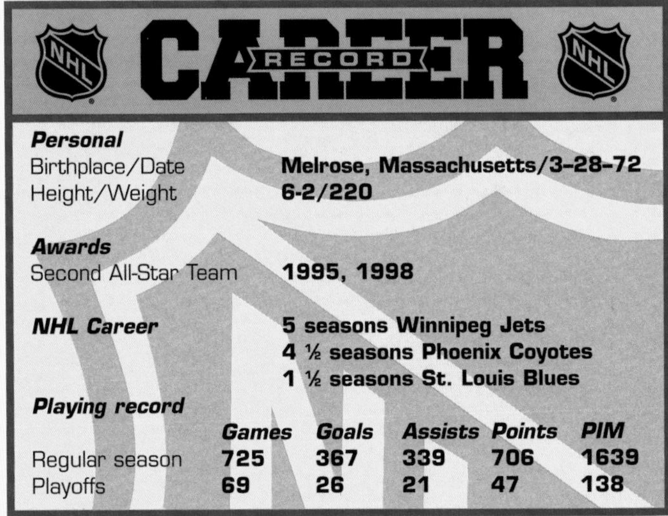

CAREER RECORD

Personal

Birthplace/Date — **Melrose, Massachusetts/3-28-72**
Height/Weight — **6-2/220**

Awards

Second All-Star Team — **1995, 1998**

NHL Career

5 seasons Winnipeg Jets
4 ½ seasons Phoenix Coyotes
1 ½ seasons St. Louis Blues

Playing record

	Games	Goals	Assists	Points	PIM
Regular season	725	367	339	706	1639
Playoffs	69	26	21	47	138

The Motor City Marvel
STEVE YZERMAN

The Red Wings inspirational captain is one of hockey's most potent two-way threat.

No player in the NHL is as closely associated with his team as Steve Yzerman is with the Detroit Red Wings. Fans in Detroit have taken to calling their city Hockeytown, USA, and Stevie Y is clearly the mayor.

Yzerman came to the Motor City in 1983 as a fresh-faced 18-year-old whom the Wings had selected with the fourth overall pick that summer. He brought an arsenal of offensive skills and made an immediate impact, scoring 39 goals as a rookie and finishing second to Buffalo goalie Tom Barrasso in voting for the Calder Trophy.

Back in his early days with the team, the Red Wings were derisively called the Dead Things. They had missed the playoffs 15 of the 17 seasons prior to Yzerman's debut. Although Detroit earned a playoff berth in each of his first two pro seasons—making a quick, first-round exit both times.

The Captain

There was only one way for the team to go—up. And it would be a long and often frustrating climb for the Wings' franchise player. But Yzerman and the team would eventually reach the NHL summit. The ascent began when Jacques Demers came in as coach in 1986–87. He installed a young Yzerman as captain, and No. 19 has worn the "C" on his sweater ever since, making him the longest-serving captain in NHL history.

Starting in 1987–88, Yzerman posted five straight 100-point seasons. The Wings made it to the conference final in 1987 and 1988, losing both times to eventual Stanley Cup champions Edmonton. In 1988–89, Yzerman notched an incredible 65 goals and 90 assists to earn the coveted Lester B. Pearson Award—league MVP as voted by the players. His 155 points that year is the highest total ever for a player not named Wayne Gretzky or Mario Lemieux.

In the early and mid 1990s, the Wings were consistently one of the best regular-season teams, but Detroit couldn't break through in the playoffs, suffering first-round ousters in 1993 and 1994 despite 100-point seasons, and being swept in the Finals in 1995 by New Jersey. Yzerman was a target of trade rumors during this time, and there were whispers about whether Detroit would be able to win with him.

Two-way star

Any doubts were laid to waste in 1997 and 1998, when the Wings won back-to-back Stanley Cups. It was a different Yzerman who led the way. He had evolved from flashy goal scorer into the ultimate two-way star. He could still dazzle with his offense, but he was perhaps even more committed to strong defensive play.

"He does the little things that inspire other players—block shots, dishes out hits, goes into the corner for the puck," said teammate Darren McCarty. "He's what you expect in a leader."

These days, Yzerman never has to pick up a check in Detroit. He is as popular a sports hero as that town has ever had. And he's still producing—he helped will the Wings to another Stanley Cup last spring despite playing on a badly injured knee. Expect another term from Stevie Y as mayor of Hockeytown.

Steve Yzerman has been an inspirational leader in Detroit for many years, helping the Red Wings to capture three Stanley Cups.

CAREER RECORD

Personal

Birthplace/Date	**Cranbrook, British Columbia/ 5-9-65**
Height/Weight	**5-11/185**

Awards

NHL All-Rookie Team	**1984**
Lester B. Pearson Award	**1989**
Conn Smythe Trophy	**1998**
First All-Star Team	**2000**
Frank J. Selke Trophy	**2000**

NHL Career **17 seasons Detroit Red Wings**

Playing record

	Games	Goals	Assists	Points	PIM
Regular season	1362	658	1004	1662	852
Playoffs	177	67	108	175	78

2002 OLYMPICS

Salt Lake City, Utah.

Talk about going loonie. When Canada beat the United States 5–2 in the gold-medal game of the 2002 Olympics, a whole country went bonkers with joy. Canadians had waited 50 years to strike gold in the sport that they invented and perfected.

The man who assembled the 2002 version of Team Canada—Wayne Gretzky—credited a certain good-luck charm with helping making that golden dream come true. Gretzky, the NHL's all-time leading scorer, pulled out a Canadian dollar coin—known as a loonie—at the postgame press conference and explained that a Canadian on the ice-making crew had buried the coin in the ice for good luck.

Of course, when it mattered most, it was the Canadian players who buried their opponents on the ice. The gold-medal triumph came 50 years to the day since the country's previous Olympic title. Despite a star-studded roster that included Mario Lemieux, Steve Yzerman and Paul Kariya up front, Rob Blake and Al MacInnis on the blue line and Martin Brodeur in goal, Canada struggled in the round-robin portion of the tournament. It went 1–1–1 in that round, before turning things up with a win over Finland in the quarterfinals and Belarus in the semifinals, leading up to the gold-medal showdown.

The finale was a dream matchup for many fans. The United States' roster was as star-studded as Canada's, and the border nations were playing on U.S. soil in Salt Lake City, Utah. Plus there was the revenge factor for Team Canada, as Team USA had dispatched the Canadians to win the 1996 World Cup of Hockey. Many of the same players for both teams were representing their countries six years later.

In the gold-medal tussle in Salt Lake, Joe Sakic scored two goals and set up another and was named tournament MVP. Despite the loss, the U.S. was well-represented on the all-tournament team, with four of the six positions: goalie Mike Richter, defensemen Brian Leetch and Chris Chelios and forward John LeClair. Sakic and Sweden's Mats Sundin filled out other two spots.

There were several other Olympic teams laden with NHL talent, including Russia, Sweden, Finland and the Czech Republic. The bronze-medal game featured a surprise team, Belarus, which upset Sweden in the quarterfinals. Russia took the bronze with a 7–2 win, powered by two goals and an assist from Alexei Kovalev.

The 2002 Olympics were the second to feature NHL stars, following the 1998 Games when the Czech Republic, Russia and Finland took the gold, silver and bronze, respectively. The NHL shut down operations for a couple weeks in February to accommodate the Salt Lake event.

MEDALS
Gold—Canada
Silver—United States
Bronze—Russia

THE STANLEY CUP

THE ULTIMATE GOAL

It's known as the National Hockey League's second season and it may well be the most exciting post-season tournament in professional sports. The Stanley Cup playoffs stretch from mid-April to mid-June as 16 of the NHL's 30 teams compete for the Stanley Cup, one of the most cherished pieces of sporting silverware in the world. The champion must win four best-of-seven series—16 games out of a possible 28 in total, all played after the 82-game regular season concludes in mid-April.

This annual North American Rite of Spring has unfolded, in various formats, since 1893, one year after Lord Stanley, the Earl of Preston and Governor-General of Canada, donated the challenge cup to symbolize the hockey championship of Canada.

Lord Stanley returned to England without ever seeing a championship game or personally presenting the trophy that bears his name. He wasn't around when the Montreal Amateur Athletic Association hockey club became the first winner of the trophy. He certainly could not have foreseen that his trophy would become the property of the National Hockey League, which did not exist until 1917 and did not assume control of the Stanley Cup competition until the 1926-27 season.

Still, the rich and colorful history attached to the cup that Lord Stanley purchased for 10 guineas ($48.67 Cdn) more than lives up to the spirit of the annual hockey competition he envisioned more than 100 years ago.

The institution of the trophy kicked off a parade of legendary performances. In 1904, One-Eyed Frank McGee scored a record five goals in an 11–2 victory for the Ottawa Silver Seven over the Toronto Marlboros. The following year, McGee scored 14 goals for the Silver Seven, who demolished the Dawson City Nuggets 23–2. The Nuggets had journeyed to Ottawa via dogsled, boat and train to challenge for Lord Stanley's Cup.

Alberta Magic: Few would have guessed that Wayne Gretzky's fourth Stanley Cup in Edmonton would be his last in an Oiler uniform.

A special time

The quality of competition has tightened considerably since those early days, and transportation is decidedly less rustic, also. But the mystique of the best four-out-of-seven game final series still holds powerful appeal for hockey fans.

The Stanley Cup final can pit speed and finesse against size and toughness, slick offense versus stingy defense, age against youth and, sometimes, brother against brother. The first time that happened was March 16, 1923 when the Denneny brothers, Cy and Corb, and the Boucher siblings, George and Frank, faced off against each other. Cy and George were members of the Ottawa Senators, Corb and Frank played for the Vancouver Maroons. Ottawa won that game 1–0 and went on to capture the Stanley Cup.

In a playoff game between the Montreal Canadiens and the Quebec Nordiques in the 1980s, Montreal's Mark Hunter missed a golden opportunity to pot an overtime winner at one end, then watched, crestfallen as older brother Dale put the game away for the Nordiques (now the Colorado Avalanche) at the other end.

The Stanley Cup tournament is a special event, when there's no time for injuries to heal, so the great ones simply play through the pain, no matter how excruciating. Hall of Fame defenseman Jacques Laperriere once played the finals with a broken wrist, and goaltender John Davidson gritted his teeth and played with a wonky knee in the 1979 finals. Montreal left winger Bob Gainey once completed a playoff series against the New York Islanders with not one but two shoulder separations. And in 1964, Toronto Maple Leafs defenseman Bob Baun scored an overtime winner with a broken ankle in Game 6, then played Game 7 without missing a shift. He then spent two months on crutches recuperating. No doubt, the Stanley Cup ring helped soothe his pain.

The Stanley Cup is about unlikely heroes, like Montreal goalie Ken Dryden being called up from the minors to backstop the Canadiens to a first-round upset over the heavily favored Boston Bruins in 1971, then going on to win the Conn Smythe Trophy, not to mention the Stanley Cup, both before winning the Calder Trophy as rookie-of-the-year the following season.

It's a showcase for the game's greatest stars, like Maurice (Rocket) Richard, who once scored five goals in a playoff game in 1944. Richard's record of six career playoff overtime goals has stood up for 36 years.

A fitting showcase

In the 1990s, the first round of the playoff tournament has captivated hockey fans, providing some stunning upsets, like the expansion San Jose Sharks knocking out the Detroit Red Wings in seven games in 1994. The Sharks rolled right to the Western Conference semifinal, extending the Toronto Maple Leafs to seven games before losing.

In 1993, the New York Islanders surprised the Washington Capitals in the opening round, then stunned the two-time defending champion Pittsburgh Penguins in the division final, a series victory that helped pave the way for Montreal's surprising Stanley Cup triumph. The Canadiens had fallen behind 2-0 to the talent-rich Quebec Nordiques before winning four straight games to eliminate their provincial rivals from the tournament.

There are those who criticize the Stanley Cup playoffs as far too long, who suggest, not without justification, that hockey is simply not meant to be played in June, taxing the ice-making machinery, the fans' attention span and the players' fitness level.

Few would dare to suggest, however, that the two-month-long tournament is not a fitting showcase for professional hockey. Boring is something the Stanley Cup playoffs most certainly are not.

Lord Stanley never knew what he missed; nor had he any idea how rich a sporting tradition he initiated all those years ago.

1997 Stanley Cup Finals

Red Wings Soar

A dominating total team effort swept Detroit from 42 years of disappointment to a Stanley Cup victory for Hockeytown, USA.

Detroit put 42 years of Stanley Cup disappointment behind it in June 1997 by sweeping away the listless Philadelphia Flyers to win their first championship since 1955. In that bygone time, the heroes were the legendary Gordie Howe, Terry Sawchuk, (Terrible) Ted Lindsay and Sid Abel.

The 1997 champions were led by Steve Yzerman, their classy captain, goaltender Mike Vernon, who won the Conn Smythe Trophy as the most valuable player in the playoffs, and Sergei Fedorov.

But, just as the Red Wings had suffered an embarrassing collective collapse in 1995 when the New Jersey Devils swept them in four straight in the Stanley Cup final series, this time their dominance over the Flyers was a total team effort, as well.

It had been 42 years since the Red Wings and their fans shared a Stanley Cup moment, so the Joe Louis Arena faithful and their heroes savored the thrill of ultimate victory in grand style.

As frequently happens in the Stanley Cup playoffs, unlikely heroes emerged and shone brightly for the Red Wings and their incomparable head coach, Scotty Bowman.

Rising to the occasion

In Game 1, the Red Wings grabbed a 2–0 lead on a pair of Flyers defensive lapses. On the first, checking line center Kris Draper stripped Flyers captain Eric Lindros of the puck and sped away on a two-on-nothing break with Kirk Maltby during a Flyers power play. The pair of speedy Wings exchanged passes before Maltby finished off the rush by lifting a shot over a spread-eagled Ron Hextall to give the Wings an early lead.

On the second goal Philadelphia defenseman Kjell Samuelsson made an ill-conceived pass that Joey Kocur intercepted just inside the Flyers' blue line. He then danced in, with Yzerman alongside as a decoy. Hextall guessed that Kocur would pass to the future Hall of Famer Yzerman. Instead, Kocur held the puck and flicked a shot high over Hextall, and it was 2–0.

Detroit's fourth goal of the game, scored on a routine shot from just inside the blue line by Steve Yzerman, had the biggest impact on the series, though. That goal apparently convinced Philadelphia head coach Terry Murray to switch to backup goalie Garth Snow for the second game of the series.

Snow didn't last long. He, too, was victimized on a pair of long-range shots as Detroit won Game 2.

Hextall was back in goal for Game 3, when Detroit's offensive gears meshed smoothly, and the Red Wings whacked the Flyers 6–1. The next day, Flyers coach Murray suggested his players were "choking" in an apparent attempt to motivate his over-matched team.

The Flyers, who held the lead in the series for just two minutes, certainly brought more intensity to Game 4 of the series, but to little avail.

The coup de grace was applied by unlikely scoring hero Darren McCarty, who scored the Cup-winning goal on a sublime rush on which he feinted magically past Flyers defenseman Janne Niinimaa, then swept the puck past a sliding Hextall on the backhand.

This prompted a dance of ecstasy by McCarty, a foreshadowing of a night-long party by the long-suffering Detroit fans.

Finally, the Stanley Cup had come back to stay, for a while at least, in the city that bills itself as Hockeytown, USA.

RESULTS

	Game	Site	Winner	Score	GWG
May 31	Game 1	Philadelphia	Detroit	4-2	Sergei Fedorov
June 3	Game 2	Philadelphia	Detroit	4-2	Kirk Maltby
June 5	Game 3	Detroit	Detroit	6-1	Sergei Fedorov
June 7	Game 4	Detroit	Detroit	2-1	Darren McCarty

1998 Stanley Cup Finals

THE WONDER WINGS

The Detroit Red Wings repeated their Cup success of 1997 and confirmed their status as one of the teams of the decade.

This time, the wait between Stanley Cups was much shorter for the Detroit Red Wings. When the team won the Cup in 1997, they ended a 42-year drought. When the Red Wings won the Cup again in 1998, they became just the second team of the decade to win back-to-back championships, joining the 1991/1992 Pittsburgh Penguins as members of the exclusive club.

The Wings were a team of destiny. Any complacency that might have settled in after their first Cup victory was wiped away six days later when star defenseman Vladimir Konstantinov and team masseur Sergei Mnatsakanov were seriously injured in a limo accident.

The Wings dedicated the season to their comrades and duly swept the Washington Capitals in the Stanley Cup Finals. It was the fourth straight Finals to end in a sweep, with Detroit having started the trend by losing to the New Jersey Devils in four games in 1995.

Brilliant Bowman

Detroit's win gave coach Scotty Bowman eight Stanley Cup rings as a coach, which tied him for the most ever with his mentor and idol Toe Blake, the great Montreal Canadiens' bench boss. Bowman got his eighth Cup thanks to a complete team effort.

The Wings boasted throughout the playoffs that they could roll four lines at any team and that held true. Evidence came in Game 1, when Grind Line winger Joe Kocur started off the scoring with his fourth goal of the playoffs. Star defenseman Nick Lidstrom added a second goal in the first period and that would be all the scoring Detroit would need in the 2–1 win at home. Wings goalie Chris Osgood faced the pressure of stepping in for the 1997 Conn Smythe Trophy winner Mike Vernon, who moved on to San Jose after the Wings' 1997 triumph. Although he let in three long goals in the first three rounds of the playoffs, he started the Finals magnificently, making 16 saves.

In Game 2, the Capitals seemed to be in control of the game in the third period. Washington led 3–1 after two periods, but even when Steve Yzerman cut the gap to 3–2 on a short-handed goal, the Caps responded 28 seconds later to stretch the lead to 4–2. Washington forward Esa Tikkanen, seemed ready to ice the game when he faked Osgood and had an open net to shoot at late in the third with the Caps ahead 4-3. But he missed the shot, and the Wings' Doug Brown scored shortly thereafter and the game headed to overtime. In the extra session, Grind Line center Kris Draper became the hero with his first goal of the playoffs.

Game 3 was played on the anniversary of the limo crash, and Detroit came out flying, outshooting the Caps 13–1 in the first period. But they only managed one goal, and Washington stayed in the game thanks to outstanding goaltending by Olaf Kolzig.

RESULTS

	Game	Site	Winner	Score	GWG
June 9	Game 1	Detroit	Detroit	2-1	Nicklas Lidstrom
June 11	Game 2	Detroit	Detroit	5-4	Kris Draper
June 13	Game 3	Washington	Detroit	2-1	Sergei Fedorov
June 16	Game 4	Washington	Detroit	4-1	Martin Lapointe

Brian Bellows tied the game in the third, but Detroit's Sergei Fedorov made a spectacular one-on-one rush to net the game-winner with five minutes to play.

Game 4 seemed more a formality than anything. Detroit got the first two goals and never looked back. Doug Brown scored twice. Konstantinov was on hand, and he made his way down to the ice in his wheelchair for the postgame celebration. The first person Yzerman handed the Stanley Cup to was an easy choice – Konstantinov. Destiny had become reality.

Detroit Red Wings Captain Steve Yzerman drinks from the Stanley Cup as he celebrates a second straight Cup victory for his team, this time a four-game sweep of the Washington Capitals.

1999 Stanley Cup Finals

Dallas Reach the Stars

Controversy reigned as the Dallas Stars claimed their first Stanley Cup, thanks to a triple-overtime goal from Brett Hull, a 1998 free-agent signing

After four straight years of sweeps in the Stanley Cup Finals, everyone who loves NHL hockey was hoping for a tight series between the Dallas Stars and Buffalo Sabres. And that's exactly what the Stars and Sabres provided.

What no one wanted was controversy. Unfortunately, that's exactly what Dallas winger Brett Hull's left skate provided.

In triple-overtime of Game 6 in Buffalo, with Dallas leading the series three games to two, Hull whacked home his own rebound to give the Stars the win and their first-ever Stanley Cup championship. Replays, however, showed that Hull's left skate was in the crease prior to the puck on the winning score.

The Stars players streamed onto the ice to celebrate while Buffalo coach Lindy Ruff fumed. He felt he never got the review of the play his team deserved, and felt that had the play been reviewed, the goal would have been disallowed. But Bryan Lewis, NHL director of officiating, insisted during a heated news conference that the goal was reviewed. "Having looked at it, the determination by those of us upstairs in the goal judge's location, including myself, was in fact that Hull played the puck," he explained. "Hull had possession and control of the puck, the rebound off the goalie does not change anything. It is his puck then to shoot and score, albeit a foot may or may not be in the crease prior to it."

The Stars shine

That goal ended the second-longest game in Finals history (just 22 seconds shy of the record) and capped a brilliant season for Dallas. With their smothering defensive style, the Stars won their second straight Presidents' Trophy for compiling the most points during the regular season. They continued to apply the brakes in the Finals, holding Buffalo to a mere nine goals in six games. Ed Belfour, who many said couldn't win the big one, was brilliant throughout, outdueling his former Chicago Blackhawks backup Dominik Hasek, a two-time league MVP.

It was the lowest-scoring six-game Finals ever. It was also extremely tight. The two teams were within one goal of each other for all but six minutes of the 400-plus minutes of the series. Joe Nieuwendyk earned the Conn Smythe Award as playoff MVP by leading the league with 11 postseason goals, including both of Dallas' tallies in Game 3 of the Finals, which the Stars won 2–1. In that game, Dallas held Buffalo to a Finals-record-low 12 shots.

It was the third time in the 1990s a team from Dallas beat a Buffalo team in a major championship. The Dallas Cowboys scored two Super Bowl wins over the Buffalo Bills.

RESULTS

	Game	Site	Winner	Score	GWG
June 8	Game 1	Dallas	Buffalo	3-2 (OT)	Jason Woolley
June 10	Game 2	Dallas	Dallas	4-2	Brett Hull
June 12	Game 3	Buffalo	Dallas	2-1	Joe Nieuwendyk
June 15	Game 4	Buffalo	Buffalo	2-1	Dixon Ward
June 17	Game 5	Dallas	Dallas	2-0	Darryl Sydor
June 19	Game 6	Buffalo	Dallas	2-1 (3OT)	Brett Hull

The big-name players kept making big plays for the Stars. Center Mike Modano assisted on all five of the Stars' goals in Games 4–6, despite an extremely painful wrist injury. Hull provided the final heroics, despite serious injuries of his own.

Said Dallas coach Ken Hitchcock after Game 6: "I think the story on Brett Hull when the dust settles is going to be an incredible story. He has a grade III full-blown (torn) MCL. He has a torn groin. He came back and played on one leg and no groins the last three shifts. He limped around the ice. The goal he scored, if you watch the shift, he limped into the corner, he limped in front of the net."

Sabre rattling: The area in front of Dominik Hasek's net is very crowded as the Stars go looking for a goal in Game 6. Brett Hull's controversial triple-overtime score gave Dallas the Cup.

2000 Stanley Cup Finals

Devils outshine Stars

New Jersey had been considered unfashionable Stanley Cup champions in 1995, but there was no doubt about their style in winning in 2000.

So much for the "Wizard of Oz" theory that there's no place like home. In the 2000 Stanley Cup Finals, the road was the place to be as the defending champion Dallas Stars and the 1995 Cup-winners New Jersey Devils combined to lose at home five times.

While the series went only six games, there was over seven games worth of hockey played. The two proud clubs made it a marathon in the final two contests. Down three games to one, the Stars be-Deviled New Jersey with a Mike Modano goal in the third overtime session. That was the first and only goal scored in more than 106 minutes of play.

Game 6 had a similar plot line. Dallas still faced elimination, and there was a lot of tight defense and many spectacular saves by the Stars' Ed Belfour and the Devils' Martin Brodeur. Patrik Elias threw a backhand pass into the slot and Jason Arnott buried the shot 8:20 into the second overtime, giving the Devils a 2–1 win and their second Stanley Cup.

Bone crusher

The Conn Smythe Trophy for playoff MVP usually goes to a prolific scorer or an impenetrable goaltender. In 2000, the award went to a punishing, physical player who set the tone for his team's style of play. Devils defenseman Scott Stevens passed out crunching bodycheck after crunching bodycheck throughout the playoffs. The captain even collected an assist on the Cup-winning goal.

It was the first Stanley Cup as a head coach for Larry Robinson – a six-time champion as a player – and it was unexpected. He started the season as Robbie Ftorek's assistant, and took over the division-leading but disgruntled Devils when Ftorek was let go with just eight games left in the season. Robinson guided New Jersey to an improbable comeback in the Eastern Conference finals, where it trailed Philadelphia three games to one.

The Finals started easy for New Jersey—a 7–3 to the Devils in Game 1—but it got very difficult after that. Game 2 was close throughout, and Brett Hull scored with less than five minutes to play to give Dallas a 2-1 victory. Game 3 went 2–1 in the Devils' favor, and game four was tight until New Jersey scored on three consecutive shots in the third period to win 3–1. Then it was on to the overtime classics.

The final game had to be stopped three times in the first period for injuries. Stars defenseman Darryl Sydor hurt his left ankle spinning away from a check and he did not return. Teammate Joe Nieuwendyk, the 1999 Conn Smythe winner, was dumped on a faceoff by Arnott and lay on the ice dazed for a few moments, though he did not miss a shift. Devils forward Petr Sykora was crunched by Derian Hatcher after skating the puck over the Dallas blue line. Sykora went to hospital for observation, but he was OK. Czech linemate Elias wore Sykora's jersey during postgame celebrations and the team planned to take the Cup to the hospital.

The two stars of the series were Belfour and Brodeur, who seemed impossible to beat. But Arnott got to live out the fantasy of the overtime goal to win the Cup.

"It feels great," said Arnott, who was extra thankful because his teammates killed off his cross checking penalty, the only power-play in the two overtimes. "It's a dream come true. Every player dreams about this. The last couple of years, we had something to prove."

RESULTS

	Game	Site	Winner	Score	GWG
May 30	Game 1	New Jersey	New Jersey	7-3	Scott Stevens
June 1	Game 2	New Jersey	Dallas	2-1	Brett Hull
June 3	Game 3	Dallas	New Jersey	2-1	Petr Sykora
June 5	Game 4	Dallas	New Jersey	3-1	John Madden
June 8	Game 5	New Jersey	Dallas	1-0 (3OT)	Mike Modano
June 10	Game 6	Dallas	New Jersey	2-1 (2OT)	Jason Arnott

Jason Arnott's (25) Stanley Cup-winning goal came 8:20 into the second overtime period of Game 6. The Finals showcased outstanding goaltending from New Jersey's Martin Brodeur and Dallas' Eddie Belfour.

Avalanche cool Devils

Colorado outlasted New Jersey in a classic 7-game confrontation to finally reward Ray Bourque with a Stanley Cup championship.

Joe Sakic displayed his usual playmaking brilliance in leading the Colorado Avalanche past the New Jersey Devils in a long, grueling Stanley Cup Finals. But the Avs center saved his best assist for the on-ice ceremony following Game 7. As per tradition, commissioner Gary Bettman presented the Stanley Cup to the winning captain. Sakic then did an immediate handoff to the man who had waited longer than anyone to hoist the Cup, Ray Bourque.

Twenty-two seasons into his storied NHL career, Bourque got the fairy tale ending. The superstar defenseman had been in the Finals before with the Boston Bruins, with whom he had spent more than 20 of his seasons. But the ultimate team prize eluded the man who had been named the NHL's best blueliner five times. Emotion carried the moment not only for Bourque, but for everyone associated with the Avs, all of whom seemed more happy for No. 77 than for themselves. The Stanley Cup was the ultimate retirement gift.

The ultimate playoff goaltender became the first player to win the Conn Smythe Trophy as postseason MVP three times. Patrick Roy, whose previous Conn Smythes came as a Montreal Canadien in 1986 and 1993, allowed just one goal over the final two games of the series.

RESULTS

	Game	Site	Winner	Score	GWG
May 26	Game 1	Denver	Colorado	5-0	Joe Sakic
May 29	Game 2	Denver	New Jersey	2-1	Turner Stevenson
May 31	Game 3	New Jersey	Colorado	3-1	Ray Bourque
June 2	Game 4	New Jersey	New Jersey	3-2	Petr Sykora
June 4	Game 5	Denver	New Jersey	4-1	Alexander Mogilny
June 7	Game 6	New Jersey	Colorado	4-0	Adam Foote
June 9	Game 7	Denver	Colorado	3-1	Alex Tanguay

Seven-game battle

The Finals featured two teams familiar with success. New Jersey was the defending Stanley Cup champion and Colorado had taken honors in 1996, the year after the Devils' first Cup triumph. The Avalanche kicked things off with a rout at home in Game 1. The 5–0 win featured two goals from Sakic. The Devils bounced back in Game 2 with a workman-like 2–1 victory. Grinders Bob Corkum and Turner Stevenson tallied for New Jersey and the team recommitted to defense.

Bourque provided heroics when the series shifted east to New Jersey. In Game 3, he scored the game winner on the power play early in the third period. The Devils' Jason Arnott scored the first goal of the series for the vaunted A-Line (Arnott, Patrick Elias, Petr Sykora), but it wasn't enough. The A-Line came to the rescue in New Jersey's next home game, even without Arnott for most of the game. The big centerman took a puck to the left temple early on and was taken to the hospital for tests. Elias and Sykora each scored in the 3–2 win, Sykora's breaking a deadlock with less than three minutes to play.

The Devils carried that momentum out to Denver, winning handily in Game 5, 4–1. While Arnott sat out the game, Elias opened the scoring on an assist from Sykora. Alexander Mogilny broke a personal 14-game scoring drought with the game-winner late in the first.

Facing elimination on the road, the Avs came up big in Game 6. Roy posted his record 19th career shutout in the 4–0 whitewash. Stay-at-home defenseman Adam Foote had a goal and two assists. Among the scarce good news for New Jersey was the fact that Arnott was back in the lineup. In Game 7, Colorado scored the first three goals en route to a 3–1 win to make the most of home-ice advantage. The Avs became the first team since the 1971 Montreal Canadiens to rally from a 3–2 series deficit. Colorado also became the second team in three years, joining the 1999 Dallas Stars, to win the Stanley Cup in the same season as the Presidents Trophy for most regular-season points.

Colorado's Adam Foote tests New Jersey's Martin Brodeur in game six. The Avalanche won 4-0 to take the series to a game seven decider.

2002 Stanley Cup Finals

WINGS FLY HIGH

Scotty Bowman becomes the first coach to win nine Stanley Cups as his Detroit Red Wings prove too strong for the Carolina Hurricanes.

RESULTS

	Game	Site	Winner	Score	GWG
June 4	Game 1	Detroit	Carolina	3-2(OT)	Ron Francis
June 6	Game 2	Detroit	Detroit	3-1	Nicklas Lidstrom
June 8	Game 3	Carolina	Detroit	3-1(3OT)	Igor Larionov
June 10	Game 4	Carolina	Detroit	3-0	Brett Hull
June 13	Game 5	Detroit	Detroit	3-1	Brendan Shanahan

Expectations were high in the Motor City when the Detroit Red Wings added three future Hall of Famers to their already star-studded lineup during the summer of 2001.

Nothing less than a Stanley Cup championship would be satisfactory when scoring stars Brett Hull and Luc Robitaille and all-world goaltender Dominik Hasek joined a team that already boasted the likes of Steve Yzerman, Sergei Fedorov, Brendan Shanahan, Chris Chelios and Nicklas Lidstrom, not to mention the winningest coach in hockey history, Scotty Bowman.

Detroit lived up to its billing during the regular season, posting 116 points, best in the league by 15 points. But with so many experienced—read "old"—players, many observers wondered if the Red Wings could withstand the grind of a two-month playoff tournament.

Things did not get off to a rosy start. In the opening series against the red-hot Vancouver Canucks, Detroit dropped the first two games at home. But the Wings kicked things into gear and won four straight, then disposed of St. Louis in round two. The Western Conference final was the best series of the 2002 postseason, featuring powerhouse arch-rivals Detroit and Colorado. It went to a game seven, when the Red Wings ousted the Avalanche.

Tobacco road

In the Stanley Cup Finals, the upstart Carolina Hurricanes drew first blood. Ron Francis, the only sure-fire future Hall of Famer not wearing a Red Wings jersey in this series, scored the winner less than a minute into overtime of game one. Carolina had made an impressive journey to the finals after finishing with just the seventh-best record in the Eastern Conference.

Game one would provide the first and final win for the Canes, however. Detroit took game two at home thanks to two late-third-period goals from Lidstrom and Grind Line center Kris Draper 13 seconds apart which broke a 1–1 tie. Game three shifted the venue to the Deep South of Raleigh, North Carolina, where fans got their first taste of Stanley Cup Finals hockey.

That first game was almost a double-header, as it went to 14:47 of the third overtime before Igor Larionov, the oldest player in the league at 41, solved standout Carolina netminder Arturs Irbe. The game came within 30 seconds of being the longest in Finals history.

The marathon session of game three did not negatively affect the older Detroit club. Five of the six goals Detroit scored in games four and five came from 30- and 40-somethings Shanahan, Hull and Larionov. Hoisting the Stanley Cup was a cherished moment for long-time veterans and first-time champions Hasek, Robitaille, Steve Duchesne and Fredrik Olausson.

Bowman went out on top, announcing his retirement immediately after passing his idol Toe Blake to become the only man to coach nine Stanley Cup winners.

Goaltender Arturs Irbe of the Carolina Hurricanes misses the puck as Detroit captures a dramatic Game 3 in triple overtime.

Stanley Cup Results 1927-2002 (NHL assumed control of the Cup in 1927)

Year	W/L	Winner	Coach	Runner-up	Coach
2002	4-1	Detroit	Scotty Bowman	Carolina	Paul Maurice
2001	4-3	Colorado	Bob Hartley	New Jersey	Larry Robinson
2000	4-2	New Jersey	Larry Robinson	Dallas	Ken Hitchcock
1999	4-2	Dallas	Ken Hitchcock	Buffalo	Lindy Ruff
1998	4-0	Detroit	Scotty Bowman	Washington	Ron Wilson
1997	4-0	Detroit	Scotty Bowman	Philadelphia	Terry Murray
1996	4-0	Colorado	Marc Crawford	Florida	Doug MacLean
1995	4-0	New Jersey	Jacques Lemaire	Detroit	Scotty Bowman
1994	4-3	NY Rangers	Mike Keenan	Vancouver	Pat Quinn
1993	4-1	Montreal	Jacques Demers	Los Angeles	Barry Melrose
1992	4-0	Pittsburgh	Scotty Bowman	Chicago	Mike Keenan
1991	4-2	Pittsburgh	Bob Johnson	Minnesota	Bob Gainey
1990	4-1	Edmonton	John Muckler	Boston	Mike Milbury
1989	4-2	Calgary	Terry Crisp	Montreal	Pat Burns
1988	4-0	Edmonton	Glen Sather	Boston	Terry O'Reilly
1987	4-3	Edmonton	Glen Sather	Philadelphia	Mike Keenan
1986	4-1	Montreal	Jean Perron	Calgary	Bob Johnson
1985	4-1	Edmonton	Glen Sather	Philadelphia	Mike Keenan
1984	4-1	Edmonton	Glen Sather	NY Islanders	Al Arbour
1983	4-0	NY Islanders	Al Arbour	Edmonton	Glen Sather
1982	4-0	NY Islanders	Al Arbour	Vancouver	Roger Neilson
1981	4-1	NY Islanders	Al Arbour	Minnesota	Glen Sonmor
1980	4-2	NY Islanders	Al Arbour	Philadelphia	Pat Quinn
1979	4-1	Montreal	Scotty Bowman	NY Rangers	Fred Shero
1978	4-2	Montreal	Scotty Bowman	Boston	Don Cherry
1977	4-0	Montreal	Scotty Bowman	Boston	Don Cherry
1976	4-0	Montreal	Scotty Bowman	Philadelphia	Fred Shero
1975	4-2	Philadelphia	Fred Shero	Buffalo	Floyd Smith
1974	4-2	Philadelphia	Fred Shero	Boston	Bep Guidolin
1973	4-2	Montreal	Scotty Bowman	Chicago	Billy Reay
1972	4-2	Boston	Tom Johnson	NY Rangers	Emile Francis
1971	4-3	Montreal	Al MacNeil	Chicago	Billy Reay
1970	4-0	Boston	Harry Sinden	St. Louis	Scotty Bowman
1969	4-0	Montreal	Claude Ruel	St. Louis	Scotty Bowman
1968	4-0	Montreal	Toe Blake	St. Louis	Scotty Bowman
1967	4-2	Toronto	Punch Imlach	Montreal	Toe Blake
1966	4-2	Montreal	Toe Blake	Detroit	Sid Abel
1965	4-3	Montreal	Toe Blake	Chicago	Billy Reay
1964	4-3	Toronto	Punch Imlach	Detroit	Sid Abel
1963	4-1	Toronto	Punch Imlach	Detroit	Sid Abel
1962	4-2	Toronto	Punch Imlach	Chicago	Rudy Pilous
1961	4-2	Chicago	Rudy Pilous	Detroit	Sid Abel
1960	4-0	Montreal	Toe Blake	Toronto	Punch Imlach
1959	4-1	Montreal	Toe Blake	Toronto	Punch Imlach
1958	4-2	Montreal	Toe Blake	Boston	Milt Schmidt
1957	4-1	Montreal	Toe Blake	Boston	Milt Schmidt
1956	4-1	Montreal	Toe Blake	Detroit	Jimmy Skinner
1955	4-3	Detroit	Jimmy Skinner	Montreal	Dick Irvin
1954	4-3	Detroit	Tommy Ivan	Montreal	Dick Irvin
1953	4-1	Montreal	Dick Irvin	Boston	Lynn Patrick
1952	4-0	Detroit	Tommy Ivan	Montreal	Dick Irvin
1951	4-1	Toronto	Joe Primeau	Montreal	Dick Irvin
1950	4-3	Detroit	Tommy Ivan	NY Rangers	Lynn Patrick
1949	4-0	Toronto	Hap Day	Detroit	Tommy Ivan
1948	4-0	Toronto	Hap Day	Detroit	Tommy Ivan
1947	4-2	Toronto	Hap Day	Montreal	Dick Irvin
1946	4-1	Montreal	Dick Irvin	Boston	Dit Clapper
1945	4-3	Toronto	Hap Day	Detroit	Jack Adams
1944	4-0	Montreal	Dick Irvin	Chicago	Paul Thompson
1943	4-0	Detroit	Jack Adams	Boston	Art Ross
1942	4-3	Toronto	Hap Day	Detroit	Jack Adams
1941	4-0	Boston	Cooney Weiland	Detroit	Ebbie Goodfellow
1940	4-2	NY Rangers	Frank Boucher	Toronto	Dick Irvin
1939	4-1	Boston	Art Ross	Toronto	Dick Irvin
1938	3-1	Chicago	Bill Stewart	Toronto	Dick Irvin
1937	3-2	Detroit	Jack Adams	NY Rangers	Lester Patrick
1936	3-1	Detroit	Jack Adams	Toronto	Dick Irvin
1935	3-0	Mtl. Maroons	Tommy Gorman	Toronto	Dick Irvin
1934	3-1	Chicago	Tommy Gorman	Detroit	Herbie Lewis
1933	3-1	NY Rangers	Lester Patrick	Toronto	Dick Irvin
1932	3-0	Toronto	Dick Irvin	NY Rangers	Lester Patrick
1931	3-2	Montreal	Cecil Hart	Chicago	Dick Irvin
1930	2-0	Montreal	Cecil Hart	Boston	Art Ross
1929	2-0	Boston	Cy Denneny	NY Rangers	Lester Patrick
1928	3-2	NY Rangers	Lester Patrick	Mtl. Maroons	Eddie Gerard
1927	2-0-2	Ottawa	Dave Gill	Boston	Art Ross

The All-Star Game

It's ironic that the NHL All-Star Game, sometimes labeled a non-contact version of hockey, came into being because of an unfortunate incident that ended a player's career. The first unofficial All-Star game was a benefit for Ace Bailey, who had been gravely injured in a regular-season game between the Toronto Maple Leafs and the Boston Bruins on December 12, 1933.

Bruins' star Eddie Shore had been knocked down while carrying the puck up the ice. Enraged, he charged Bailey, who had not been the culprit, and upended him viciously. Bailey's head struck the ice, knocking him unconscious. Bailey never played again.

On February 14, 1934, the Maple Leafs played a team of NHL All-Stars at Maple Leaf Gardens in a benefit for Bailey. More than $23,000 Cdn. was raised for Bailey, but the format did not exactly capture the imagination of the league's governors.

Two more unofficial All-Star games were staged, both owing to personal tragedy. In November 1937, a game was organized after the death following complications from a broken leg of Montreal Canadiens star Howie Morenz.

And in 1939, a similar game was held to benefit the widow of Babe Siebert, who had drowned that summer.

It's official

The first official All-Star Game was held in 1947, with the reigning Stanley Cup champions, the Toronto Maple Leafs, playing an All-Star team. The Stars won 4–3, establishing the format that would remain for most of the next two decades.

The Dream Game notion was that the true test of just how good the Stanley Cup champions were was to pit the best players from around the league against them. There was one obvious flaw with this set-up. The All-Star team selections often were dominated, understandably, by members of the Stanley Cup champions.

In 1958–59, for example, the Montreal Canadiens placed four players on the first All-Star team and two on the second team. Inevitably, the All-Star team that faced the champions took the ice minus several of its best players.

The league experimented with a different format for two years in the early 1950s, pitting the first All-Star team against the Second Team, but otherwise did not deviate from the Stars against the Stanley Cup champions until 1969.

This was the first All-Star Game following the first major expansion in NHL history, a project that doubled the size of the league from six to 12 teams.

From 1969 through 1971, the All-Star Game pitted the stars from the so-called Original Six against the stars from the six expansion clubs. That period featured the first All-Star Game held in an expansion city when St. Louis played host to the game in 1970.

The established stars of the East won that game 4–1, but the expansion stars surprised the Original Six when they won the 1971 game in Boston 2–1.

In 1972, the first of a series of realignments shifted the established Chicago Blackhawks into the West Division, and further expansion would continue to alter the makeup of the division.

By 1975, the league had grown to 18 teams, organized into two nine-team conferences: the Prince of Wales Conference and the Clarence Campbell Conference, named after the longtime president of the NHL.

The Wales did All-Star battle with the Campbells until 1994, when the NHL realigned its conferences and divisions geographically, replacing the Campbell with the Western Conference, and the Wales with the Eastern. The Central and Pacific Divisions comprise the Western Conference, while the Atlantic and Northeast Divisions make up the Eastern.

New trends

The league also had new uniforms designed, in teal and violet colors, and placed new emphasis on the skills competition, a fan-friendly feature the NHL had borrowed from a highly successful skills format used in the National Basketball Association.

The game itself remains an exhibition, a non-contact shootout which showcases plenty of offensive flash but involves little or no bodychecking and little commitment to defense. The goaltenders often have to perform at their best, and just as often they are buried in an avalanche of shots.

Injuries are rare in the All-Star Game, since no one is dishing out any bodychecks. Penalties are rare, too. The 1992 and 1994 games were penalty-free, while the 1993 game involved a single infraction, a minor penalty handed out to defenseman Dave Manson.

The marketing-savvy NHL front office sees the All-Star Game as a chance to market its stars and win new fans. Not content with resting on its laurels, the league altered the All-Star Game's format the past several seasons, eager to continue the growth of the game through reinvention and fresh ideas.

To add some sense of rivalry to the exhibition, the NHL has pitted a team of North American stars from Canada and the United States against a World team of players from the rest of the globe, replacing the previous Eastern Conference vs Western Conference match-up.

The format has proved a success with fans and has provided the game with some added spice as the two sets of players compete for bragging rights. It was the North America All-Stars who won those rights in 1998, 1999 and 2001, while in 2000 and 2002 the World team members earned the right to beat their chests.

The NHL, it seems, has got the rivalry it wanted.

1999 All-Star Game

Gretzky does it one last time

North America All-Stars 8 - World All-Stars 6

No one knew it at the time, but the 1999 All-Star Game in Tampa Bay was a swan song for the player many consider to be the greatest in NHL history. And Wayne Gretzky went out in style, winning his third All-Star Game MVP award in what proved to be his final NHL season before retiring.

The NHL kept with the successful 1998 All-Star Game format—pitting a North America team of Canadian and American stars against a World team composed of the top players from the rest of the globe. The North America squad won, 8–6, an almost identical score to its 8–7 triumph in 1998.

Gretzky recorded a goal and two assists for the winning side to claim the Dodge Durango given to the game's MVP. "It was a wonderful weekend," said The Great One after the game. North America jumped to a 4–1 lead in the first period on goals by Mike Modano, Luc Robitaille, Paul Kariya and Mark Recchi. Both teams scored three goals in the second period. The World team outscored the North American squad in the third period, 2–1, but it wasn't enough to overcome its big, early deficit.

Hitchcock gets his win

Nobody was more relieved with the North American victory than the team's coach, Ken Hitchcock, head man of the Dallas Stars. Heading into the game he was 0–11 as a coach in All-Star Games, including 0–2 in the NHL. Ending the streak was special, but the coach could not resist praising the MVP after the game.

"It's not just his game. It's the professionalism that he exhibits," said Hitchcock of Gretzky. "Just little things—there were some special people who came in the dressing room and he made sure every player was there. He pulled guys out of the changing rooms to make sure that people like Vladimir Konstantinov (a former player seriously injured in a limo accident in 1997) and the young kids were greeted by everyone. He just loves the game."

Neither team was shy about shooting either, and once again the six All-Star goalies saw plenty of rubber. The successful North America team fired 49 shots, and the World team countered with 36.

Nobody knew it at the time, but MVP Wayne Gretzky was playing in his 18th and final All-Star Game before his retirement in April 1999.

Russians rock in Toronto

World All-Stars 9 - North America All-Stars 4

It was World domination in the new millennium. Fans at Toronto's Air Canada Centre were treated to a close-fought game until it was blown open in the final period as the World team scored four unanswered goals.

The NHL changed the format for the All-Star Game in 1998 from Eastern Conference vs. Western Conference to North America (players from the United States and Canada) vs. the World (non-North American players). And in the first two years of the new alignment, the World team won the SuperSkills competition (fastest skater, puck control relay, hardest shot, etc.) on All-Star Game eve but lost the game itself.

Not so in the year 2000. Powered by Panthers star and native Russian Pavel Bure, the World team not only won the SuperSkills for the third straight year, it also blew out the North America squad in the All-Star Game, 9–4. The score was no fluke either, as the World squad outshot the North Americans, 48–32.

Brothers in arms

Bure netted a hat trick and added an assist to take MVP honors in the 50th edition of the annual classic. And he wasn't the only Bure to figure prominently in the scoring. His younger brother Valeri, a Calgary Flames forward playing in his first All-Star Game, assisted on both of his big brother's second-period goals.

"It was great," said Pavel. "It couldn't get any better. When I heard Bure scored from Bure, that was unbelievable."

The World team also got a pair of goals from St. Louis Blues sniper Pavol Demitra, the second of which ignited a 4–0 third period which buried the North America squad. The North Americans had gained some life by scoring a pair of goals (Chicago's Tony Amonte and Florida's Ray Whitney) to close the second period, bringing the score from 5–2 to 5–4. But the North Americans couldn't carry that momentum into the third.

Just like the first All-Star Game in 1947, the 50th event took place in Toronto, but this time in the year-old Air Canada Centre rather than historic Maple Leaf Gardens. Wayne Gretzky, who grew up in nearby Brantford and retired after the 1999 season, got a huge ovation when he dropped the ceremonial opening face-off.

Pavel Bure, left, shone brightest in the 2000 NHL All-Star Game at Toronto, netting a hat-trick and providing an assist too.

Guerin shines in Colorado

North America All-Stars 14 - World All-Stars 12

For the first three years of the North America vs. World All-Star Game format, the average total score—both teams combined—was 14 goals. In the format's fourth season, the winning side got 14 goals all by itself.

The North America squad outgunned the World team 14–12 in the highest-scoring All-Star Game in NHL history. The 26 goals smashed the old record of 22 set in 1993. Leading the way for the North America side was Boston Bruins winger Bill Guerin, who tallied three goals and two assists in his first All-Star Game. The Massachusetts native's five-point night earned him game MVP honors.

There were plenty of highlight moments to go around, unless you were one of the six goalies participating in the game. Eighteen players found the back of the net. Guerin's linemate Tony Amonte (Chicago Blackhawks) had a pair of goals, as did fellow North Americans Simon Gagne, Theo Fleury and Luc Robitaille and World team centers Sergei Fedorov and Mats Sundin. In fact, the scoring was so fast and furious that Gagne's second goal came while ABC-TV was in a commercial break.

Tough night for the masked men

Only in such a shootout would it be possible for Martin Brodeur to be credited with the win. The New Jersey netminder manned the North American pipes in the third period and surrendered five goals on 23 shots. He was quoted afterward as saying: "I know it's hard to believe in a game like this, but I made some great saves. It was exhausting out there for a goalie. Once a year for this is enough."

The host Colorado Avalanche were represented by five hometown heroes—forward Joe Sakic, defenseman Ray Bourque and goalie Patrick Roy for the North America side and forwards Peter Forsberg and Milan Hejduk for the World team. It was the 19th and final All-Star Game appearance for Bourque.

On All-Star Saturday the day before the game, the North Americans started a sweep of weekend activities by besting the World squad for the first time in the SuperSkills competition. North America boasted the fastest skater (Guerin), top goalie (Phoenix's Sean Burke) and most accurate shooter (Bourque, his eighth accuracy title).

The Bruins' Bill Guerin was awarded MVP honors thanks to a five-point performance.

The Bulin Wall stands tall

World All-Stars 8 - North America All-Stars 5

For someone who played in just two NHL games over the previous two seasons, Nikolai Khabibulin was decidedly short on rust in 2001–02. That was never more evident than in the All-Star Game in Los Angeles. The Tampa Bay Lightning goalie pitched a shutout in the third period for the World team, which rallied from a two-goal deficit in the final frame to beat the North American squad, 8–5. Khabibulin, nicknamed "The Bulin Wall," faced 20 shots, the most of any of the six goalies who played in the game. The Russian joined Patrick Roy, Martin Brodeur and Olaf Kolzig on the short list of backstoppers who have posted a shutout period in the last 14 All-Star Games.

Vancouver's Markus Naslund scored with under two minutes to go to break a 5-5 tie in favor of the World team, and Chicago's Alexei Zhamnov and Carolina's Sami Kapanen finished the World scoring with empty-netters. The game-winner, Naslund's second on the day, came just over a minute after Detroit's Sergei Fedorov evened up the score. San Jose's right winger Teemu Selanne also scored two goals for the winning World All-Stars.

A blistering start

It looked like the 2002 All-Star Game was going to be as wild and high scoring as the record-setting 2001 game when North America's Vincent Damphousse scored 35 seconds in. But the defensive intensity turned up and the final total of 13 goals was exactly half of the previous year's number. There was even a body check registered when Philadelphia's Jeremy Roenick dumped unsuspecting World defenseman Alexei Zhitnik.

Khabibulin's stellar play wasn't enough to earn MVP honors. That went to Chicago's Eric Daze, who scored twice and recorded an assist for the losing North Americans. In his postgame comments, Daze, playing in his first All-Star Game, was slightly dazed—but thrilled—by his coronation: "I was surprised because we lost the game and [Khabibulin] played a pretty good game."

Pittsburgh's Mario Lemieux made history when he scored early in the second period to give the North Americans a 4–2 lead. It was Super Mario's 13th career All-Star Game goal, tying him with Wayne Gretzky for first all-time in that category.

The Coyotes' Sean Burke foils another World attack but it was Nikolai Khabibulin in the opposite net who stole the show.

All-Star Game Results 1947-2002

Year	Venue	Score	Coaches
2002	Los Angeles	World 8, North America 5	Scotty Bowman; Pat Quinn
2001	Denver	North America 14, World 12	Joel Quenneville; Jacques Martin
2000	Toronto	World 9, North America 4	Scotty Bowman; Pat Quinn
1999	Tampa Bay	North America 8, World 6	Ken Hitchcock; Lindy Ruff
1998	Vancouver	North America 8, World 7	Scotty Bowman; Ken Hitchcock
1997	San Jose	Eastern 11, Western 7	Doug MacLean; Marc Crawford
1996	Boston	Eastern 5, Western 4	Doug MacLean; Scotty Bowman
1994	New York	Eastern 9, Western 8	Jacques Demers; Barry Melrose
1993	Montreal	Wales 16, Campbell 6	Scotty Bowman; Mike Keenan
1992	Philadelphia	Campbell 10, Wales 6	Bob Gainey; Scotty Bowman
1991	Chicago	Campbell 11, Wales 5	John Muckler; Mike Milbury
1990	Pittsburgh	Wales 12, Campbell 7	Pat Burns; Terry Crisp
1989	Edmonton	Campbell 9, Wales 5	Glen Sather; Terry O'Reilly
1988	St. Louis	Wales 6, Campbell 5(OT)	Mike Keenan; Glen Sather
1986	Hartford	Wales 4, Campbell 3(OT)	Mike Keenan; Glen Sather
1985	Calgary	Wales 6, Campbell 4	Al Arbour; Glen Sather
1984	New Jersey	Wales 7, Campbell 6	Al Arbour; Glen Sather
1983	NY Islanders	Campbell 9, Wales 3	Roger Neilson; Al Arbour
1982	Washington	Wales 4, Campbell 2	Al Arbour; Glen Sonmor
1981	Los Angeles	Campbell 4, Wales 1	Pat Quinn; Scotty Bowman
1980	Detroit	Wales 6, Campbell 3	Scotty Bowman; Al Arbour
1978	Buffalo	Wales 3, Campbell 2 (OT)	Scotty Bowman; Fred Shero
1977	Vancouver	Wales 4, Campbell 3	Scotty Bowman; Fred Shero
1976	Philadelphia	Wales 7, Campbell 5	Floyd Smith; Fred Shero
1975	Montreal	Wales 7, Campbell 1	Bep Guidolin; Fred Shero
1974	Chicago	West 6, East 4	Billy Reay; Scotty Bowman
1973	New York	East 5, West 4	Tom Johnson; Billy Reay
1972	Minnesota	East 3, West 2	Al McNeill; Billy Reay
1971	Boston	West 2, East 1	Scotty Bowman; Harry Sinden
1970	St. Louis	East 4, West 1	Claude Ruel; Scotty Bowman
1969	Montreal	East 3, West 3	Toe Blake; Scotty Bowman
1968	Toronto	Toronto 4, All-Stars 3	Punch Imlach; Toe Blake
1967	Montreal	Montreal 3, All-Stars 0	Toe Blake; Sid Abel
1965	Montreal	All-Stars 5, Montreal 2	Billy Reay; Toe Blake
1964	Toronto	All-Stars 3, Toronto 2	Sid Abel; Punch Imlach
1963	Toronto	All-Stars 3, Toronto3	Sid Abel; Punch Imlach
1962	Toronto	Toronto 4, All-Stars1	Punch Imlach; Rudy Pilous
1961	Chicago	All-Stars 3, Chicago 1	Sid Abel; Rudy Pilous
1960	Montreal	All-Stars 2, Montreal 1	Punch Imlach; Toe Blake
1959	Montreal	Montreal 6, All-Stars 1	Toe Blake; Punch Imlach
1958	Montreal	Montreal 6, All-Stars 3	Toe Blake; Milt Schmidt
1957	Montreal	All-Stars 5, Montreal 3	Milt Schmidt; Toe Blake
1956	Montreal	All-Stars 1, Montreal 1	Jim Skinner; Toe Blake
1955	Detroit	Detroit 3, All-Stars 1	Jim Skinner; Dick Irvin
1954	Detroit	All-Stars 2, Detroit 2	King Clancy; Jim Skinner
1953	Montreal	All-Stars 3, Montreal 1	Lynn Patrick; Dick Irvin
1952	Detroit	1st Team 1, 2nd Team 1	Tommy Ivan; Dick Irvin
1951	Toronto	1st Team 2, 2nd Team 2	Joe Primeau; Hap Day
1950	Detroit	Detroit 7, All-Stars 1	Tommy Ivan; Lynn Patrick
1949	Toronto	All-Stars 3, Toronto 1	Tommy Ivan; Hap Day
1948	Chicago	All-Stars 3, Toronto 1	Tommy Ivan; Hap Day
1947	Toronto	All-Stars 4, Toronto 3	Dirk Irvin; Hap Day

The Hockey Hall of Fame

The building that houses the state-of-the-art Hockey Hall of Fame in Toronto is a former Bank of Montreal that was built in the previous century. It's appropriate that the National Hockey League showcases its rich history in a vintage 1885 building. After all, the first recorded advertisement for a hockey game comes from the same era, having been placed in the *Montreal Gazette* in 1875.

The game that came to be known as hockey had been played for decades across Canada by that time, in a variety of forms, with a variety of names. Its 'invention' was a product of rural isolation and the need for some activity to enliven the months-long winter.

Unlike baseball, though, hockey has no Abner Doubleday, no personage who can be said, however inaccurately, to have invented the game, no bucolic equivalent of Cooperstown to cherish as the cradle of the game.

Numerous hockey historians make cases for the game originating in, variously, Kingston, Ontario, or Montreal, or a certain rural pond in Nova Scotia. Which claim is the most legitimate? Flip a coin.

But if there is no one mythology surrounding the location of the Hockey Hall of Fame it doesn't seem to matter. The ultra-modern facility is fraught with lore, rich in tradition, bursting with memories.

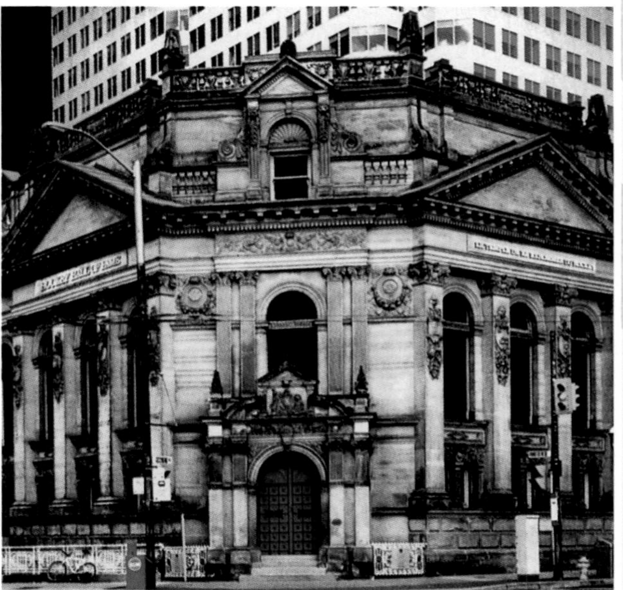

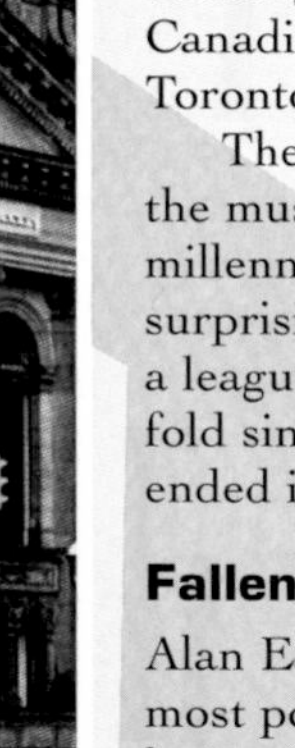

Hall of Honor: The great rotunda in the imposing Hockey Hall of Fame in Toronto is a fitting setting for the array of plaques honoring all the greats of the NHL game.

Golden memories

The Hall fills 51,000 square feet of space at BCE Place in downtown Toronto, a modern skyscraper that incorporates the century-old former bank building into its sprawling complex.

The displays include a surprisingly life-like re-creation of the fabled Montreal Canadiens dressing room in the old Forum, a large collection of the many strikingly artistic protective masks worn by the league's goaltenders over the years, and interactive displays that enable visitors, for example, to try their hand at play-by-play description of some of the game's golden moments.

The centerpiece of the building, which opened on 18 June 1993, is the Great Hall, a magnificent dome-ceilinged room that proudly showcases the plaques honoring the members as well as the NHL's glittering family of trophies.

The most famous trophy in the collection, of course, is the Stanley Cup, donated by Lord Stanley in 1893, the oldest trophy continuously competed for by professional athletes in North America.

The plaques honor the Hall of Fame's 324 members: 222 players, 88 builders (coaches, general managers, owners) and 14 referees and linesmen.

There are also 66 members from the media—broadcasters and print reporters—whose work helped raise awareness about, and helped foster the mythology of the game.

Honor for a league

The Hall of Fame was first established in 1943, its early members first honored in 1945. But a permanent location to house the legacy of the game wasn't found until 26 August 1961, when the collection was set up in a building on the grounds of the Canadian National Exhibition on Toronto's lakeshore.

The current location updates the museum for the new millennium. Which is not surprising for the Hall of Fame of a league that has expanded five-fold since the Original Six era ended in 1967.

Fallen Eagleson

Alan Eagleson, once one of the most powerful men in pro hockey, became the first person to resign from the Hockey Hall of Fame. He did so in March 1998 under heavy pressure. There were strong indications that if he did not resign he would be removed from the Hall's roster after former hockey stars such as Bobby Orr, Brad Park and Ted Lindsay threatened to quit the Hall had Eagleson been allowed to stay.

Eagleson was elected to the builders' category of the Hall of Fame in 1989 for his role in the formation of the NHL Players' Association and international hockey tournaments like the 1972 Canada-Soviet Union 'Summit Series'. His misdeeds included stealing Canada Cup tournament rinkboard advertising money between 1984 and 1991. He was also found guilty of fraud involving player pensions, player career-ending disability insurance money and overcharging players as head of their union. "I do not wish the board of directors to be forced to consider a review of my status and membership in the Hall of Fame under the circumstances of threatened renunciation of membership by a number of players," the disgraced Eagleson wrote in his resignation letter

Inspirational Leader: Bobby Clarke overcame limited natural ability and diabetes through sheer hard work and dedication to become the key player on the Philadelphia Flyers in the 1970s.

JEAN BELIVEAU: center. A native of Victoriaville, Quebec, Beliveau became a star center with the Quebec Aces of the Quebec Senior League. Le Colisée in Quebec, where the Aces played their games, was nicknamed the House that Beliveau Built, but it wasn't his hockey home for long. In 1952, Beliveau joined the Montreal Canadiens, who held his pro rights. He remained with them for his entire 18-year NHL career, and led the Canadiens to ten Stanley Cup victories. He was the first winner of the Conn Smythe Trophy as the most valuable player in the playoffs and twice won the Hart Trophy. He retired after leading the Canadiens to the Stanley Cup in 1970-71, having played 1125 NHL games and scored 507 goals.

HECTOR (TOE) BLAKE: left winger, coach. Blake played 578 NHL games, scoring 235 goals and adding 292 assists. The left wing beside center Elmer Lach and right winger Maurice Richard on the legendary Punch Line, Blake was nicknamed the Old Lamplighter for his scoring prowess. Many regard him as the best coach in the history of the NHL. For 13 seasons he coached the Canadiens, who won eight Stanley Cups under his regime, including five straight from 1956–60. He retired after coaching his eighth Cup victory in 1968.

MIKE BOSSY: right winger. As a junior star, Bossy was considered a soft player, a one-dimensional scorer whose offensive skills would be muted in the NHL, whose defensive skills would be a liability. The Montreal Canadiens, among other teams, passed on Bossy in the Entry Draft and lived to regret it. Bossy became the best right winger in the NHL in the 1980s, scoring 573 goals in just 752 regular-season games. For nine straight years, he scored 50 or more goals. He was the sniper on the Trio Grande—a line with Bryan Trottier at center and Clark Gillies at left wing. Bossy added 85 goals in 129 playoff games as he helped the New York Islanders win four straight Stanley Cup championships from 1980–83. Chronic back trouble forced him into retirement in 1987.

JOHNNY BOWER: goaltender. Scar-faced Bower didn't make it to the NHL for good until he was 34. He played 11 seasons for the Toronto Maple Leafs, helping them win four Stanley Cups, including the fabled upset in 1967 when an aging Toronto team beat the favored Montreal Canadiens. Bower and Terry Sawchuck shared the goaltending duties that season, as well as the Vezina Trophy as the best netminding duo in the league. He retired after the 1969–70 season, the only one in which he wore a protective mask.

SCOTTY BOWMAN: coach, general manager. He apprenticed in the Montreal Canadiens system under Sam Pollock before becoming the coach of the expansion St. Louis Blues, whom he led to three straight Stanley Cup finals. Repatriated to the Canadiens as head coach in 1971, Bowman led them to five Stanley Cup victories. He worked for the Sabres from 1979 to 1987 but didn't return to the Stanley Cup final until 1992, with the Penguins, replacing the late Bob Johnson as head coach. Now the head coach of the Detroit Red Wings, Bowman is the most successful coach in NHL history with well over 1,000 victories.

CLARENCE CAMPBELL: NHL president, 1947–78. Campbell was a Rhodes Scholar and won the Order of the British Empire after working as a prosecutor with the Canadian War Crimes Commission in Germany. He is remembered mostly as the man who suspended Maurice (Rocket) Richard after he slugged linesman Cliff Thompson in March 1955. Campbell's presence at the Forum on March 16, 1955 touched off a riot by outraged Montreal fans. But Campbell withstood that storm. In 1968, when he oversaw the expansion of the NHL from six to 12 teams. When he retired in 1978, the league had grown to 18 teams.

GERRY CHEEVERS: goaltender. Starting goalie for the Boston Bruins in the Bobby Orr-Phil Esposito era. Known as a great money goaltender, Cheevers was at his best in the playoffs. He helped Boston win the Stanley Cup in 1970 and 1972.

Straight On: Al Arbour coached one of the best teams in the history of the NHL during the New York Islanders' run of four straight Stanley Cups in the 1980s.

BOBBY CLARKE: center, coach, general manager. In 1968–69, Clarke piled up 137 points with the Flin Flon Bombers of the Western Hockey League, but many teams were leery of his diabetic condition and he was taken 17th overall in the NHL entry draft. He proved the skeptics wrong, playing 15 NHL seasons for the Philadelphia Flyers, winning the Hart Trophy three times and leading the Flyers to two straight Stanley Cups in the early 1970s. He was the first player on a post-1967 expansion team to score 100 or more points in a season. His grit, determination and leadership were central to the Flyers becoming the first expansion club ever to win the Stanley Cup.

Yvan Cournoyer: right winger. Cournoyer's speed earned him the nickname 'The Roadrunner,' but he was anything but birdlike. His speed came from thickly muscled legs that teammate Ken Dryden once compared to "two enormous roasts spilling over his knees." When he joined the Montreal Canadiens in 1963–64, Cournoyer was used as a power-play specialist. He developed into one of the most explosive forwards in the game, scoring 428 goals in 16 seasons, and helping Montreal win ten Stanley Cups. He was the Canadiens captain for their four-straight Stanley Cup run in the 1970s.

Marcel Dionne: center. Dionne was chosen second overall behind Guy Lafleur in the 1970 entry draft and played most of his career in brilliant obscurity. After racking up 366 points in four seasons with Detroit, Dionne was traded to the Los Angeles Kings, where he quietly piled up points for years, centering the Triple Crown Line with wingers Charlie Simmer and Dave Taylor. He won a scoring championship with the Kings and ended his 18-year career with 731 goals and 1,040 assists, but no Stanley Cup victories.

Ken Dryden: goaltender. Dryden, 23-year-old law student and a 6-foot-4, 210-pound giant, backstopped the Montreal Canadiens to a surprise Stanley Cup victory in 1970-71 after playing just six regular-season games with the club. He was awarded the Conn Smythe Trophy as the most valuable player in the playoffs, and followed that up by winning the Calder Trophy (rookie-of-the-year) the next season. Dryden played eight seasons for the Canadiens, helping them win six Stanley Cups, while winning the Vezina Trophy five times. He retired after the 1978–79 season, after helping the Canadiens win a fourth straight Cup. On March 2, 1971, he made hockey history when he faced brother Dave Dryden of the Buffalo Sabres. The pair were the first goaltending brothers ever to face each other in goal.

Phil Esposito: center, coach, general manager. Esposito was a competent, but unremarkable center for the Chicago Blackhawks when he was traded, with Ken Hodge and Fred Stanfield, to the Boston Bruins in 1967 for Hubert (Pit) Martin, Jack Norris and Gilles Marotte. Esposito blossomed as a Bruin, becoming the first player to score more than 100 points in a season. He won five scoring titles in eight-and-a-half seasons in Boston, where he and Bobby Orr led the Bruins to two Stanley Cups. He won two Hart Trophies and scored 55 goals or more in five straight seasons. He played 18 seasons in all, scoring 717 goals and adding 873 assists. He retired in 1981, finishing his career as a New York Ranger.

The Roadrunner: Montreal Canadiens sniper Yvan Cournoyer used blazing speed to zoom past opponents and score big goals.

Bill Gadsby: defenseman. Gadsby played standout defense for Chicago, New York Rangers and the Detroit Red Wings for 20 seasons over three decades, stretching from 1946–47 to 1965–66. Gadsby was fortunate to have a career at all. When he was 12, he and his mother were returning from England when the ship they were traveling on was torpedoed and sunk. He was rescued after spending five hours in the frigid Atlantic. In 1952, he overcame a bout of polio so severe doctors told him he would never play again. He played—well enough to be named an All-Star seven times. Strangely, he never won a Stanley Cup.

Bernard (Boom-Boom) Geoffrion: left wing. Geoffrion earned his nickname by becoming the first to consistently use the slap shot as an offensive weapon in the 1950s. He won the Calder Trophy in 1952 and led the NHL in scoring in 1955. He was the second player, after teammate Maurice Richard, to score 50 goals in a season and helped Montreal win five Stanley Cups. He frequently played the point (defense) on the power play to take advantage of his booming shot. He also coached, briefly, for the New York Rangers, Atlanta Flames and Montreal Canadiens.

Wayne Gretzky: center. The man known as The Great One certainly lived up to his nickname. In a 20-year NHL career starting with the Edmonton Oilers in 1979 and ending with the New York Rangers in 1999, Gretzky dominated the game. He held or shared 61 league records at retirement and won four Stanley Cups (all with the Oilers). The blockbuster trade that sent him to the Los Angeles Kings in 1988 made hockey hip in Southern California. Since that trade, Sun Belt states like Texas, Florida, North Carolina and Arizona have become part of the NHL family. In a comprehensive poll by the *Hockey News*, Gretzky was named the game's greatest ever player.

Doug Harvey: defenseman. Many consider Harvey, who played 20 NHL seasons from 1947–48 to 1968–69, the best defenseman in the history of the game. He won the Norris Trophy as the league's best defenseman seven times and helped the Montreal Canadiens win six Stanley Cups. He was the point man on the great Montreal power-play unit that included Jean Beliveau, Maurice (Rocket) Richard, Dickie Moore and Bernard (Boom-Boom) Geoffrion. The power-play unit was so effective that the NHL altered its rules so that a penalized player could leave the penalty box before his two minutes was up if the opposing team scored a goal. It was said of Harvey that he was so skilled he could control the tempo of a game, speeding its pace or slowing it down to suit the situation.

Gordie Howe: right winger. Howe, a physically powerful, awesomely talented but shy and humble farm boy from Floral, Saskatchewan, fully earned the nickname Mr. Hockey. Howe played 26 seasons, 34 pro seasons in all, covering five decades from 1946–47 to 1979–80. He played 1767 NHL games, scored 801 goals, added 1049 assists. At one time, he held NHL records for most games played, most goals, assists, and points in both regular season and playoffs. He became the first NHLer over the age of 50 to score a goal and the first to play on a line with his sons, Mark and Marty.

GLENN HALL: goaltender. The man who became known as Mr. Goalie didn't earn the title for nothing. Hall played 18 seasons—ten with Chicago—and was named an All-Star 11 times. He led the NHL in shutouts for six seasons, played in 115 Stanley Cup playoff games and set a league record for most consecutive games by a goalie—502, stretching from 1955 to November 7, 1962. He finished his remarkable career sharing goaltending duties with fellow Hall of Famer Jacques Plante in St. Louis, where he backstopped the Blues to three straight Stanley Cup final appearances.

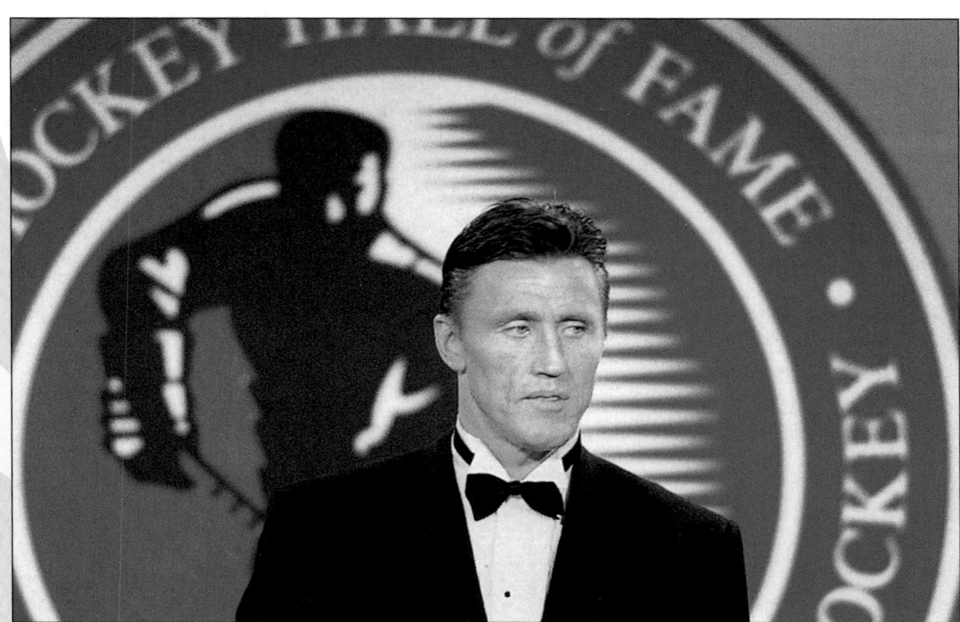

Old World Flash: Swedish defenseman Borje Salming brought an elegant skating stride and a large basket of skills to the Toronto Maple Leafs in the early 1970s. He was the first true European superstar in the NHL.

BOBBY HULL: left winger. Blond-haired and dimple-cheeked handsome and built like an Adonis, Hull also had blazing speed (29.7 mph top speed) and a frighteningly hard slap shot that once was clocked at 118.3 mph. Hull quickly became known as The Golden Jet in the NHL. He scored 610 goals in a 16-year NHL career during which he became the first player ever to record more than one 50-goal season (he had five). He won the Art Ross Trophy as the league's top scorer three times, the Lady Byng Trophy once, the Hart twice. He led the Blackhawks to the Stanley Cup in 1961, the first of his 50-goal seasons. He was the first big-name superstar to jump to the World Hockey Association when he signed a $1 million Cdn. contract with the Winnipeg Jets.

GEORGE (PUNCH) IMLACH: coach, general manager, Toronto Maple Leafs, Buffalo Sabres. Imlach was a bundle of superstitions and hockey acumen who piloted the Maple Leafs to four Stanley Cups in the 1960s. In 1970–71 he gave the expansion Buffalo Sabres instant credibility when he became their first coach and general manager. Imlach was instantly recognized by his trademark lucky fedoras. His superstition prevented him from changing suits when his team was on a winning streak.

GUY LAFLEUR: right winger. Lafleur, lightning-fast, creative and possessed of a wicked slap shot, was the NHL's dominant scorer of the 1970s. He was the first to score 50 goals or more in six consecutive seasons and six straight 100-point seasons. He also was the youngest player in history to score 400 goals and attain 1,000 points. He helped the Canadiens win five Stanley Cups, including four straight during his heyday from 1976–79.

MARIO LEMIEUX: center. Super Mario is one of the most gifted players the game has ever seen, but his magnificent playing career was cut short by chronic back problems and a battle with Hodgkin's disease. When he retired in 1997, he earned the rare honor of having the three-year waiting period waived, so that he could immediately be inducted into the Hockey Hall of Fame. Lemieux was the first player taken in the 1984 draft, by the struggling Pittsburgh Penguins. It took a while for a talented team to be built around him, but led by Lemieux, Pittsburgh won back-to-back titles in 1991 and '92. The tall centerman moved into ownership during retirement. In December of 2000, the six-time NHL scoring champ unretired as a player, becoming just the third person to be an active player and a Hall of Fame member simultaneously (Gordie Howe and Guy Lafleur were the previous two).

FRANK MAHOVLICH: left winger. The man better known to hockey fans as The Big M possessed a booming slap shot and perhaps the smoothest, most powerful skating stride the game has ever seen. He scored 48 goals as a 23-year-old with Toronto in 1961 and helped the Maple Leafs win four Stanley Cups in the 1960s. Traded to Detroit in 1968, Mahovlich played on a line with Gordie Howe and Alex Delvecchio. Detroit traded him to Montreal in 1971 and The Big M set a playoff scoring record with 27 points and 14 goals to lead the Canadiens to the Stanley Cup. He also helped the Canadiens win the Cup in 1973.

LANNY MCDONALD: right winger. McDonald scored 500 goals and added 506 assists in his 16-year career with Toronto, Colorado and Calgary. McDonald teamed up with Sittler as a potent one-two punch with the Maple Leafs until club owner Harold Ballard traded him to Colorado, largely out of spite. McDonald concluded a distinguished career in style, scoring a goal in Calgary's Cup-winning game against the Montreal Canadiens in 1989, the only Cup victory of his career.

STAN MIKITA: center. Born in Czechoslovakia, Mikita entered the NHL as a feisty, clever centerman, but he underwent a transformation into a gentlemanly player winning the Art Ross, Hart and Lady Byng trophies in 1967 and 1968, the first player ever to win all three in a single season. He is credited with introducing the curved stick blade to the NHL, by accident, it turns out. An angry Mikita tried to snap his stick blade by closing the door to the team bench on it. The stick bent, but did not break, and Mikita discovered it enhanced his shooting immensely.

FRANK NIGHBOR: center, defenseman. They called Nighbor the Pembroke Peach and he is credited with perfecting the poke check. He played 13 seasons in the NHL, from 1917–18 to 1929–30. He won five Stanley Cups, one with the Vancouver Millionaires in 1915, four more with the Ottawa Senators. In 1923, he became the first winner of the Hart Trophy as the NHL's most valuable player. In 1925, he was the first recipient of the Lady Byng Trophy, awarded to the league's most sportsmanlike player.

BOBBY ORR: defenseman. Played junior hockey for the Oshawa Generals and joined the Boston Bruins, at age 18, in 1966–67. Orr, one of the fastest skaters in the NHL in his time, revolutionized the defense position. With his quick acceleration, excellent straightahead speed and lateral mobility, Orr played defense like a point guard in basketball. More often than not, it was Orr who led the Bruins' offensive attacks, dishing a pass off to a teammate, or going end to end to take a shot on goal. He scored 296 goals in his 13 NHL seasons and was the first defenseman to score more than 40 goals and record more than 100 points in a season. He was the first defenseman to win the Conn Smythe Trophy. He also won the Norris Trophy eight times, the Hart three times and twice won the league scoring championship. He led the Bruins to two Stanley Cups. His career was foreshortened by a series of knee injuries.

BRAD PARK: defenseman. Contemporary of Orr and Potvin. Park played 17 years in the NHL, never for a team that missed the playoffs; but never for a team that won the Stanley Cup. He was named a first-team All-Star five times and became the second defenseman in NHL history to record 500 assists—after Orr. He scored 213 goals and added 683 assists in his career, which, like Orr's, was plagued by knee injuries. Early in his career, Park revived the seemingly lost art of the open-ice body check. Often cast in the shadow of first Orr, then Denis Potvin, Park was a superb two-way defenseman.

GILBERT PERREAULT: center. Won two Memorial Cups while a member of the Montreal Junior Canadiens. Perreault was the first draft pick of the Buffalo Sabres, for whom he played his entire 17-year career. Perreault centered the dangerous French Connection line with wingers Rene Robert and Richard Martin, amassing 1,336 points (512 goals) in his brilliant career. A virtuoso performer, Perreault was a strong, fast, slightly bow-legged skater, whose head and shoulder fakes and quicksilver stickhandling mystified opponents. The Sabres built a credible NHL franchise in Buffalo around Perreault, who retired after the 1987–88 season.

JACQUES PLANTE: goaltender. Plante redefined his position. He was the first to roam away from the goal crease to handle loose pucks in the corners and along the end boards. After he suffered a nasty facial cut in a game in 1959, Plante donned a protective mask of his own design and, over the protests of his coach, Toe Blake, wore one from then on. Plante played 19 years in the NHL, with Montreal, New York, Toronto, St. Louis and Boston, but his years in Montreal were his finest. He won seven Vezina Trophies, six Stanley Cups and one Hart Trophy during his career.

DENIS POTVIN: defenseman. After a brilliant five-year junior career with the Ottawa 67s that Potvin began as a 14-year-old, the defenseman joined the New York Islanders as their indisputable franchise player. He led the Islanders to four straight Stanley Cups in the early 1980s. Potvin, a rugged, highly skilled player, chafed at comparisons with Orr. When his 15-year career was over, Potvin had recorded more goals (310), assists (742) and points (1,052) than any defenseman in NHL history.

Big Bird: Larry Robinson was one of the famous Big Three defenseman in Montreal, with Guy Lapointe and Serge Savard in the 1970s.

MAURICE RICHARD: right winger. The Rocket, as he was known, was a passionate presence on the ice who often saved his most brilliant performances for the most dramatic of circumstances. Among the 82 playoff goals he scored, 18 were game-winners, six of those in sudden-death overtime. He was the first player to score 50 goals in 50 games in a single season and the first to score 500 in his career. He scored 544 goals during his career, won eight Stanley Cups and won the Hart Trophy. Ironically, the man many consider the league's best-ever pure scorer, never won the Art Ross Trophy as the NHL's leading scorer.

TERRY SAWCHUK: goaltender. Many consider Sawchuk to be the best goalie who ever played in the NHL. He posted an NHL-record 103 shutouts during his 21-year career, which saw him play for Detroit, Toronto, Boston, Los Angeles and New York Rangers. In 1952, Sawchuk carried the Red Wings to a Stanley Cup, posting four shutouts in Detroit's eight straight victories, and allowing just five goals overall. Sawchuk won the Vezina Trophy three times, including one award he shared with Johnny Bower for Toronto in 1967.

DARRYL SITTLER: center. Sittler was the heart and soul of some exciting Toronto Maple Leafs teams in the 1970s. He is remembered, as much as anything, for one brilliant night when he scored six goals and added four assists in an 11-4 Maple Leafs victory over the Boston Bruins in 1976. The same year, he scored five goals in a playoff game against the Flyers. He was the first member of the Maple Leafs to score 100 points in a season. He finished his career with 484 goals.

VLADISLAV TRETIAK: goaltender. In a perfect world, Tretiak, the brilliant goaltender for the Soviet Red Army and Soviet national teams, might have played for the Montreal Canadiens, who held his NHL rights. As a 20-year-old, Tretiak established himself as an excellent goaltender in the eight-game Canada-Soviet Summit Series in 1972. Viktor Tikhonov, the legendary Soviet coach, pulled Tretiak after the first period in the famous Miracle on Ice loss to the US team at the Winter Olympics in 1980 in Lake Placid. Tikhonov would admit later this was his biggest regret as a coach.

Glossary of Hockey Terms

Art Ross Trophy: Awarded to the player who wins the scoring championship during the regular season.
Assist: A pass that leads to a goal being scored. One or two, or none, may be awarded on any goal.
Backchecking: Skating with an opponent through the neutral and defensive zones to try to break up an attack.
Backhand: A pass or shot, in which the player cradles the puck on the off- or backside of the stick blade and propels it with a shoveling motion.
Back pass: A pass left or slid backwards for a trailing teammate to recover.
Blocker: A protective glove worn on the hand a goaltender uses to hold his stick so that the goalie can deflect pucks away from the net.
Blue lines: The lines, located 29 feet from each side of the center red line, which demarcate the beginning of the offensive zone.
Boarding: Riding or driving an opponent into the boards. A two- or five-minute penalty may be assessed, at the referee's discretion.
Boards: Wooden structures, 48 inches high, topped by plexiglass fencing, that enclose the 200 feet by 85 feet ice surface.
Bodycheck: Using the hips or shoulders to stop the progress of the puck carrier.
Breakaway: The puck carrier skating toward the opposition's net ahead of all the other players.
Butt-Ending: Striking an opponent with the top end of the hockey stick, a dangerously illegal act that brings a five-minute penalty.
Calder Memorial Trophy: Awarded to the goaltender, defenseman or forward judged to be the best first-year, or rookie, player.
Central Scouting Bureau: An NHL agency that compiles statistical and evaluative information on all players eligible for the Entry Draft. The information, which includes a rating system of all players, is distributed to all NHL teams.
Charging: Skating three strides or more and crashing into an opponent. Calls for a two-minute or five-minute penalty at the referee's discretion.
Conn Smythe Trophy: Awarded to the top performer throughout the Stanley Cup playoffs.
Crease: A six-foot semicircular area at the mouth of the goal that opponents may not enter. Only the goaltender may freeze the puck in this space.
Crossbar: A red, horizontal pipe, four feet above the ice and six feet long across the top of the goal cage.
Crosschecking: Hitting an opponent with both hands on the stick and no part of the stick on the ice. Warrants a two-minute penalty.
Defensemen: The two players who form the second line of defense, after the goalie. Defensemen try to strip opponents of the puck in their own zone and either pass to teammates or skate the puck up-ice themselves to start an attack. When retreating from the opponent's zone, defensemen move back toward their zone by skating backwards, facing the oncoming opponents.
Deflection: Placing the blade of the stick in the path of a shot on goal, causing the puck to change direction and deceive the goaltender. A puck may also deflect off a player's skate or pads.
Delay of game: Causing the play to stop by either propelling the puck outside the playing surface or covering it with the hand. Warrants a two-minute penalty.
Delayed penalty: An infraction, signaled by the referee's upraised right hand, but not whistled until the offending team regains possession of the puck. During the delay, the other team can launch a scoring attack, sometimes by replacing their goaltender with a skater. If the team scores during the delay, the penalized player does not sit out his penalty.
Elbowing: Striking an opponent with the elbow. Calls for a two-minute penalty.
Entry Draft: An annual event, at which all 30 NHL teams submit claims on young players who have not signed professional contracts. The talent pool consists of players from the Canadian junior leagues, U. high schools and universities and European elite and junior leagues.
Faceoff: A play that initiates all action in a hockey game, in which the referee or a linesman drops the puck onto a spot between the poised stick blades of two opponents. Marks the start of every period, also occurs after every goal and every play stoppage.
Fighting: Players dropping their gloves and striking each other with their fists. Calls for a five-minute penalty and ejection for the player who instigated the fisticuffs.
Forechecking: Harassing opponents in their own zone to try to gain possession of the puck.
Forwards: Three players—the center and the left and right wingers—comprise a hockey team's forward line. The forwards are primarily attackers whose aim is to score goals.
Frank J. Selke Trophy: Awarded to the player judged the best defensive forward in the NHL.
Goal: A goal is scored when the puck completely crosses the red goal line and enters the net.
Goals-Against-Average (GAG): Average number of goals a goaltender surrenders per game. Determined by multiplying the total number of goals allowed by 60 and dividing that figure by the total number of minutes played.
Goaltender: A heavily padded player who protects his team's goal.
Hart Memorial Trophy: Awarded to the player judged the most valuable to his team during the NHL regular season.
Hat Trick: One player scoring three goals in one game. A player who scores three consecutive goals in one period is said to have scored a 'natural' hat trick.
High sticking: Carrying the stick above the shoulder level. Calls for a faceoff if a player strikes the puck in this fashion. Calls for a two- or five-minute penalty if a player strikes an opponent with his stick.
Holding: Using the hands to impede the progress of an opponent. Two-minute penalty.
Hooking: Using the blade of the stick to impede an opponent. Two-minute penalty.
Icing the puck: Shooting the puck from one side of the center red line so that it crosses the opponent's red goal line. Calls for a play stoppage and a faceoff in the offending team's zone.
Interference: Using the body or stick to impede an opponent who is not in possession of the puck or was the last one to touch it. Two-minute penalty.
James Norris Memorial Trophy: Awarded annually to the player who is judged to be the best defenseman in the NHL.
Kneeing: Using the knee to check an opponent. Two-minute penalty.
Lady Byng Trophy: Awarded to the player who best combines playing excellence with sportsmanship.
Linesmen: Two on-ice officials responsible for calling offside, icing and some infractions, such as too many men on the ice. Linesmen drop the puck for faceoffs excluding those after a goal has been scored.
Neutral zone: The area of the ice surface between the two blue lines and bisected by the center red line.
Neutral-zone trap: Also called the delayed forecheck. A checking system designed to choke off offensive attacks in the neutral zone and enable the defensive team to regain possession of the puck.
Offside: A player who crosses the opposition blue line before the puck does is offside. Play is stopped when this occurs and a faceoff is held outside the blue line. A player also is offside if he accepts a pass that has crossed two lines (e.g. his team's blue line and the center red line). When this occurs, play is stopped and a faceoff is held at the point where the pass was made.
Original Six: In common usage, it refers to the six NHL teams in the pre-1968 expansion era: Toronto Maple Leafs; Montreal Canadiens; Boston Bruins; New York Rangers; Chicago Blackhawks; Detroit Red Wings.
Overtime: During regular-season play, teams play a five-minute, sudden-death overtime period if the score is tied at the end of regulation time. Teams play as many 20-minute sudden-death overtime periods as is necessary to reach a final result during the entire playoff schedule. Sudden-death means the game is over as soon as a goal is scored.
Penalty: A rules infraction which results in a player serving a two- or five-minute penalty in the penalty box, or in expulsion from the game. The penalized player's team must play one man short while he serves a minor or major penalty, but is not so handicapped if the player is assessed a ten-minute misconduct. The player cannot play until his time is up, but the team continues at full on-ice strength. A player assessed a game misconduct penalty cannot play for the rest of the game.
Penalty kill: A four- or three-man unit of players assigned to prevent the opposition from scoring while a teammate serves a two- or five-minute penalty.
Penalty Shot: Called when an attacking player, on a breakaway, is illegally prevented from getting a shot on goal. The puck is placed at center ice and the fouled player skates in alone on the goaltender.
Period: A 20-minute segment, during which time the clock stops at every play stoppage. A hockey game consists of three stop-time periods.
Playing Roster: A team may only dress 18 skaters and two goaltenders for each NHL game.
Plus-Minus: A 'plus' is credited to a player who is on the ice when his team scores an even-strength or shorthanded goal. A 'minus' is given to a player who is on the ice when an opponent scores an even-strength or shorthanded goal. A player's plus-minus total is the aggregate score of pluses and minuses. It is a barometer of a player's value to his team.
Point man: A player, usually a defenseman, who positions himself along the blue line near the boards and orchestrates an attacking team's offensive zone strategy. Often teams try to isolate the point man for a shot on goal.
Pokecheck: A sweeping or poking motion with the stick used to take the puck away from an opponent. Perfected by Frank Nighbor of the Ottawa Senators teams in the 1920s.
Power play: A situation in which one team has one or two more players on the ice than the other team, owing to penalties assessed. It provides the attacking team with an excellent opportunity to create quality scoring chances.
Puck: A vulcanized rubber disk, three inches wide and one inch thick. Game pucks are kept on ice before and during a game, which hardens them even more and helps prevent them from bouncing.
Rebound: A puck bouncing off the boards, the goaltender or the goalposts. A rebound gives an attacker a second chance for a dangerous shot on goal.
Red line: The red, center line dividing the ice surface in half. In junior and professional hockey, the red line is used to determine icing calls and offside passes. It is not used in US college hockey.
Referee: The chief on-ice official at a hockey game. The referee calls all penalties except too many men on the ice and controls the flow of the game.
Roughing: Excessive pushing and shoving that has not escalated to the level of fisticuffs. Two-minute penalty.
Rink: A surface 200 feet by 85 feet on which a game of hockey is played.
Save: Occurs when a goalie uses his blocker, goalie stick, catching glove or pads to prevent a puck from entering the goal.
Scout: A man or woman who travels to junior, college and high school games, evaluating players who will be available in the Entry Draft. NHL teams also have pro scouts, who evaluate the play of opposing teams.
Shift: The period of time—usually 35-45 seconds—that a player spends on the ice playing the game. Normally a player will play several shifts each period. Some players log as much as 30 minutes in ice time in any given game.
Shot On Goal: Any deliberate attempt by a player to shoot the puck into an opponent's net that, without the intervention of the goaltender, would have scored a goal. Therefore, a shot that hits a goalpost or the crossbar and bounces away, is not a shot on goal.
Shutout: A game result in which the opponent does not score a goal, usually owing to excellent work by the goaltender.
Slap shot: Shooting the puck by swinging the hockey stick through the disk, in a manner similar to a golf swing, except with the hands several inches apart on the stick.
Slashing: Swinging a stick at an opponent. Two-minute penalty.
Slot, The: The area in the offensive zone directly in front of the crease, extending back between the two faceoff circles, about halfway toward the blue line. Teams work hard to create scoring opportunities inside this area.
Spearing: Using a stick as a weapon, jabbing it, like a spear, into an opponent. Five-minute penalty, with expulsion at the discretion of the referee.
Stanley Cup: A silver trophy, originally donated by Lord Stanley, Earl of Preston in 1893 to be emblematic of Canadian hockey supremacy. Since 1926 only NHL teams have competed for the trophy.
Stickhandle: Manipulating the puck back and forth, or any direction, with the blade of the stick in order to deceive an opponent and carry the puck up the ice.
Tip-In: A goal that results when one player shoots on net and a teammate, positioned near the crease, uses his stick to redirect the puck past the goaltender.
Vezina Trophy: Awarded annually to the player judged to be the best goaltender in the NHL.
Wrist shot: Shooting the puck by sweeping the stick along the ice, snapping the wrists on the follow-through.
Zamboni: The box-like, motor-powered vehicle used to resurface the ice in all NHL arenas. The machine collects the snow that builds up during a period of play and lays down a fresh coat of water, providing a smooth ice sheet to begin each period.

INDEX

Picture captions are in bold type, forward lines are in italics

Hockey Hall of Fame Membership Roster
(Players Only)

Sid Abel: center, Detroit Red Wings (1938-43 and 1945-52), Chicago Blackhawks (1952-54). Inducted 1969.

Jack Adams: forward, Toronto Arenas (1917-19), Toronto St. Pats (1922-26), Ottawa Senators (1926-27). Inducted 1959.

Syl Apps: center, Toronto Maple Leafs (1936-43 and 1945-48). Inducted 1961.

George Armstrong: center, Toronto Maple Leafs (1949-71). Inducted 1975.

Irvine (Ace) Bailey: forward, Toronto Maple Leafs (1926-34). Inducted 1975.

Dan Bain: forward, Winnipeg Victorias (1895-1902). Inducted 1945.

Hobey Baker: forward, Princeton University (1910-1914). Inducted 1945.

Bill Barber: forward, Philadelphia Flyers (1972-84). Inducted 1990.

Marty Barry: forward, NY Americans (1927-28), Boston Bruins (1929-35), Detroit Red Wings (1935-39), Montreal Canadiens (1939-40). Inducted 1965.

Andy Bathgate: right winger, NY Rangers (1952-64), Toronto Maple Leafs (1964-65), Detroit Red Wings (1965-67), Pittsburgh Penguins (1967-68 and 1970-71). Inducted 1978.

Bobby Bauer: right winger, Boston Bruins (1936-42, 1945-47 and 1951-52). Inducted 1996.

Jean Beliveau: center, Montreal Canadiens (1950-51 and 1952-71). Inducted 1972.

Clint Benedict: goaltender, Ottawa Senators (1912-24), Montreal Maroons (1924-30). Inducted 1965.

Doug Bentley: forward, Chicago Blackhawks (1939-44 and 1945-52), NY Rangers (1953-54). Inducted 1964.

Max Bentley: forward, Chicago Blackhawks (1940-43 and 1945-47), Toronto Maple Leafs (1947-53), NY Rangers (1953-54). Inducted 1966.

Hector (Toe) Blake: left winger, Montreal Maroons (1934-35), Montreal Canadiens (1935-48). Inducted 1966.

Leo Boivin: defenseman, Toronto Maple Leafs (1951-54), Boston Bruins (1954-66), Detroit Red Wings (1966-67), Pittsburgh Penguins (1967-69), Minnesota North Stars (1969-70). Inducted 1986.

Dickie Boon: defenseman, Montreal AAAs (1899-03), Montreal Wanderers (1904-06). Inducted 1952.

Mike Bossy: right winger, New York Islanders (1977-87). Inducted 1991.

Emile (Butch) Bouchard: defenseman, Montreal Canadiens (1941-1956). Inducted 1966.

Frank Boucher: forward, Ottawa Senators (1921-22), NY Rangers (1926-38 and 1943-44). Inducted 1958.

George Boucher: defenseman, Ottawa Senators (1915-1929), Montreal Maroons (1928-31), Chicago Blackhawks (1931-32). Inducted 1960.

Johnny Bower: goaltender, NY Rangers (1953-55 and 1956-57), Toronto Maple Leafs (1958-70). Inducted 1976.

Russell (Dubbie) Bowie: forward, Montreal Victorias (1898-1908). Inducted 1945.

Frank Brimsek: goaltender, Boston Bruins (1938-43 and 1945-49), Chicago Blackhawks (1949-50). Inducted 1966.

Harry (Punch) Broadbent: forward, Ottawa Senators (1912-15 and 1918-24 and 1927-28), Montreal Maroons (1924-27), NY Americans (1928-29). Inducted 1962.

Walter (Turk) Broda: goaltender, Toronto Maple Leafs (1936-43 and 1945-52). Inducted 1967.

John Bucyk: left winger, Detroit Red Wings (1955-57), Boston Bruins (1957-78). Inducted 1981.

Billy Burch: forward, Hamilton Tigers (1922-25), NY Americans (1925-32), Boston Bruins (1932-33), Chicago Blackhawks (1933). Inducted 1974.

Harry Cameron: defenseman, Toronto Blue Shirts (1912-16), Toronto 228th Battalion (1916-17), Montreal Wanderers (1917), Toronto Arenas (1917-19), Ottawa Senators (1919), Toronto St. Pats (1919-20 and 1921-23), Montreal Canadiens (1920). Inducted 1962.

Gerry Cheevers: goaltender, Toronto Maple Leafs (1961-62), Boston Bruins (1965-72 and 1975-80). Inducted 1985.

Francis (King) Clancy: defenseman, Ottawa Senators (1921-30), Toronto Maple Leafs (1930-37). Inducted 1958.

Aubrey (Dit) Clapper: right winger/defenseman, Boston Bruins (1927-47). Inducted 1947.

Bobby Clarke: center, Philadelphia Flyers (1969-84). Inducted 1987.

Sprague Cleghorn: defenseman, Montreal Wanderers (1911-17), Ottawa Senators (1918-21), Toronto St. Pats (1921), Montreal Canadiens (1921-25), Boston Bruins (1925-28). Inducted 1958.

Neil Colville: center/defenseman, NY Rangers (1935-42 and 1944-49). Inducted 1967.

Charlie Conacher: forward, Toronto Maple Leafs (1929-38), Detroit Red Wings (1938-39), NY Americans (1939-41). Inducted 1961.

Lionel Conacher: defenseman, Pittsburgh Pirates (1925-38), NY Americans (1926-30), Montreal Maroons (1930-33 and 1934-37,) Chicago Black Hawks (1933-34). Inducted 1994.

Roy Conacher: left winger, Boston Bruins (1938-42 and 1945-46), Detroit Red Wings (1946-47), Chicago Black Hawks (1947-52). Inducted 1998.

Alex Connell: goaltender, Ottawa Senators (1924-31 and 1932-33), Detroit Falcons (1931-32), NY Americans (1933-34), Montreal Maroons (1934-35 and 1936-37). Inducted 1958.

Bill Cook: forward, NY Rangers (1926-37). Inducted 1952.

Fred (Bun) Cook: forward, NY Rangers (1926-36), Boston Bruins (1936-37). Inducted 1995.

Art Coulter: defenseman, Chicago Blackhawks (1931-36), NY Rangers (1936-42). Inducted 1974.

Yvan Cournoyer: right winger, Montreal Canadiens (1963-79). Inducted 1982.

Bill Cowley: forward, St. Louis Eagles (1934-35), Boston Bruins (1935-47). Inducted 1968.

Rusty Crawford: forward, Quebec Bulldogs (1912-17), Ottawa Senators (1917-18), Toronto Arenas (1918-19). Inducted 1962.

Jack Darragh: forward, Ottawa Senators (1910-1924). Inducted 1962.

Allan (Scotty) Davidson: forward, Toronto Blueshirts (1912-14). Inducted 1950.

Clarence (Hap) Day: defenseman, Toronto St. Pats (1924-26), Toronto Maple Leafs (1926-37), NY Americans (1937-38). Inducted 1961.

Alex Delvecchio: center, Detroit Red Wings (1950-74). Inducted 1977.

Cy Denneny: forward, Toronto Shamrocks (1914-15), Toronto Blueshirts (1915-16), Ottawa Senators (1916-28), Boston Bruins (1928-29). Inducted 1959.

Marcel Dionne: center, Detroit Red Wings (1971-75), LA Kings (1975-87), NY Rangers (1987-89). Inducted 1992.

Gordie Drillon: forward, Toronto Maple Leafs (1936-42), Montreal Canadiens (1942-43). Inducted 1975.

Graham Drinkwater: forward, Montreal AAAs (1892-93), Montreal Victorias (1894-99). Inducted 1950.

Ken Dryden: goaltender, Montreal Canadiens (1970-73 and 1974-79). Inducted 1983.

Woody Dumart: forward, Boston Bruins (1935-42 and 1945-54). Inducted 1992.

Tommy Dunderdale: forward, Winnipeg Victorias (1906-08), Toronto Shamrocks (1909-10), Quebec Bulldogs (1910-11), Victoria Aristocrats 1911-15 and 1918-23), Portland Rosebuds (1915-18), Saskatoon/Edmonton (1923-24). Inducted 1974.

Bill Durnan: goaltender, Montreal Canadiens (1943-50). Inducted 1964.

Mervyn (Red) Dutton: defenseman, Montreal Maroons (1926-30), NY Americans (1930-36). Inducted 1958.

Cecil (Babe) Dye: forward, Toronto St. Pats (1919-26), Hamilton Tigers (1920), Chicago Blackhawks (1926-28), NY Americans (1928-29), Toronto Maple Leafs (1930-31). Inducted 1970.

Phil Esposito: center, Chicago Blackhawks (1963-67), Boston Bruins (1967-75), NY Rangers (1975-81). Inducted 1984.

Tony Esposito: goaltender, Montreal Canadiens (1968-69), Chicago Blackhawks (1969-84). Inducted 1988.

Arthur Farrell: forward, Montreal Shamrocks (1896-1901). Inducted 1965.

Viacheslav Fetisov: defenseman, New Jersey Devils (1989-95), Detroit Red Wings (1995-98). Inducted 2001.

Fernie Flaman: defenseman, Boston Bruins (1944-50 and 1954-61), Toronto Maple Leafs (1950-54). Inducted 1990.

Frank Foyston: forward, Toronto Blueshirts (1912-15), Seattle Metros (1915-24), Victoria Aristocrats (1924-26), Detroit Cougars (1926-28). Inducted 1958.

Frank Fredrickson: forward, Victoria Aristocrats (1920-26), Boston Bruins (1926-29), Detroit Falcons (1926-27 and 1930-31), Pittsburgh Pirates (1928-30). Inducted 1958.

Bill Gadsby: defenseman, Chicago Blackhawks (1946-54), NY Rangers (1954-61), Detroit Red Wings (1961-66). Inducted 1970.

Bob Gainey: left winger, Montreal Canadiens (1973-89). Inducted 1992.

Chuck Gardiner: goaltender, Chicago Blackhawks (1927-34). Inducted 1945.

Herb Gardiner: defenseman, Montreal Canadiens (1926-29), Chicago Blackhawks (1928-29). Inducted 1958.

Jimmy Gardner: forward, Montreal AAAs (1900-03), Montreal Wanderers (1903-11), New Westminster Royals (1911-13), Montreal Canadiens (1913-15). Inducted 1962.

Michael Alfred Gartner: right winger, Washington Capitals (1979-89), Minnesota North Stars (1989-90), NY Rangers (1990-94), Toronto Maple Leafs (1994-96), Phoenix Coyotes (1996-98). Inducted 2001.

Bernard (Boom Boom) Geoffrion: right winger, Montreal Canadiens (1951-64), NY Rangers (1966-68). Inducted 1972.

Eddie Gerard: leftwinger/defenseman, Ottawa Victorias (1907-08), Ottawa Senators (1913-23). Inducted 1945.

Eddie Giacomin: goaltender, NY Rangers (1965-75), Detroit Red Wings (1975-78). Inducted 1987.

Rod Gilbert: forward, NY Rangers (1960-78). Inducted 1982.

Billy Gilmour: forward, Ottawa Senators (1902-06 and 1908-09 and 1915-16), Montreal Victorias (1907-08). Inducted 1962.

Frank (Moose) Goheen: defenseman, St. Paul Athletic Club (1914-28). Inducted 1952.

Ebbie Goodfellow: center/defenseman, Detroit Cougars (1929-30), Detroit Falcons (1930-32), Detroit Red Wings (1932-43). Inducted 1963.

Wayne Gretzky: center, Edmonton Oilers (1979-88), LA Kings (1988-96), St. Louis Blues (1996), NY Rangers (1996-99). Inducted 1999.

Michel Goulet: left winger, Quebec Nordiques (1979-90). Chicago Blackhawks (1990-94). Inducted 1998.

Mike Grant: defenseman, Montreal Victorias (1893-1902). Inducted 1950.

Wilf (Shorty) Green: forward, Hamilton Tigers (1923-25), NY Americans (1925-27). Inducted 1962.

Si Griffis: forward/defenseman, Rat Portage Thistles (1902-06), Kenora Thistles (1906-07), Vancouver Millionaires (1911-19). Inducted 1950.

George Hainsworth: goaltender, Montreal Canadiens (1926-33 and 1936-37), Toronto Maple Leafs (1933-36). Inducted 1961.

Glenn Hall: goaltender, Detroit Red Wings (1952-53 and 1954-57), Chicago Blackhawks (1957-67), St. Louis Blues (1967-71). Inducted 1975.

Joe Hall: defenseman, Quebec Bulldogs (1910-17), Montreal Canadiens (1917-19). Inducted 1961.

Doug Harvey: defenseman, Montreal Canadiens (1947-61), NY Rangers (1961-64), Detroit Red Wings (1966-67), St. Louis Blues (1967-69). Inducted 1973.

Dale Hawerchuk: center, Winnipeg Jets (1981-90), Buffalo Sabres (1990-95), St. Louis Blues (1995-96), Philadelphia Flyers (1996-97). Inducted 2001.

George Hay: forward, Chicago Blackhawks (1926-27), Detroit Cougars (1927-30), Detroit Falcons (1930-31), Detroit Red Wings (1932-34). Inducted 1958.

Riley Hern: goaltender, Montreal Wanderers (1906-11). Inducted 1962.

Bryan Hextall: forward, NY Rangers (1936-44 and 1945-48). Inducted 1969.

Harry (Hap) Holmes: goaltender, Toronto Blue Shirts (1912-16), Seattle Metros (1915-17 and 1918-24), Toronto Arenas (1917-19), Victoria Aristocrats (1924-26), Detroit Cougars (1926-28). Inducted 1972.

Tom Hooper: forward, Rat Portage Thistles (1901-05), Kenora Thistles (1906-07), Montreal Wanderers (1907-08), Montreal AAAs (1907-08). Inducted 1962.

G. Reginald (Red) Horner: defenseman, Toronto Maple Leafs (1928-40). Inducted 1965.

Tim Horton: defenseman, Toronto Maple Leafs, 1949-70), NY Rangers (1970-71), Pittsburgh Penguins (1971-72), Buffalo Sabres (1972-74). Inducted 1977.

Gordie Howe: right winger, Detroit Red Wings (1946-71), Houston Aeros (1973-77), New England Whalers (1977-79), Hartford Whalers (1979-80). Inducted 1972.

Syd Howe: forward, Ottawa Senators (1929-30 and 1932-34), Philadelphia Quakers (1930-31), Toronto Maple Leafs (1931-32), St. Louis Eagles (1934-35), Detroit Red Wings (1935-46). Inducted 1965.

Harry Howell: defenseman, NY Rangers (1952-69), Oakland Seals (1969-71), LA Kings (1971-73). Inducted 1979.

Robert Marvin (Bobby) Hull: left winger, Chicago Blackhawks (1957-72), Winnipeg Jets (1972-80), Hartford Whalers (1980). Inducted 1983.

Bouse Hutton: goaltender, Ottawa Senators (1898-1904). Inducted 1962.

Harry Hyland: forward, Montreal Shamrocks (1908-09), Montreal Wanderers (1909-11 and 1912-18), New Westminster Royals (1911-12), Ottawa Senators (1918). Inducted 1962.

Dick Irvin: forward, Portland Rosebuds (1916-17), Regina Capitals (1921-25), Portland Capitals (1925-26), Chicago Blackhawks (1926-29). Inducted 1958.

Harvey (Busher) Jackson: forward, Toronto Maple Leafs (1929-39), NY Americans (1939-41), Boston Bruins (1941-44). Inducted 1971.

Ernie Johnson: forward, Montreal Victorias (1903-05), Montreal Wanderers (1905-11), New Westminster Royals (1911-14), Portland Rosebuds (1914-18), Victoria Aristocrats (1918-22). Inducted 1952.

Ivan Wilfrid (Ching) Johnson: defenseman, NY Rangers (1926-37), NY Americans (1937-38). Inducted 1958.

Tom Johnson: defenseman, Montreal Canadiens (1947-48 and 1949-63), Boston Bruins (1963-65). Inducted 1970.

Aurel Joliat: forward, Montreal Canadiens (1922-38). Inducted 1947.

Gordon (Duke) Keats: forward, Toronto Blueshirts (1915-17), Edmonton Eskimos (1921-26), Boston Bruins (1926-27), Detroit Cougars (1927) Chicago Black Hawks (1927-29). Inducted 1958.

Leonard (Red) Kelly: defenseman, center, Detroit Red Wings (1947-60), Toronto Maple Leafs (1960-67). Inducted 1969.

Ted (Teeder) Kennedy: forward, Toronto Maple Leafs (1942-55 and 1956-57). Inducted 1966.

Dave Keon: center, Toronto Maple Leafs (1960-75), Hartford Whalers (1979-82). Inducted 1986.

Jari Pekka Kurri: right winger, Edmonton Oilers (1980-90), LA Kings (1991-96), NY Rangers (1996), Anaheim Mighty Ducks (1996-97), Colorado Avalanche (1997-98). Inducted 2001.

Elmer Lach: center, Montreal Canadiens (1940-54). Inducted 1966.

Guy Lafleur: right winger, Montreal Canadiens (1971-85), NY Rangers (1988-89), Quebec Nordiques (1989-91). Inducted 1988.

Edouard (Newsy) Lalonde: forward, Montreal Canadiens (1909-11 and 1912-22), NY Americans (1926-27). Inducted 1950.

Jacques Laperriere: defenseman, Montreal Canadiens (1962-74). Inducted 1987.

Edgar Laprade: center, NY Rangers (1945-55). Inducted 1993.

Guy Lapointe: defenseman, Montreal Canadiens (1968-82), St. Louis Blues (1982-83), Boston Bruins (1983-84). Inducted 1993.

Jack Laviolette: defenseman/right winger, Montreal Nationals (1903-04), Michigan Soo Indians (1904-07), Montreal Shamrocks (1907-09), Montreal Canadiens (1909-18). Inducted 1962.

Hugh Lehman: goaltender, New Westminster Royals (1911-14), Vancouver Millionaires (1914-26), Chicago Blackhawks (1926-28). Inducted 1958.

Jacques Lemaire: left winger, center, Montreal Canadiens (1967-79). Inducted 1984.

Mario Lemieux: center, Pittsburgh Penguins (1984-94, 1995-97 and 2000-present) Inducted 1997.

Percy LeSueur: goaltender, Ottawa Senators (1905-14), Toronto Shamrocks (1914-15), Toronto Blueshirts (1915-16). Inducted 1961.

Herbie Lewis: forward, Detroit Cougars (1928-30), Detroit Falcons (1930-33), Detroit Red Wings (1933-39). Inducted 1989.

Ted Lindsay: left winger, Detroit Red Wings (1944-57 and 1964-65), Chicago Blackhawks (1957-60). Inducted 1966.

Harry Lumley: goaltender, Detroit Red Wings (1943-50), Chicago Blackhawks (1950-52), Toronto Maple Leafs (1952-56), Boston Bruins (1957-60). Inducted 1980.

Mickey MacKay: forward, Vancouver Millionaires (1914-19 and 1920-24), Vancouver Maroons (1924-26), Chicago Blackhawks (1926-28), Pittsburgh Pirates (1928), Boston Bruins (1928-30). Inducted 1952.

Frank Mahovlich: left winger, Toronto Maple Leafs (1956-68), Detroit Red Wings (1968-71), Montreal Canadiens (1971-74). Inducted 1981.

Joe (Phantom) Malone: forward, Quebec Bulldogs (1908-09, 1910-17 and 1919-20), Waterloo (1909-10), Montreal Canadiens (1917-19, 1920-21 and 1922-24), Hamilton Tigers (1921-22). Inducted 1950.

Sylvio Mantha: defenseman, Montreal Canadiens (1923-36), Boston Bruins (1936-37). Inducted 1960.

Jack Marshall: forward, Winnipeg Victorias (1900-01), Montreal Victorias (1901-03), Montreal Wanderers (1903-05 and 1906-07 and 1909-12 and 1915-17), Montreal Montagnards (1905-06), Montreal Shamrocks (1907-09), Toronto Tecumsehs (1912-13), Toronto Ontarios (1913-14), Toronto Shamrocks (1914-15). Inducted 1965.

Fred Maxwell: forward, Winnipeg Monarchs (1914-16), Winnipeg Falcons (1918-25). Inducted 1962.

Lanny McDonald: right winger, Toronto Maple Leafs (1973-79), Colorado Rockies (1979-81), Calgary Flames (1981-89). Inducted 1992.

Frank McGee: forward, Ottawa Senators (1902-06). Inducted 1945.

Billy McGimsie: forward, Rat Portage Thistles (1902-03 and 1904-06), Kenora Thistles (1906-07). Inducted 1962.

George McNamara: defenseman, Montreal Shamrocks (1907-09), Halifax Crescents (1909-12), Waterloo (1911), Toronto Tecumsehs (1912-13), Ottawa (1913-14), Toronto Shamrocks (1914-15), Toronto Blueshirts (1915-16), 228th Battalion (1916-17). Inducted 1958.

Stan Mikita: center, Chicago Blackhawks (1958-80). Inducted 1983.

Richard (Dickie) Moore: left winger, Montreal Canadiens (1951-63), Toronto Maple Leafs (1964-65), St. Louis Blues (1967-68). Inducted 1974.

Paddy Moran: goaltender, Quebec Bulldogs (1901-09 and 1910-17), Halleybury Comets (1909-10). Inducted 1958.

Howie Morenz: forward, Montreal Canadiens (1923-34 and 1936-37), Chicago Blackhawks (1934-36), NY Rangers (1936). Inducted 1945.

Bill Mosienko: forward, Chicago Blackhawks (1941-55). Inducted 1965.

Joseph Mullen: right winger, St. Louis Blues (1980, 1981-86), Calgary Flames (1986-1990), Pittsburgh Penguins (1990-1995 and 1996-97), Boston Bruins (1995-96). Inducted 2000.

Frank Nighbor: center, Ottawa Senators (1915-30), Toronto Maple Leafs (1930). Inducted 1947.

Reginald Noble: forward/defenseman, Toronto Arenas (1917-19), Toronto St. Patricks (1919-24), Montreal Maroons (1924-27), Detroit Cougars (1927-30), Detroit Falcons (1930-32), Montreal Maroons (1932-33). Inducted 1962.

Buddy O'Connor: forward, Montreal Canadiens (1941-47), NY Rangers (1947-51). Inducted 1988.

Harry Oliver: forward, Boston Bruins (1926-34), NY Americans (1934-37). Inducted 1967.

Bert Olmstead: left winger, Chicago Blackhawks (1948-50), Montreal Canadiens (1950-58), Toronto Maple Leafs (1958-62). Inducted 1985.

Robert (Bobby) Orr: defenseman, Boston Bruins (1966-76), Chicago Blackhawks (1976-79). Inducted 1979.

Bernard Parent: goaltender, Boston Bruins (1965-67), Philadelphia Flyers (1967-71 and 1973-79), Toronto Maple Leafs (1970-72). Inducted 1984.

Brad Park: defenseman, NY Rangers (1968-75), Boston Bruins (1975-83), Detroit Red Wings (1983-85). Inducted 1988.

Joseph Lynn Patrick: forward, NY Rangers (1934-43 and 1945-46). Inducted 1980.

Lester Patrick: defenseman, Brandon (1903-04), Westmount (1904-05), Montreal Wanderers (1905-07), Edmonton (1907-08), Renfrew Creamery Kings (1909-10), Victoria Aristocrats (1911-16 and 1918-22), Spokane (1916-17), Seattle Metros (1917-18), Victoria Cougars (1925-26), NY Rangers (1926-27). Inducted 1947.

Gilbert Perreault: center, Buffalo Sabres (1970-87). Inducted 1990.

Tom Phillips: forward, Montreal AAAs (1902-03), Toronto Marlboroughs (1903-04), Rat Portage Thistles (1904-06), Kenora Thistles (1906-07), Ottawa Senators (1907-08), Vancouver Millionaires (1911-12). Inducted 1945.

Pierre Pilote: defenseman, Chicago Blackhawks (1955-68), Toronto Maple Leafs (1968-69). Inducted 1975.

Didier Pitre: forward/defenseman, Montreal Nationals (1903-05), Montreal Shamrocks (1907-08), Renfrew Creamery Kings (1908-09), Montreal Canadiens (1909-13 and 1914-23), Vancouver Millionaires (1913-14). Inducted 1962.

Jacques Plante: goaltender, Montreal Canadiens (1952-63), NY Rangers (1963-65), St. Louis Blues (1968-70), Toronto Maple Leafs (1970-73), Boston Bruins (1972-73). Inducted 1978.

Denis Potvin: defenseman, NY Islanders (1973-88). Inducted 1991.

Walter (Babe) Pratt: defenseman, NY Rangers (1935-42), Toronto Maple Leafs (1942-46), Boston Bruins (1946-47). Inducted 1966.

Joe Primeau: center, Toronto Maple Leafs (1927-36). Inducted 1963.

Marcel Pronovost: defenseman, Detroit Red Wings (1949-65), Toronto Maple Leafs (1965-70). Inducted 1978.

Bob Pulford: forward, Toronto Maple Leafs (1956-70), LA Kings (1970-72). Inducted 1991.

Harvey Pulford: defenseman, Ottawa Senators (1893-1908). Inducted 1945.

Bill Quackenbush: defenseman, Detroit Red Wings (1942-49), Boston Bruins (1949-56). Inducted 1976.

Frank Rankin: forward, Stratford (1906-09), Eaton's Athletic Association (1910-12), St. Michaels' (1912-14). Inducted 1961.

Jean Ratelle: center, NY Rangers (1960-75), Boston Bruins (1975-81). Inducted 1985.

Chuck Rayner: goaltender, NY Americans (1940-41), Brooklyn Americans (1941-42), NY Rangers (1945-53). Inducted 1973.

Kenneth Joseph Reardon: defenseman, Montreal Canadiens (1940-42 and 1945-50). Inducted 1966.

Henri Richard: center, Montreal Canadiens (1955-75). Inducted 1979.

Maurice (Rocket) Richard: right winger, Montreal Canadiens (1942-60). Inducted 1961.

George Richardson: forward, 14th Regiment (1906-13), Queens University (1908-09). Inducted 1950.

Gordon Roberts: forward, Ottawa Senators (1909-10), Montreal Wanderers (1910-16), Vancouver Millionaires (1916-17 and 1919-20), Seattle Metropolitans (1917-18). Inducted 1971.

Larry Robinson: defenseman, Montreal Canadiens (1972-89), Los Angeles Kings (1989-92). Inducted 1995.

Art Ross: defenseman, Westmount (1904-05), Brandon (1906-07), Kenora Thistles (1906-07), Montreal Wanderers (1907-09 and 1910-14 and 1916-18), Halleybury Comets (1909-10), Ottawa Senators (1914-16). Inducted 1945.

Blair Russel: forward, Montreal Victorias (1899-1908). Inducted 1965.

Ernie Russell: forward, Montreal AAAs (1904-05), Montreal Wanderers (1905-08 and 1909-14). Inducted 1965.

Jack Ruttan: defenseman, Armstrong's Point (1905-06), Rustler (1906-07), St. Johns College (1907-08), Manitoba Varsity (1909-12), Winnipeg (1912-13). Inducted 1962.

Borje Salming: defenseman, Toronto Maple Leafs (1973-89), Detroit Red Wings, (1989-90). Inducted 1996.

Denis Savard: center, Chicago Blackhawks (1980-90 and 1995-97), Montreal Canadiens (1990-93), Tampa Bay Lightning (1993-95). Inducted 2000.

Serge Savard: defenseman, Montreal Canadiens (1966-81), Winnipeg Jets (1981-83). Inducted 1986.

Terry Sawchuk: goaltender, Detroit Red Wings (1949-55 and 1957-64 and 1968-69), Boston Bruins (1955-57), Toronto Maple Leafs (1964-67), LA Kings (1967-68), NY Rangers (1969-70). Inducted 1971.

Fred Scanlan: forward, Montreal Shamrocks (1897-1901), Winnipeg Victorias (1901-03). Inducted 1965.

Milt Schmidt: center, Boston Bruins (1936-42 and 1945-55). Inducted 1961.

Sweeney Schriner: forward, NY Americans (1934-39), Toronto Maple Leafs (1939-43 and 1944-46). Inducted 1962.

Earl Seibert: defenseman, NY Rangers (1931-36), Chicago Blackhawks (1936-45), Detroit Red Wings (1945-46). Inducted 1963.

Oliver Seibert: forward, Berlin Rangers (1900-06). Inducted 1961.

Eddie Shore: defenseman, Boston Bruins (1926-40). Inducted 1947.

Steve Shutt: left winger, Montreal Canadiens (1972-1984), LA Kings (1984-85). Inducted 1993.

Albert Charles (Babe) Siebert: left winger/ defenseman, Montreal Maroons (1925-32), NY Rangers (1932-33), Boston Bruins (1933-36), Montreal Canadiens (1936-39). Inducted 1964.

Joe Simpson: defenseman, Edmonton Eskimos (1921-25), NY Americans (1925-31). Inducted 1962.

Darryl Sittler: center, Toronto Maple Leafs (1970-82), Philadelphia Flyers (1982-84), Detroit Red Wings (1984-85). Inducted 1989.

Alf Smith: forward, Ottawa Senators, 1894-97 and 1903-08), Kenora Thistles (1906-07). Inducted 1962.

Billy Smith: goaltender: LA Kings (1971-72), NY Islanders (1972-89). Inducted 1993.

Clint Smith: forward, NY Rangers (1936-43), Chicago Blackhawks (1943-47). Inducted 1991.

Reginald (Hooley) Smith: forward, Ottawa Senators (1924-27), Montreal Maroons (1927-36), Boston Bruins (1936-37), NY Americans (1937-41). Inducted 1972.

Tommy Smith: forward, Ottawa Victorias (1905-06), Ottawa Senators (1906), Brantford Indians (1908-10), Cobalt Silver Kings (1909-10), Galt (1910-11), Moncton (1911-12), Quebec Bulldogs (1912-16 and 1919-20), Ontarios (1914-15), Montreal Canadiens (1916-17). Inducted 1973.

Allan Stanley: defenseman, NY Rangers (1948-54), Chicago Blackhawks (1954-56), Toronto Maple Leafs (1958-68), Philadelphia Flyers (1968-69). Inducted 1981.

Barney Stanley: forward, Vancouver Millionaires (1914-19), Calgary Tigers (1921-22), Regina Capitals (1922-24), Edmonton Eskimos (1924-26). Inducted 1962.

Peter Stastny: center, Quebec Nordiques (1980-90), New Jersey Devils (1990-93), St. Louis Blues (1994-95). Inducted 1998.

Jack Stewart: defenseman, Detroit Red Wings (1938-43 and 1945-50), Chicago Blackhawks (1950-52). Inducted 1964.

Nelson Stewart: forward, Montreal Maroons (1925-32), Boston Bruins (1932-35 and 1936), NY Americans (1935-40). Inducted 1962.

Bruce Stuart: forward, Ottawa Senators (1898-1900, 1901-02 and 1908-11), Quebec Bulldogs (1900-01), Montreal Wanderers (1907-08). Inducted 1961.

William Hodgson (Hod) Stuart: defenseman, Ottawa Senators (1898-1900), Quebec Bulldogs (1900-02), Montreal Wanderers (1906-07). Inducted 1945.

Frederic (Cyclone) Taylor: forward/defenseman, Ottawa Senators (1907-09), Renfrew Cream Kings (1909-11), Vancouver Millionaires (1912-21 and 1922-23). Inducted 1947.

Cecil R. (Tiny) Thompson: goaltender, Boston Bruins (1928-38), Detroit Red Wings (1938-40). Inducted 1959.

Vladislav Tretiak: goaltender, Central Red Army (1969-84), Soviet National Team (1969-84). Inducted 1989.

Harry Trihey: forward, Montreal Shamrocks (1896-1901). Inducted 1950.

Bryan Trottier: center, New York Islanders (1979-90), Pittsburgh Penguins (1990-92 and 1993-94). Inducted 1997.

Norm Ullman: center, Detroit Red Wings (1955-68), Toronto Maple Leafs (1968-75), Edmonton Oilers (1975-77). Inducted 1982.

Georges Vezina: goaltender, Montreal Canadiens (1910-26). Inducted 1945.

Jack Walker: forward, Toronto Blueshirts (1912-15), Seattle Metros (1915-24), Victoria Cougars (1924-26), Detroit Cougars (1926-28). Inducted 1960.

Marty Walsh: forward, Ottawa Senators (1907-12). Inducted 1962.

Harry (Moose) Watson: left winger, St. Andrews (1915), Aura Lee Juniors (1918), Toronto Dentals (1919), Toronto Granites (1920-25), Toronto Sea Fleas (1931). Inducted 1962.

Harry (Whipper) Watson: left winger, Brooklyn Americans (1941-42), Detroit Red Wings (1942-46), Toronto Maple Leafs (1946-54), Chicago Blackhawks (1954-57). Inducted 1994.

Ralph (Cooney) Weiland: forward, Boston Bruins (1928-32 and 1935-39), Ottawa Senators (1932-33), Detroit Red Wings (1933-35). Inducted 1971.

Harry Westwick: forward, Ottawa Senators (1894-98 and 1900-08), Kenora Thistles (1906-07). Inducted 1962.

Fred Whitcroft: forward, Kenora Thistles (1906-08), Edmonton (1908-10), Renfrew Cream Kings (1909-10). Inducted 1962.

Gordon Allan (Phat) Wilson: defenseman, Port Arthur War Veterans (1918-20), Iroquois Falls Eskimos (1921), Port Arthur Bearcats (1923-33). Inducted 1962.

Lorne (Gump) Worsley: goaltender, NY Rangers (1952-63), Montreal Canadiens (1963-70), Minnesota North Stars (1970-74). Inducted 1980.

Roy Worters: goaltender, Pittsburgh Pirates (1925-28), NY Americans (1928-37), Montreal Canadiens (1930). Inducted 1969.